D1478923

Roman Imperialism

DEBATES AND DOCUMENTS IN ANCIENT HISTORY

GENERAL EDITORS

Emma Stafford, *University of Leeds* and
Shaun Tougher, *Cardiff University*

Focusing on important themes, events or periods throughout ancient
history, each volume in this series is divided into roughly equal parts. The
first introduces the reader to the main issues of interpretation. The second
contains a selection of relevant evidence supporting different views.

PUBLISHED

Diocletian and the Tetrarchy
Roger Rees

Julian the Apostate
Shaun Tougher

Rome and its Empire, AD 193–284
Olivier Hekster with Nicholas Zair

Roman Imperialism
Andrew Erskine

IN PREPARATION

The Family in the Roman World
Mary Harlow and Tim Parkin

Sex and Sexuality in Classical Athens
James Robson

King and Court in Ancient Persia (559–331 BC)
Lloyd Llewellyn-Jones

Justinian and the Sixth Century
Fiona Haarer

The Emperor Nero
Steven Green

Roman Imperialism

Andrew Erskine

Edinburgh University Press

© Andrew Erskine, 2010

Edinburgh University Press Ltd
22 George Square, Edinburgh

www.euppublishing.com

Typeset in Minion
by Servis Filmsetting Ltd, Stockport, Cheshire, and
printed and bound in Great Britain by
CPI Antony Rowe, Chippenham and Eastbourne

A CIP record for this book is available from the British Library

ISBN 978 0 7486 1962 7 (hardback)
ISBN 978 0 7486 1963 4 (paperback)

For Michelle

Contents

Series Editors' Preface

Debates and Documents in Ancient History is a series of short books on central topics in Greek and Roman history. It will range over the whole period of classical history from the early first millennium BC to the sixth century AD. The works in the series are written by expert academics and provide up-to-date and accessible accounts of the historical issues and problems raised by each topic. They also contain the important evidence on which the arguments are based, including texts (in translation), archaeological data and visual material. This allows readers to judge how convincing the arguments are and to enter the debates themselves. The series is intended for all those interested in the history of the Greek and Roman world.

In this volume Andrew Erskine focuses on the topic of Roman imperialism, spanning a broad chronological period, from Rome's domination of Italy to the fall of the western empire in the fifth century AD. How Rome acquired an empire, why she did so, and how she maintained it are questions of the first interest, but as Erskine shows interpretations of the motivations of Roman imperialism have varied greatly. Did Rome expand as a method of defence, or was she aggressively seeking empire? Was she simply acting as any other empire of the times would have done? What part did economic interests play in her thinking? Erskine addresses such key debates by engaging with the range of source material available, both Roman and non-Roman: histories, chronicles, biographies, speeches, letters, handbooks, religious and moral tracts, oracles, legislation, inscriptions and monuments. What emerges especially clearly is that the example of Rome continues to resonate today, and that interpretation of the nature of her imperialism says as much about contemporary circumstances and concerns as it does about Rome itself, making this a particularly fascinating and rewarding topic. This volume should provide an invaluable tool for students, teachers and all those interested in imperialism, Roman or otherwise.

Emma Stafford and Shaun Tougher

November 2009

Preface

The Roman empire and the wars that brought it about may now be long ago but for many modern countries an imperial past is rather more recent, whether experienced as the ruler or the ruled – and for some too it may not be the past. It is part not only of the history of countries but also of families; to take myself as an example I can point to Scottish settlers in Ireland on one side of my family and a river pilot on the Irrawaddy in Burma on the other, both aspects of British imperialism in one form or another. Consequently the study of Roman imperialism is necessarily informed by the perspectives of the present and this is something that gives the continuing debate its energy and vitality. I accepted the invitation to write this book not long after the invasions of Afghanistan and Iraq. Those events will no doubt resonate in these pages even where I am not aware of it.

In what follows I have tried to consider not merely the processes that led to the Roman empire but also its impact on the peoples subordinated to it. My own specialism is in the eastern Mediterranean and readers will probably notice that this account leans in that direction, both in what it covers and its selection of evidence. The book is divided into two halves. Part I treats some of the main issues in modern debates about Roman imperialism and opens with a narrative of Roman expansion. Part II offers a selection of evidence, references to which are given in bold in the text of Part I, thus '**Appian B, p. 92**' refers to passage B of Appian on p. 92. I make no claim to originality in the translations which owe much to earlier translators. In the case of Cicero's *Letters* and of Polybios I have loosely adapted the translations of Evelyn S. Shuckburgh (1899–1900 and 1889 respectively).

In preparing this book many people have been very helpful to me and I am very grateful to them. John Curran, John Richardson and Ursula Rothe all read large sections of the manuscript; Glenys Davies, Peter Thonemann and Shane Wallace provided me with photographs;

and Dominic Berry, Brian McGing and Keith Rutter gave much needed help and advice. Carol MacDonald at Edinburgh University Press has been quietly persistent in encouraging me to complete the book. Nicola Wood's careful copy-editing has done much to improve the manuscript I submitted. I am also indebted to the Leverhulme Trust for research leave; to Trinity College Dublin for a visiting research fellowship; and to the Backstage Theatre for providing a welcome distraction from anything academic. But it is to Michelle that I owe most and this book is dedicated to her.

Andrew Erskine
Longford, Ireland
October 2009

Illustrations

Abbreviations

App. *Mith.*	Appian, *Mithridatic Wars*
Caes. *BG.*	Caesar, *Gallic War*
*CAH*²	*Cambridge Ancient History*, 2nd edn. Cambridge, 1961–
Cic. *Att.*	Cicero, *Epistulae ad Atticum* (*Letters to Atticus*)
Cic. *Cat.*	Cicero, *In Catilinam* (*Against Catiline*)
Cic. *Fam.*	Cicero, *Epistulae ad familiares* (*Letters to Friends*)
Cic. *Leg.*	Cicero, *De legibus* (*On Laws*)
Cic. *Off.*	Cicero, *De officiis* (*On Duties*)
Cic. *Phil.*	Cicero, *Philippics*
Cic. *Prov. cons.*	Cicero, *De provinciis consularibus* (*On the Consular Provinces*)
Cic. *Rep.*	Cicero, *De Republica* (*On the Republic* or *On the Commonwealth*)
Dion. Hal. *Ant. Rom*	Dionysios of Halikarnassos (Dionysius of Halicarnassus), *Roman Antiquities*
ILS	Dessau, H. *Inscriptiones Latinae Selectae.* Berlin 1892–1916
IOSPE	Latyschev, B. *Inscriptiones antiquae orae septentrionalis Ponti Euxini Graecae et Latinae.* St Petersburg 1885–1901
Jos. *Jewish War*	Josephus, *The Jewish War*
JRS	*Journal of Roman Studies*
Milet	*Milet, Ergebnisse der Ausgrabung seit dem Jahren 1899.* Berlin 1906–36
Moretti *ISE*	Moretti, L. *Iscrizioni storiche ellenistiche.* Florence 1967–76
Pliny, *NH*	Pliny the Elder, *The Natural History*

Plut. *Aem.*	Plutarch, *Aemilius Paullus*
Plut. *Cato Mai.*	Plutarch, *Cato the Elder*
Plut. *Luc.*	Plutarch, *Lucullus*
Plut. *Pomp.*	Plutarch, *Pompey*
Plut. *Pyrrh.*	Plutarch, *Pyrrhus*
Polyb.	Polybios (Polybius)
RDGE	Sherk, R. K. *Roman Documents from the Greek East*: Senatus Consulta *and* Epistulae *to the Age of Augustus.* Baltimore 1969.
RG	*Res Gestae Divi Augusti* (*The Achievements of the Deified Augustus*)
Sall. *Iug.*	Sallust, *Bellum Iugurthinum* (*The Jugurthine War*)
SIG³	Dittenberger, W. *Sylloge Inscriptionum Graecarum.* 3rd edn. Leipzig 1915–24.
Suet. *Aug.*	Suetonius, *Augustus*
Suet. *Caes.*	Suetonius, *Caesar*
Tac. *Ann.*	Tacitus, *The Annals*
Tac. *Hist.*	Tacitus, *The Histories*
Vell. Pat.	Velleius Paterculus
Verg. *Aen.*	Vergil (or Virgil), *The Aeneid*
ZPE	*Zeitschrift für Papyrologie und Epigraphik*

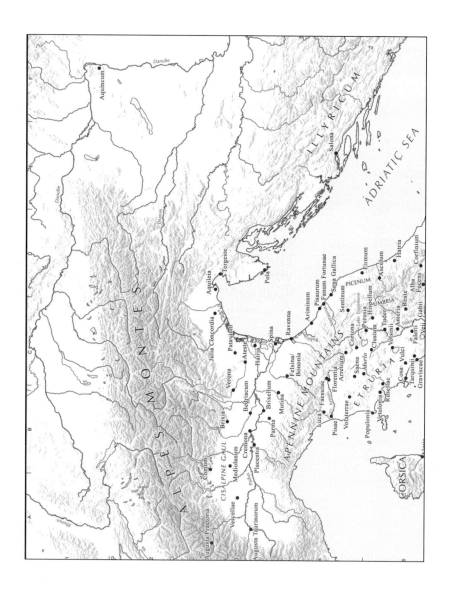

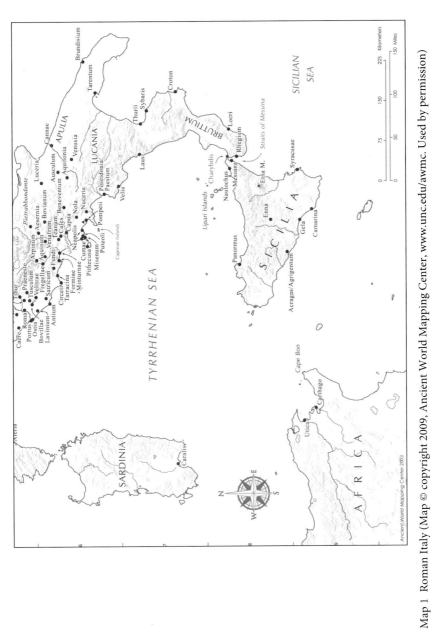

Map 1 Roman Italy (Map © copyright 2009, Ancient World Mapping Center, www.unc.edu/awmc. Used by permission)

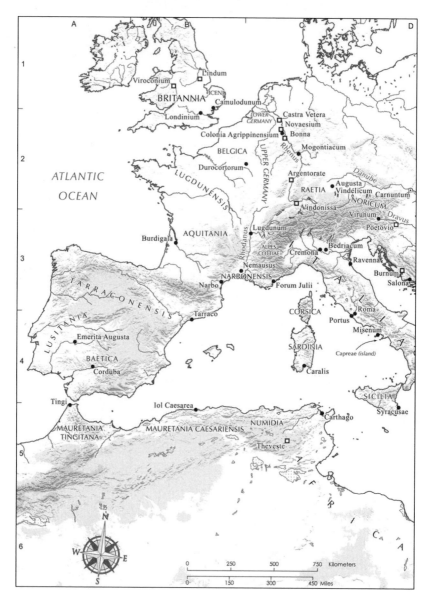

Map 2 The Roman Empire in AD 69 (Map © copyright 2009, Ancient World
Mapping Center, www.unc.edu/awmc. Used by permission)

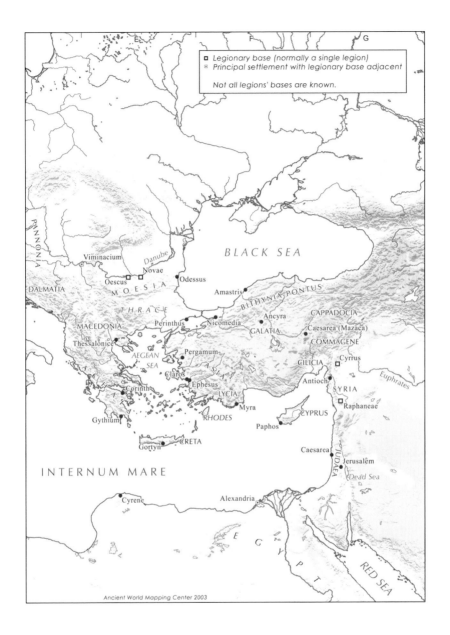

Timeline

This guide is inevitably very selective and the early dates in particular are often approximate.

BC

814	Traditional date for foundation of Carthage (archaeological evidence later)
776	Traditional date for foundation of the Olympic games
753	Traditional date for foundation of Rome
753–509	Rome, according to its own tradition, ruled by kings (Romulus, Numa Pompilius, Tullius Hostilius, Ancus Marcius, L. Tarquinius Priscus, Servius Tullius and finally L. Tarquinius Superbus)
750–580	Greek colonisation in the Mediterranean and Black Sea
700–500	Etruscan ascendancy in Italy
509	First year of the Roman republic after the expulsion of the kings.
494	First plebeian secession at Rome; beginning of the tribunate
493	Treaty of Spurius Cassius between the Romans and the Latins
451–449	Decemvirate and publication of the Twelve Tables at Rome, followed by secession of the Plebs in Rome
390 (or 387)	Gauls capture Rome
343–341	First Samnite War
341–338	Roman conquest of Latium
336–323	Reign of Alexander the Great and the Macedonian conquest of the Persian empire
328	Rome founds colony of Fregellae
326–304	Second Samnite War
321	Defeat of Rome at Caudine Forks

312	Construction of Via Appia begins
307	Construction of Via Valeria begins
298–290	Third Samnite War
295	Roman victory at battle of Sentinum
287	End of 'Conflict of Orders' at Rome
280–275	Pyrrhos of Epiros aids Tarentum against Rome; campaigns in Italy and Sicily
c. 270	Romans complete conquest of Italian peninsula
264–241	First Punic War
240–237	Carthage's Mercenaries War, following their defeat in First Punic War
230s	Romans campaign in Sardinia, Corsica, Liguria and against Gauls of northern Italy
229–228	First Illyrian War
225–222	Romans at war with Gauls of north Italy
225	Battle of Telamon: Romans defeat Gauls
220	Construction of Via Flaminia
219	Second Illyrian War
218	Rome founds colonies in northern Italy at Cremona and Placentia
218–202	Second Punic War
218	Battle of Trebia: Hannibal defeats Romans
217	Battle of Trasimene: Hannibal defeats Romans
216	Battle of Cannae: Hannibal defeats Romans
215	Alliance between Hannibal and Philip V of Macedon
214–205	First Macedonian War
211	Roman alliance with Aitolian League
210–206	P. Scipio Africanus seizes control of Spain from the Carthaginians
202	Battle of Zama: Scipio defeats Hannibal in North Africa
200–196	Second Macedonian War
197	Battle of Kynoskephalai: Flamininus defeats Philip V
196	Flamininus declares the freedom of the Greeks at the Isthmian games
195–175	Spanish wars including those against Celtiberians and Lusitanians
194	Romans withdraw from Greece
192–189	War with Antiochos III
189	Battle of Magnesia: Romans defeat Antiochos
188	Peace of Apamea between Rome and Antiochos

19	Death of Vergil
16 BC–AD 6	Danube provinces (Raetia, Noricum, Pannonia, Moesia) added to Roman empire

AD

6	Judaea becomes Roman province
9	Arminius destroys three Roman legions under Varus in the Teutoburg Forest in Germany
14	Death of Augustus
14–69	Julio-Claudian Dynasty
14–37	Tiberius emperor
37–41	Gaius Caligula emperor
41–54	Claudius emperor
43	Claudius' invasion of Britain
54–68	Nero emperor
60–61	Revolt of Boudicca in Britain
64	The Great Fire of Rome; Nero's persecution of Christians
66–70	Revolt in Judaea
69	Year of the four emperors after fall of Nero; Batavian revolt
69–96	Flavian Dynasty
69–79	Vespasian emperor
79–81	Titus emperor
79	Eruption of Mt Vesuvius and burial of Pompeii and Herculaneum
80	Inauguration of the Colosseum
81–96	Domitian emperor, followed briefly by Nerva
98–117	Trajan emperor
101–106	Campaigns against Dacians
110	Pliny governor of Bithynia and Pontus
113–117	Campaigns against Parthians
117–138	Hadrian emperor
122–126	Construction of Hadrian's Wall
132–135	Bar Kokhba revolt in Judaea
138–161	Antoninus Pius emperor
161–180	Marcus Aurelius emperor (until 169 with Lucius Verus)
162–166	Roman campaigns against Parthia
166–168	German tribes invade across the Danube
180–192	Commodus emperor
193–194	Civil war

193–211	Septimius Severus emperor
211–17	Caracalla emperor
212	Antonine Constitution gives Roman citizenship to all free men and women in the Roman empire
284–305	Diocletian and (from 293) the Tetrarchy
306–337	Constantine emperor
330	Dedication of new city of Constantinople
410	Sack of Rome by Alaric and the Goths
429	Vandals invade Africa
450s–470s	End of the Roman empire in the West

Part I

Debates

Debates

CHAPTER 1

Approaching Roman Imperialism

The perfect settlement of the Roman empire was preceded by ages of violence and rapine.

Edward Gibbon

1. Imperialism and empire

The transformation of Rome from a small central Italian city-state into the sole Mediterranean superpower has long proved fascinating and controversial. Its interest lies not merely in the scale and significance of what the Romans did but in its relevance to our understanding of the present: powerful states continue to impose their will on weaker states. This works both ways. Just as commentators on latterday imperialism look to Rome, so the scholarship on Rome has been and continues to be shaped by perceptions of contemporary international power relations, in particular by recent and current imperial experiences. It is Roman imperialism that is the theme of this book. It is not, therefore, about the Roman empire in general but about how that empire was acquired, conceived and maintained and how the subject responded to it.

At its height the Roman empire extended from Britain in the North to Libya in the South and from Spain in the West to Syria in the East. It has impressed not only by its extent but also by its longevity. If we give it a rough span from the conquest of Italy in the third century BC to the barbarian invasions of the fifth century AD, then it lasted for around seven centuries. Some too would see it as persisting in the form of the Byzantine empire centred on Constantinople. Yet, although the Romans may have liked to present themselves as rulers of the world, theirs was essentially a Mediterranean empire, notwithstanding the inclusion of some more northerly regions; at its heart was the Mediterranean, 'our sea', as the Romans called it. Rome resonates so powerfully in the Western tradition that it is easy to overlook other contemporary empires. Among the most prominent and influential of these was the vast Chinese empire of the Han dynasty, which lasted for some four centuries from 202 BC to AD 220 and ruled a population of similar size.

In the West, however, it is the influence of Rome that has been far-reaching; even the very word for empire is derived from the Latin *imperium*. States and leaders with imperial aspirations have regularly invoked the name of Rome, whether directly or through some form of imitation, thus the Holy Roman Empire or the new Rome of Napoleon with its Roman-style monuments, imagery and titles. In Victorian Britain the classically-trained elite looked to Rome as a model of empire and saw themselves as continuing its civilising mission. Pliny the Elder (*NH* 27.1.1) had written of the 'tremendous majesty of the *pax Romana*' (Roman peace), now the British spoke of the *pax Britannica*. In the twentieth century Mussolini staged an elaborate, if unsuccessful, revival of the Roman empire. But the Roman empire was not only a model and an aspiration; it could also be used as a means to criticise. When Queen Victoria took the title of empress of India, those opposed to it pointed to the example of the debauched emperors of Rome. When Robert F. Kennedy wanted to attack President Lyndon Johnson's policy in Vietnam, he borrowed from Tacitus, 'They made a desert and they called it peace.'

There are numerous theories of imperialism that define it in different ways and emphasise different aspects. It was only in the early twentieth century that the term came to be part of the vocabulary of scholarly discussion and then, initially, with reference to modern European empires. Early theorists related imperialism closely to capitalism. Fundamental were J. A. Hobson in his *Imperialism: A Study* (1902) and V. I. Lenin in *Imperialism, the Highest Stage of Capitalism* (1917), both of whom stressed the economic character of imperialism. Joseph Schumpeter, on the other hand, in his essay 'The Sociology of Imperialisms' (1919) tended to present the imperial power as a self-perpetuating war machine in pursuit of unlimited but unreasoned expansion. Some interpretations of imperialism see empire as necessarily territorial, emphasising the formal structures of direct control, but such approaches are often unhelpful, especially for understanding the development of the Roman empire. Preferable is a broader interpretation of imperialism which allows for less formal ways of exerting power. Although now we may think of Rome as a territorial empire, in the early years of its development the annexation of territory played only a limited role but Rome very clearly exercised a considerable amount of control over other states, first in Italy and then beyond the peninsula. For all their differences what imperial powers have in common is a willingness and capacity to change the world they encounter to work in their own interests. Rome may not have annexed territory immediately but it shaped the world to suit itself.

The dissolution of the European empires, especially those of Britain and France, during the twentieth century has led scholars to talk of postcolonialism, a misleading term in that it suggests that empire is somehow a thing of the past and that scholars today are free of its influence. Certainly the century saw a shift in attitudes about imperialism, presaged already in the anti-imperialist writings of Hobson and Lenin. Where previously empire was something to be celebrated, now imperial powers became rather more circumspect, the United States for example adopting what has been called the 'imperialism of anti-imperialism'. Yet what has happened is not so much the end of empire as a change in the way that imperial power is exercised, informal means frequently being preferred to the direct control of territory; even in the case of the recent occupation of Afghanistan and Iraq the professed intention is to withdraw. The Roman empire may have arisen in very different conditions from those of modern times but in its development it employed a variety of strategies for the exercise of power over others. In Greece in 196 BC it publicised itself as liberator and withdrew after arranging affairs to suit itself; in Spain at the same time it maintained occupying forces and established the structures of direct control. No empire is the same, but all this makes Rome good to think with and shows too that imperialism often defies easy categorisation.

2. The language of empire

The Latin term *imperium* may have given rise to the English words 'empire' and 'imperialism', but any sense approximating to what is today meant by 'empire' was a relatively late development in the Latin and there is no equivalent for 'imperialism'. The essence of *imperium* was the issuing of orders or commands; thus it could be used to mean an 'order' or, in a more technical sense, to refer to the power held by Roman officials, whether magistrates, such as consuls or praetors, or those appointed as pro-magistrates. Over the course of time its meaning came to be extended so that by the first century BC it was being used to express power more broadly, as in the phrase, *imperium populi Romani*, which could denote the power or authority of the Roman people over others. Here the idea of empire is approached but it is empire conceived in terms of orders rather than territory. Only in the early first century AD is *imperium* used to signify the Roman empire as a territorial entity (Richardson 2008). Roman orders are still integral to the conception of empire; this is an area where Rome is obeyed. The development of the word *imperium* thus tracks the way that the empire itself developed with Roman rule becoming increasingly formalised. This range of meanings, however, makes *imperium* a difficult word to translate satisfactorily and that much more vulnerable to scholarly interpretation. A similar process can be seen at work in another key term, *provincia*, which began as a task assigned to a magistrate and ended as a unit of empire, the province.

It might seem that the Romans took rather a long time to develop a territorial idea of their empire but this is only so if we start with the presupposition that this is what an empire should be; as section 1 above suggests, however, this is rather a limited conception of empire. Romans and Greeks often talked of peoples rather than places, a way of thinking that lent itself to understanding empire primarily in terms of power rather than territory. This is sometimes lost in the translation of Latin and Greek texts, where the translator might substitute a place-name (e.g. Ephesos) for a people (e.g. the Ephesians) and so subtly alter the way the ancients thought about civic identity and inter-state relations. To say that the Romans ruled the Syracusans is different from saying that Rome ruled Syracuse, the former expressing a relation in which the Syracusans are expected to obey the Romans, the latter introducing a territorial, geographical dimension not there in the original Latin or Greek.

There is an ambiguity in the modern English word, 'empire', when applied to Rome, which for those coming to Roman history for the first time can be confusing. It is the term used for Rome's domination of other states but it also has a narrower political meaning. The expansion of Roman power over the Mediterranean largely took place when it was ruled by a Republic, that is to say by the institutions of the Senate and popular assemblies. In the first century BC, however, a series of destructive civil wars led to the emergence of what was in effect a monarchy, the rule of the emperor, beginning with the emperor Augustus. Consequently the period from Augustus onwards is known as the Empire, usually capitalised and sometimes divided into sub-sections such the early Empire and the late Empire. Historians, therefore, talk of the transition from Republic to Empire, which is a change in the political structure of the Roman state and independent of the acquisition of the empire that is the subject of this book. Rome had an empire before it had an emperor.

Language is relevant to empire in another way. The ruling power can use its own language to assert itself over its subjects. For example, in the 1830s when the British army began mapping Ireland, itself an exercise in control, Irish placenames were converted into English equivalents, an episode that was the subject of Brian Friel's play *Translations*. Modern scholarship is not immune from such practices. It has been common for writers on ancient history, especially Roman history, to Latinise Greek place names and personal names, thus Ephesos becomes Ephesus in Latin, Isokrates becomes Isocrates. This in part reflects the importance of Latin in the Renaissance but it has the effect of asserting the view of the imperial power, Rome's perspective rather than that of those faced with Rome. In the process they are stripped of one aspect of their Greek identity. The spellings Ephesos and Isokrates, on the other hand, attempt to render the Greek script by transliteration. Consequently in what follows I have preferred to avoid Latinised spelling, except in cases where names are so familiar it would be perverse to change them. In the West, however, the lack of extensive texts in the indigenous languages means that it is the Latin names that are used today.

3. Sources

A selection of source material is collected in the second half of this book, each source prefaced with a short introduction, but it is useful here to review briefly some of the more significant evidence for Roman imperialism, together with its strengths and limitations. The focus will be on the development of the empire; further discussion of evidence for particular themes, such as explanations for Rome's rise to power, the effects of Roman rule on the subject and Roman ideas of empire can be found in Chapters 3, 4 and 5 respectively, especially in their opening sections.

The narrative of Rome's rise to empire, at least until second century BC, largely rests on two historians, Polybios and Livy. In spite of their common subject matter these were two very different historians, writing from very different perspectives. Polybios was a Greek politician, active in the second century BC, who observed the Roman take-over of his homeland and was a participant in some of the events he describes. Livy, on the other hand, was a Roman citizen, born in northern Italy, and writing around the end of the first century BC at a time when Roman rule of the Mediterranean was long established. In interpreting what they wrote, it is important to keep these contrasting backgrounds in mind.

Polybios' history is a remarkable document, the earliest surviving account of Rome and one written from the perspective of an outsider. A work of high quality, it was begun during some fifteen years spent as a political detainee in Rome. His object was to explain to his fellow Greeks how Rome came to bring the whole inhabited world under its sole rule; significantly he believed that this had already happened by the mid-second century BC. Unfortunately, however, although he wrote forty books, only the first five survive complete. These treat events in the third century including the first war with Carthage and the beginning of the second; the remainder which extend to the 140s BC are known through extracts, albeit sometimes quite substantial extracts. Consequently we only get glimpses of how Polybios covered the Roman interventions in the Greek world, the region with which he was most familiar and most involved. The number of selections from Polybios in Part II of this book reflects his importance for understanding early Roman expansion. Not only did he narrate it, he asked fundamental questions about it.

Livy's project, extending to 142 books, was equally ambitious but in some ways more traditional; it was the history of a single city from its foundation to his own day but that city was Rome and so its scope widens as the history progresses. Again much does not survive. Importantly his account of the Roman conquest of Italy in the fourth century BC does survive, although, as he was writing some three centuries or more after the events he was describing, there may have been a certain elaboration in the telling (Cornell 1995: 1–25 considers possible sources). The books that follow, covering much of the third century, are lost, but those treating the second war with Carthage and the first thirty years or so of the second century BC do survive. This is especially important for our knowledge of events in the East because Livy used Polybios as his main source for these. Where their two accounts both survive, it is possible to see how Livy reshapes Polybios, sometimes for literary effect, sometimes to project a more appropriate image of Rome. Livy, therefore, should never be mistaken for Polybios, but his account does help us to situate the surviving extracts of Polybios in their proper place in the narrative. With the conclusion of the forty-fifth book in 167 BC Livy's text also comes to end; of the remaining books we now possess only summaries, which are known as the *Periochae*.

The narrative of Rome's subsequent wars is often supplied by those writing considerably later, prominent among whom are Plutarch, Appian and Dio Cassius, all Greeks working in the period of the Empire in the first to third centuries AD. Among Plutarch's many works were a series of paired biographies of distinguished Greeks and Romans. The Roman biographies included many of the leading figures of the late Republic, notably the Gracchi, Marius, Sulla, Lucullus, Pompey, Cicero, Caesar and Antony. There are also lives of earlier figures such as Flamininus, the elder Cato and Aemilius Paullus which offer useful supplements to Polybios and Livy. More historical in approach is Appian who, rather than providing a unified narrative centred on Rome, treats each theatre of war separately and so offers a history of the development of the Roman empire structured geographically; he is particularly important for wars such as those against Mithridates that are less well-documented. Dio wrote a long history of Rome from its foundation until AD 229, of which the section from 69 BC to AD 46 is largely extant while other parts are known in various excerpted, summarised or fragmented forms. Such historical works offer valuable insights into the way that Rome was perceived by Greeks living in the established empire but they are written in a very different context from the events described; there is a cultural, political and temporal gulf that needs to be borne in mind when reading them. Another important source for the modern historian of the Roman empire is the *Geography* of Strabo, a detailed survey of the known world written at the time of Augustus. It could be argued that what Polybios and his history are to the expansionary Rome of the second century BC Strabo and his geography are to the established empire of the time of Augustus. Polybios wrote universal history to explain how the whole inhabited world came under Roman control, Strabo wrote universal geography to depict the world Rome ruled (cf. Clarke 1999; for the subjects' perspective on Rome, see further Chapter 4, section 1).

The first century BC, however, does give us something that is lacking earlier, genuine contemporary Roman perspectives on empire, stemming not only from historians but also from some of the leading participants in the events of the time. Roman historians such as Livy and to a lesser extent Sallust may have been writing about the past but their way of thinking about empire reflected their present, a world in which Rome had long been the dominant state. Notable among political figures is Marcus Tullius Cicero, whose voluminous writings include his political and court speeches, his philosophical and other essays and his extensive correspondence, especially with his friend Atticus. This variety is particularly valuable because it means that we can see Cicero addressing several different types of audience and speaking with both a public and a private (or at least less public) persona. All these reveal something of the way empire was understood and conceived by a largely non-military member of the Roman elite – he was, for instance, singularly reluctant to take up a role as a provincial governor. On the other hand, C. Iulius Caesar had no such reluctance and in his commentaries on his invasion and subjugation of Gaul offers up for examination the perspective of the military commander himself. Thus, where Polybios and Strabo represent subjects coming to terms with Roman power, Cicero and Caesar represent Roman power itself. The most forceful expression of Roman power and the ideology of empire, however, is surely the voice of the emperor Augustus himself as recorded in the inscription known as the *Res Gestae Divi Augusti* (see **Res Gestae, p. 148**). By this stage it is the emperor himself who is central to the narrative of Rome and as a result the vicissitudes of the imperial family come to dominate histories as much as foreign affairs, though, as a reading of the historian and senator Tacitus shows, war was still an important part of writing history. Moreover, Tacitus takes time to reflect on the nature of the empire, not only in his major historical works, the *Annals* and the *Histories*, but also in his short biography of his late father-in-law Gnaeus Iulius Agricola who was governor of Britain.

Such literary sources might seem to reflect the views of just a small section of the elite, perhaps not even a representative selection, since writers would have been the exception rather than the norm. A different perspective can be offered through the evidence of inscriptions, the study of which is known as epigraphy. These are texts that have been inscribed on a material such as stone or bronze, the former surviving rather better than bronze, which could be easily damaged or melted down. Then as now one of the most common forms of inscription was funerary, but in antiquity inscription was practised far more widely than it is today. Short inscriptions would have included those on tombstones, milestones and the bases of statues, while longer ones included whole public documents, such as civic decrees, treaties and municipal charters. These could be very substantial documents; when the town of Irni in Spain inscribed on bronze their copy of the Flavian law giving them municipal status, it ran to around 1500 lines and filled a space nine metres in width (González 1986). Such documents are important for taking us beyond the constructed narrative of histories such as those of Polybios and Livy. Especially illuminating for our understanding of the expansion of Roman power in the Republic are the many Roman documents that were inscribed by Greek cities; these include decrees of the Roman Senate and letters sent by Roman magistrates to the cities. Texts such as these are valuable contemporary documents which in contrast to histories are composed without the benefit of hindsight so have an immediacy which a historical narrative, often composed much later, will not have. Nonetheless, they must be interpreted closely and not simply taken at face value. Political spin is not the preserve of the modern politician alone. Moreover, the inscriptions should be understood, if possible, in context, that is say in a specific location on a specific physical object.

There are many other forms of material evidence ranging from scattered potsherds to the imperial monuments of Rome. Excavation reveals military camps, villas and towns, so giving an insight into the impact of Rome in war and peace, but it is the activities of the state and the rich which will most readily show up in this way. The poor in less substantial dwellings are more easily missed. Recently survey archaeologists, gathering together surface finds such a potsherds, have been able to build up a broader picture of land use across time in particular regions (cf. Chapter 5, section 4 for the Italian countryside and Alcock 1993 for Greece under Roman rule). Then there are the monuments of Rome itself which sometimes make emphatic statements about empire and Roman military prowess. Those that survive are often from the developed city, such as Trajan's Column with its spiralling relief of the military campaign in Dacia or the Arch of Titus marking victory in Judaea. Numismatics, the study of coins, is another source of illumination. They clearly have economic significance; the fact of their minting would seem to reveal something about state expenditure, perhaps on occasions about the need to pay troops, although this is the subject of some debate (Crawford 1970 v. Howgego 1990). But the design of the coin, which would include an image and a legend (i.e. the written text on the coin), could also be meaningful, reflecting the values and aspirations of the state and its nobility; in the late Republic, for example, coins would often memorialise the achievements and virtues of the ancestors of the moneyers, the annual magistrates responsible for minting the coins (Meadows and Williams 2001).

Generally it is the elite who speak to us and who therefore have a disproportionate influence on the way Rome is viewed. The voice of those outside the elite is much less audible, although papyrus documents from Egypt or tombstones such as those of Roman soldiers can offer one means of recovering their perspective. For the most part, however, they remain anonymous, making little direct comment on the experience of empire, even though many will have made up the armies that fought in wars for or against Rome or worked the land that was devastated by the campaigns or defended cities that were sacked.

CHAPTER 2

From City to Empire

And as president, I will bring back this nation's time-honored tradition: the United States of America never goes to war because we want to; we only go to war because we have to.

John Kerry, defeated US presidential candidate, 2004

1. The conquest of Italy

Regional diversity was the hallmark of the Italian peninsula before the Roman conquest. This fragmented landscape offered a complex mix of cultures, peoples, tribes and cities. Maps of Italy in textbooks often fail to give an adequate impression of the physical geography, leaving the reader unaware of the impact of the Apennine mountain range that runs right down the peninsula dividing West from East (**Map 1**). In Italy was to be found a multitude of languages and dialects. In Latium Latin was spoken, further north in Etruria there was Etruscan, over in the North-West among the Gauls there was Celtic, while Oscan was widespread among the mountain peoples such as the Samnites, Lucanians and Bruttians. The southern coast was populated by Greek cities, such as Naples and Tarentum, and further round the coast visitors to the heel of Italy might have found themselves addressed in some form of Messapic. So dominant was Rome and its culture to become that these languages largely disappeared, at least as languages leaving a written record (Lomas 2009, Clackson and Horrocks 2007: 37–84, Häussler 2002).

Rome was one of the more northerly of the Latin cities. Its close proximity to the Etruscans and its strategic location at a bridging point on the river Tiber gave it a distinctive character that marked it out from the rest of Latium. This separateness was evident early on. Already in the 490s Rome had concluded a treaty on equal terms with a major grouping of Latin cities that we know as the Latin League.

This agreement, a defensive alliance said to have been negotiated on the Roman side by Spurius Cassius, was to govern Rome's relations with the Latin community for well over a hundred years. Fifth-century Roman history is not a little hazy but whatever the details the Romans can be observed at war on two fronts. On the one hand they fought alongside the Latins to defend the region from the incursions of the Aequi and Volsci, mountain tribes from inland, on the other hand they were in frequent conflict with their northern neighbour the Etruscan city of Veii. In comparison with the Roman empire that was to develop, all this was on a very small scale; Veii for instance was a mere ten miles from Rome. But Rome was gradually asserting itself as a significant force in central Italy, notwithstanding the temporary capture of the city by an army of marauding Gauls at the beginning of the fourth century.

Political and military changes in fourth-century Rome seem to have transformed the effectiveness of its army (Potter 2004: 66–73). Rome's growing strength eventually led in 341 to a violent reaction from the cities of the Latin League which in alliance with some non-Latin peoples such as the Campanians fought an unsuccessful three-year war with Rome. Latin resistance was shattered and the settlement of 338 was to shape Rome's relationship with Italy in the centuries that followed (**Livy B, p. 113**; Cornell 1995: 348–52).

Rome now radically restructured its relations with the defeated cities and dealt with each individually, creating in the process a spectrum of statuses. Striking is the way in which the Latin League was dissolved and Latin cities were divided from each other. Some nearby Latin cities, such as Lanuvium and Aricia, were simply incorporated into the Roman state as were some Volscian cities such as Antium. Livy represents this as Roman generosity – they were given Roman citizenship, but the reality was that they ceased to exist as separate independent cities, even if the communities themselves were still allowed an element of self-government as *municipia*. Roman treatment of the remaining Latin cities further undermined any sense of Latin unity, both on a political and on a cultural level. Each was an ally of Rome but they were forbidden political activity with one another. Gone too was the traditional Latin right to marry a citizen of another Latin state or to transact business there. Now these rights could only be exercised with Rome and Roman citizens. The Latins were effectively divided with Rome at the centre.

The most innovative aspect of this settlement was the creation of a new status, that of Roman citizenship without a vote (*civitas sine suffragio*). It was the Volscian and Campanian cities south of Latium that were the 'beneficiaries' of this development. As citizens they became part of the Roman citizen body and shared in the obligations and for the most part the rights of Roman citizenship but they were not allowed to participate politically. Their own communities operated as self-governing *municipia* within the expanding Roman state. In this way Rome could embrace the valuable and prosperous region of Campania while retaining the institutions of a city-state.

The incorporation of other communities into the Roman state and the resulting loss of independence was most likely considered by both parties to be a form of punishment. It asserted Roman power and subjugated one to the other, although it may have been considered relatively lenient; certainly it could be supplemented with more stringent measures such as loss of territory (**cf. Livy B, p. 113**). Nonetheless Rome's approach was very unusual in antiquity. Citizenship was often considered to be something closely guarded and not to be shared with others unless they had earned it. But Rome is here using citizenship as means of extending its power; it is absorbing its enemies. Citizenship thus loses its parochial and ethnic dimension. By the first century BC Roman citizenship was the common property of all Italians, a phenomenon that would have been incomprehensible to a Greek of the fifth century BC. Whatever the initial motivation many developed a loyalty to both Rome and their hometown, what Cicero would describe as their two *patriae* (fatherlands), one by birth and one by citizenship (Cic. *Leg.* 2.5; Ando 2000: 57–60). This Roman willingness to accept others was echoed in their mythology; the Rome of Romulus takes in the dispossessed of Italy. It was observed too by Rome's rivals; Philip V of Macedon in a letter which is one of the earliest surviving references to Rome seeks to encourage the Thessalian city of Larisa to copy the Romans and adopt a more open attitude to citizenship (**Inscription A, p. 104**).

The settlement of 338 helped establish the structures that enabled Roman control of Italy to spread. There are communities with full Roman citizenship, those with partial citizenship, Latin allies, and in addition to these there are other Italian allies and an increasing number of colonies, made up of Roman or allied citizens. It is in part this variety that prevents the creation of a unified opposition to Rome – one can note the failure of first Pyrrhos and later Hannibal to win over enough of Italy to undermine Rome. Instead of a sharp polarisation between Rome and Italian subjects there was a spectrum, subtle gradations that mark out difference but leave it unclear who is better off.

All these various groups had one thing in common, however, which was essential to the Roman imperial enterprise. They all had an obligation to provide troops when required, giving Rome a large and increasing pool of military manpower to draw on. Indeed in the case of the allies it was their only real obligation; in contrast to the allies in the Athenian empire Rome's allies paid no tribute. This had important consequences. First, if Rome was to benefit from these alliances, it had to demand that the allied states supply the Roman army with troops. Secondly, this demand had to be made year after year in order to re-affirm Rome's position as the leading state. In this way, the structure of Rome's relations with its allies did much to encourage continuous warfare and gave the impetus to further expansion. More wars brought more allies which in turn increased the available manpower. The allies may have joined Rome as a result of military defeat or weakness or expediency, but once they were part of the Roman alliance they too could benefit, sharing in the spoils of war, both moveable booty and land confiscated from the defeated. Thus the old victims in partnership with the Romans would divide up the possessions and territory of the new victims and so it would go on (Cornell 1995: 364–8; Momigliano 1975: 44–6).

The success against the Latins in 338 was followed by a series of wars against other Italian peoples, most importantly the power-ful Samnites, a tribal people who occupied the central southern Apennines. Provoked when the Romans founded a colony at Fregellae on the edge of Samnite territory in 328, this long and brutal war finally brought the Romans victory in 304, but only after they had endured the humiliating surrender of their army at the Caudine Forks in 321. The start of the third century saw renewed fighting against the Samnites who now joined forces with Etruscans, Umbrians and Gauls, an alli-ance that may signal Italian desperation when faced with continuing Roman pressure. Defeat for the Samnites and the Gauls at the battle of Sentinum in Umbria in 295 ended any hopes the coalition may have had and left Rome with little significant opposition in the Italian peninsula.

Even as these wars were being fought Rome was putting in place the infrastructure of power. Colonies were founded at strategic locations, such as Alba Fucens in the central Apennines (303 BC), Narnia in Umbria (299) and Hadria over towards the Adriatic coast (289). More colonies would follow, Ariminum (268) and Firmum (264), both of which strengthened Roman control on the far side of the Apennines and looked onto the Adriatic Sea. Roads too were constructed: the Via

Appia, begun in 312 and heading down to Capua in Campania, the
Via Valeria, begun in 307 and crossing the Apennines. Roads such as
these were more than a means of communication and military transport, they were also symbols of power; with their rigorous straight-
ness they demonstrated Roman control even over the landscape and
would come to be a distinctive feature of Rome's empire (Purcell 1990;
Mitchell 1999; **Milestones, esp. C, p. 119**).

The final stage of Rome's conquest of Italy came not with a war
against an Italian power but against a king from the Greek mainland.
The Samnite wars brought Rome into contact with the Greeks of
South Italy or Magna Graecia as it is often known. Here Tarentum,
the leading Greek city in the region, fearing that Rome was eroding its
influence among its Greek neighbours, called upon Pyrrhos of Epiros
to assist them against this new threat. This was Rome's first encounter
with the highly-trained armies of the Hellenistic East and with the
elephants that were so regularly a part of its warfare. Pyrrhos inflicted
two defeats on the Romans, in 280 and 279, but so heavy were his
losses that he was unable to follow up his victories (Plut. *Pyrrh.* 21).
Roman military resources and Roman resolution, on the other hand,
seemed almost undented. Side-tracked into fighting the Carthaginians
in Sicily, Pyrrhos finally abandoned the West and returned to Greece in
275, leaving South Italy to its fate. Tarentum, captured by the Romans
in 272, became a somewhat involuntary Roman ally and was forced to
accept a Roman garrison (Eckstein 2006: 157).

2. The battle for the western Mediterranean

Carthage in North Africa was a powerful trading city, founded in the
eighth century BC by the Phoenician city of Tyre, and one of the most
successful of many colonies sent out from that Lebanese homeland. In
the early third century, with its influence stretching from Sicily to the
Straits of Gibraltar (the Pillars of Hercules in antiquity), it dominated
the western Mediterranean basin. Strategically located between the
two halves of the Mediterranean and also in possession of western
Sicily, it controlled the main sea routes between East and West (**Map
2**). Sicily was crucial to Carthaginian power in the region, hence the
repeated wars between the Carthaginians and the various inhabitants
of the island, both Greek and native, as Carthage sought to maintain or
extend its hold.

The Carthaginians, or *Poeni* in Latin, had long had links with central
Italy. Indeed the Greek historian Polybios records a series of treaties

between Rome and Carthage dating back to the late sixth century which indicate amicable relations between the two cities. Even in the early 270s at the time of the war with Pyrrhos they are to be found making an agreement, Rome concerned to withstand Pyrrhos in Italy, Carthage to defend its interests against him in Sicily (Polyb. 3.22–6). Before the next decade was over, however, Rome and Carthage would be at war. When Rome's priority was the Italian mainland and Carthage's was the sea, the two could co-exist, but with the departure of Pyrrhos and the acquisition of southern Italy Rome began to look to Sicily, prompting a rapid deterioration in relations. Rome and Carthage would spend some forty years of what remained of the century fighting each other in two major wars, the First and Second Punic Wars. Victory would make the western Mediterranean Roman.

The catalyst for the war was the Greek city of Messene, strategically located on the Sicilian side of the straits that separated the island from the Italian mainland, attractive to any state who wished to control the straits or access to the island. It was in the possession of a group of Campanian mercenaries known as the Mamertines, who had seized it some years previously. Around 264 under pressure from Syracuse, the leading Greek city in Sicily, these mercenaries appealed for help to both Carthage and Rome. Both obliged. The Carthaginians already had a garrison in place when the Romans under Appius Claudius arrived, but withdrew it under circumstances that are obscure to us and also perhaps to the Carthaginians who ordered their ineffective commander to be crucified. The Romans had for the first time crossed the sea under arms and now had troops in a key Sicilian town. It is an indication of Syracusan and Carthaginian alarm that these two old enemies allied with each other, albeit briefly, against the intruder.

With this war the historical record improves somewhat, not least because this is where Polybios begins his history. Importantly he reports something of the debate in Rome about whether or not the Mamertine appeal should be accepted (**Polybios B, p. 130**). Two main reasons for accepting the appeal are put forward: first, that if Rome did not act, the Carthaginians would take Messene and then the whole of Sicily, posing a threat to Italy; secondly, that the war would be profitable. The Senate, we are told, was reluctant to go to war, not because of any doubt about the Carthaginian threat but because it would not look right to help those who had treacherously seized control of a city, especially as they themselves had recently executed a Roman garrison at nearby Rhegion for the very same offence. The lure of plunder, however, was enough to convince the people to vote for war. Some have suggested that Polybios may, with hindsight, have overstated Roman concerns about Carthage and their initial objective may have been to curb Syracuse, a city with a long history of involvement with the Greeks of South Italy. If that was a motive, however, they soon shifted their attention in the direction of Carthage. Polybios' account is often thought to derive from the history of the Roman senator Fabius Pictor whom he certainly used for his narrative of the First Punic War, but he also used the pro-Carthaginian Greek historian Philinos. The curious amalgam of justification (the Carthaginians are a threat) with suggestions of greed, opportunism and inconsistency may derive from a mix of sources combined with Polybios' own take on them.

Several of the themes of this passage turn out to be recurring features in the narrative of Roman expansion. Again and again Rome acts because there is an appeal for help, a response on its part that legitimates intervention in regions where it has had no previous presence and that could be interpreted by the existing regional powers as a challenge. Secondly, Rome is represented here and elsewhere as anxious about threats to its own or its allies' security; this appears to be not so much an explanation of Roman action as a justification and one which is perhaps too convenient. Thirdly, their reservations about helping the Mamertines reflect a preoccupation with public image, a preoccupation that may lie behind the two features already noted. Finally, plunder is clearly voiced as an important objective; here is a reason for war which is credible and which is unlikely to have been publicised among the international community, but which occurs repeatedly in accounts of the Romans (Harris 1979: 58–63, 102–4). The gulf between senatorial concern with threatening neighbours and the People's aggressive desire for booty neatly encapsulates the split personality that has bedevilled discussion of Roman imperialism (see further Chapter 3)

A Roman siege of Syracuse rapidly split the fragile Syracusan–Carthaginian alliance, allowing the Romans to concentrate their efforts against the Carthaginians with the Syracusan ruler Hiero II as their ally. With this began a long and costly war that was to last until 241 and for the most part revolve around Sicily, causing enormous damage to the cities and inhabitants of the island. The war demonstrated Rome's capacity to innovate. To fight on an island against a major sea power such as Carthage they needed to take to the sea themselves. With little apparent experience of naval warfare they not only built and manned a fleet, they also defeated the Carthaginians in several naval battles, gaining command of the sea (though their naval inexperience may

have been exaggerated: Steinby 2007). Roman pride in this achievement is evident in the inscription that marked the triumphal celebration of C. Duilius, consul of 260 and the first Roman to be victorious
at sea (*ILS* 65, trans. in Dillon and Garland 2005: 4.10). In this new
venture their enemy was not so much the Carthaginians as their own
inexperience; several fleets were virtually destroyed in storms with tremendous loss of ships and men. As with the war against Pyrrhos it was
the resources of the Italian allies that gave Rome the ability to absorb
such huge losses. Control of the sea allowed the Romans to make an
attempt on North Africa itself; the invasion led by M. Atilius Regulus
ultimately failed but this first campaign in Africa was a measure not
only of Roman daring but also of their ambition.

After a final naval defeat in 241 off the Aegates Islands to the west
of Sicily the almost bankrupt Carthaginians sued for peace. The
Romans demanded that the Carthaginians abandon Sicily and pay an
indemnity of 3,200 talents, a substantial sum, over a ten-year period.
Such indemnities by instalments had the effect of emphasising the
subordination of the defeated. At what point Sicily can be considered
a Roman province is debatable but whatever its status it was now
effectively subject to Rome (Serrati 2000). Carthage was left to regain
some control over its remaining territories, a situation not helped
by the revolt of its unpaid mercenaries. A few years later Rome took
advantage of Carthaginian weakness and with the threat of renewed
war it demanded that Carthage give up the island of Sardinia and pay
an additional 1,200 talents, an act that Polybios described as 'contrary
to all justice' (Polyb. 2.28).

War between Rome and Carthage would recommence in 218,
stirred up in part, Polybios argued, by Carthaginian resentment at
their defeat and in particular at the unjustified seizure of Sardinia. In
the intervening years both states were active. Roman troops were busy
fighting in Sardinia in the 230s, across the Adriatic against the Illyrians
in 229–228 (see next section), and against the Gauls of northern Italy
for much of the 220s. Roman victories in the north were consolidated
by the establishment of the colonies of Cremona and Placentia in the
Po Valley and the building of the great highway, the Via Flaminia,
which led from Rome over the Apennines to Ariminum (Rimini) on
the Adriatic coast.

Carthage, meanwhile, was energetically expanding its possessions
in Spain, first under its general Hamilcar Barca, then his son-in-law
Hasdrubal and finally Hamilcar's son Hannibal who took over the
Carthaginian forces there in 221. Carthaginian success in Spain did not

go unnoticed at Rome. According to Dio Cassius, in a report accepted
by some scholars and rejected by others, in 231 a Roman embassy went
to investigate Hamilcar's activities; he responded that he was fighting to pay off Carthaginian debts to the Romans (Dio Cassius 12 frag.
48). In the mid-twenties Roman concern about growing Carthaginian
power in Spain might even have led them to go to war with Hasdrubal
had they not been otherwise occupied with the Gauls, or so at least
Polybios implies. Instead they concluded a treaty with Hasdrubal that
the Carthaginians could not lead armed forces across the Ebro, a river
in north-east Spain (Polyb. 2.13). At some point the Romans made an
agreement, perhaps even an alliance, with the city of Saguntum on the
coast south of the Ebro, a move that could only have been construed as
provocative by the Carthaginians regardless of whether the Ebro treaty
had yet been drawn up.

Polybios covered the origins of the Second Punic War in some
detail but questions still multiply: at what date did Rome become
interested in Carthage's Spanish campaigns? What was the significance of the Ebro treaty? What was the nature of Rome's relationship
with Saguntum? When did it begin? None of these admits of a clear
answer (scholarly disagreement is reviewed in Richardson 1986: 20–30,
Scullard 1989a: 21–31). Nevertheless within the wider frame of Roman
expansion a pattern can be seen. Just as the Mamertines had provided
the opportunity for Roman intervention in Sicily, so it was an appeal
from Saguntum that opened the way for a new war with Carthage, an
appeal that may well have been anticipated when the agreement was
made. Saguntum fell to Hannibal before any Roman help arrived. The
response of the Romans was typical; they made a demand that no independent state could accept – Carthage should hand over Hannibal or
face war. Intending to take the war to the enemy, they assigned Spain
to one consul and Africa to the other; such a military assignment was
known as a '*provincia*', a term which would eventually come to signify
a unit of the empire. Before this plan could be acted upon, Hannibal
had outmanoeuvred them with a rapid march northwards and a daring
crossing of the Alps to descend into northern Italy, forcing Rome to
abandon its African invasion. The war is relatively well-documented;
the Roman historian Livy's highly readable and patriotic narrative survives intact, as do the early books of Polybios' more analytical account
which cover the years up to the battle of Cannae (Livy, books 21–30;
Polyb. books 2–5).

Hannibal's campaign ended in failure in spite of a series of outstanding victories that caused panic in Rome: Trebia (218), Trasimene

(217) and most memorably Cannae (216). His assault on Italy relied on speed and surprise, and its objective was to cause revolts among Rome's Italian allies, hence his favourable treatment of allied prisoners. The recently conquered Gauls did come over to his side and so too did much of the South but crucially central Italy stayed loyal, just as it had in the time of Pyrrhos. With the Carthaginians failing to gain control of the sea and the Romans increasingly successful in Spain, Hannibal's campaign lost momentum. Finally, after some fifteen years in Italy, he was forced to return to Africa to face the Roman general P. Scipio Africanus at Zama in 202. Rome did not destroy Carthage but the terms were harsh. Carthage was to relinquish its empire, give up its elephants and most of its fleet, pay an indemnity of 10,000 talents over fifty years and was prohibited from making war outside Africa and only with Rome's permission within Africa. Carthage was effectively a Roman subject. A little more than fifty years later there would be a last and one-sided war that would end in the sack of the city of Carthage; the reasons for this are as controversial now as they were then (Harris 1989: 234–40; **Polybios N, p. 146**).

The victory at Zama transformed Rome from an Italian power to a Mediterranean power, whose authority now extended well beyond the Italian peninsula to include Spain, Sicily and Sardinia. It is conventionally said that these regions were organised into provinces: Sicily (excluding Syracusan territory) and Sardinia already in 227, and Spain as two provinces in 197 (largely limited to the coastal areas of the South and South-East). Certainly the Roman empire came to be composed of regional units known as 'provinces' (*provinciae*), each under the command of a Roman governor, but the process may have been considerably more gradual and haphazard than this simple formulation implies. In the early second century the Romans were no doubt still developing ways of ruling their overseas subjects. In Spain, Sicily and Sardinia the tribes and cities acknowledged Roman power in the person of the governor and paid tribute but apart from that they ran their own affairs. The repeated wars fought by the Romans in second-century Spain, notably against the Lusitanians and Celtiberians, may suggest that *provinciae* in Spain at least still lay in the grey area between the early sense of the term as 'military assignment' and its later one as 'unit of empire'. To talk of 'provinces' in the way that we use the term of the developed empire may be anachronistic and thus import connotations that are not appropriate to Roman power at this early stage of its overseas expansion (cf. Richardson 1986: 4–10, 2008: 10–62; Kallet-Marx 1995: 18–29).

3. The Greek East

Since Alexander the Great's conquest of the Persian empire in the fourth century BC the eastern Mediterranean had been a Graeco-Macedonian domain. His successors had divided his empire up among themselves, giving rise to three main dynasties: the Antigonids in Macedon, the Ptolemies in Egypt and the Seleucids in Asia. These were supplemented later in the third century by the Attalids, an upstart dynasty based at Pergamon in Asia Minor. The royal courts and newly-founded cities were centres of Greek culture and language in this Hellenistic world. Alexandria in Egypt rapidly became the largest and most prosperous Greek city in the Mediterranean, the royal library of which housed the greatest collection of Greek books. The campaigns of Pyrrhos in Italy brought this world to the notice of Rome, and his failure made its kings aware of Rome. It is no coincidence that the first recorded diplomatic contact between a Hellenistic king and Rome occurs a couple of years after Pyrrhos abandons Italy; in 273 Ptolemy II sends an embassy to Rome and Rome in turn sends one to Egypt. To what extent the resulting friendship (*amicitia*) shaped Roman attitudes to the East must be a matter for speculation (Gruen 1984: 673–719, who plays down its long-term significance).

Rome's first substantial involvement with the Greeks across the Adriatic Sea occurs as a result of the Illyrian War of 229–228 BC. Two Roman consuls with a sizeable force of men and ships led a swift and decisive campaign against the Illyrian tribes who occupied the eastern coast of the Adriatic. In the previous decade under the leadership of Agron and, after his death, of his widow Teuta the Illyrians had been growing in power both on land and sea and increasingly coming into conflict with Greeks further south. Explanations for this unprecedented Roman intervention across the Adriatic are varied and have tended to focus on the immediate. Sources report a request from Italian traders for help against Illyrian pirates (Polyb. 2.8), an appeal from the Greek island-city of Issa in the face of an Illyrian siege (Appian, *Illyrian Wars* 7), and in both cases the subsequent murder of a Roman ambassador. Again we see the Romans drawn in by the appeals of others. Recently a new and persuasive interpretation has placed the war in the context of Roman activities on the Adriatic coast of Italy during the previous sixty or so years (Derow 2003: 51–4). As Rome consolidated its position in the Italian peninsula, so it established colonies on the far side of the Apennines from Ariminum in the North in 268 to Brundisium (Brindisi) on the heel of Italy in 244; the purpose may have been to secure its territories but the effect was to create an Adriatic coast, and by extension Adriatic Sea, that was increasingly Roman. Roman warfare in the Po valley in the 230s only made it more so. Victory against the Illyrians brought the Romans increased power in the Adriatic and in consequence strengthened their control over the eastern side of the Italian peninsula.

The significance of these events was observed by Polybios (2.2). Not only had Rome for the first time crossed the Adriatic with military forces but the war had allowed it to establish political relations with Greek cities along the western coast of the Balkans. The nature of these relationships is controversial; were there formal alliances (Derow 1991) or are we looking at something looser (Eckstein 1999)? Whatever form these relationships took Roman power was now recognised around the whole coast of the Adriatic. The war, however, had repercussions beyond the Adriatic. The expansion of Illyrian power had been viewed with considerable apprehension among the Greeks, and, conscious of its image, Rome now presented itself as a benefactor of the Greeks, ridding them of the northern menace. Embassies were sent to the major federations of mainland Greece, the Aitolian and Achaian Leagues, and to the cities of Athens and Corinth to make the Roman case. In Corinth the Romans were even given the honour of admittance to the Isthmian games (Polyb. 2.12).

No embassy, however, was sent to the leading power in Greece, the Macedonian king, an omission which can hardly have been an oversight and one that may suggest that in their choice of embassies the Romans were looking to the future. The Macedonians were likely to have viewed Roman activity in the western Balkans as an incursion into their sphere of influence, a view that would not have been dispelled by a second Roman expedition in 219 to overthrow another Illyrian dynast, Demetrios of Pharos, who subsequently took refuge at the Macedonian court. Some scholars, borrowing the language of nineteenth-century European imperial powers, have termed the Roman relationship with the region 'a Protectorate' (Badian 1958: 55–83; Scullard 1980: 193), but for the Macedonian king the Roman role was less benign. It was in part Roman interference in the area that prompted Philip V of Macedon to make an alliance with Hannibal after the battle of Cannae, setting in motion a series of wars between Rome and Macedon. The text of the treaty reveals Macedonian concerns and a rather different interpretation of Rome's involvement with the region: it laid down that the Romans should no longer be 'the masters of Corcyra, Apollonia, Epidamnos, Pharos, Dimale, Parthini or

Atintania', essentially the east coast of the Adriatic (Polyb. 7.9.13; contrast this with Livy 23.33's very Roman interpretation). Unfortunately, 216 BC and the battle of Cannae mark the point where Polybios' history breaks off and from here on we must rely on fragments of his history, often substantial but fragments nonetheless. Instead it is Livy who provides the narrative for Rome's conquest of the eastern Mediterranean, much of it based on his reading of Polybios but more Romanocentric in its approach.

The alliance, made in 215, led to an intermittent war between Philip and Rome, known in modern scholarship as the First Macedonian War, but Rome, preoccupied with the Carthaginians in Italy and Spain, did not have the resources to commit substantial forces to any new war zones. In 211, however, the Romans found an ally on the Greek mainland to do much of the fighting for them, the delay perhaps less a result of Roman indifference than of Greek reluctance to ally with a loser (as Rome seemed after Cannae). The ally was the Aitolian League, recipient of an earlier Roman embassy and regular enemy of Macedon. A summary of the alliance is given by Livy and part of the original text survives as an inscription on stone; the emphasis on plunder may reflect both Aitolian and Roman priorities (**Livy C, p. 114; Inscription B, p. 105**). Rome here tapped into longstanding Greek friendships and conflicts. Sparta, Messenia and importantly Attalos I of Pergamon aligned themselves with Aitolia and thus Rome, influenced more by local concerns than the wider world of Mediterranean politics. In 206 the Aitolians, frustrated at lack of support from Rome, negotiated a separate peace with Philip; the Romans, concerned to concentrate their efforts on the final defeat of Carthage, made peace at Phoinike a year later. Neither side may have won or lost much but Rome was now well-immersed in Greek affairs with friends as far as Asia Minor; Livy writes ominously that the Romans 'wanted for the present to be relieved of all other wars' (29.11). The war may have begun and ended in a rather desultory and half-hearted way but at its height it was marked by a brutality and viciousness rarely seen in Greek warfare, or that at least is how it is represented in a speech seeking to persuade the Aitolians to make peace (**Polybios H, p. 136**; cf. Polyb. 9.39.1–5).

In 201 the Romans made peace with Carthage; the following year they were at war with Macedon again. The Second Macedonian War has inspired vigorous and prolonged debate among ancient historians. What was it that prompted the Romans to begin a further war so soon after the long and gruelling struggle against Hannibal? Self-defence, fear, militaristic aggression, philhellenism and pride have all been suggested (the debate is reviewed by Gruen 1984: 382–98). The most influential contribution has been that of Maurice Holleaux, who argued that prior to the Second Macedonian War Rome had no real interest in the East. Once such a political about-turn has been posited an explanation is required and finding it has continued to exercise scholars ever since. Holleaux himself found it in an anti-Ptolemaic pact between Philip V and the Seleucid king Antiochos the Great, which he believed so alarmed the Romans that they took action against Philip before this coalition could grow too dangerous (Holleaux 1921, revived by Eckstein 2008: 121–80). It can, however, be doubted that this new war against Macedon reflected any change in Roman policy. It may be preferable to see it as a continuation of the First. Maybe the Romans wished to demonstrate to the Mediterranean world that no one makes an alliance against Rome with impunity. The opportunity was provided by the Greeks themselves. Philip, perhaps to avoid conflict with Rome, was focusing his military activity on the Aegean Sea, much to the dismay of Attalos of Pergamon and the Rhodians, who responded by appealing to Rome for assistance. Rome's attitude to Philip was clear from the beginning. It issued an ultimatum to Philip through his general Nikanor; either he refrained from making war on the Greeks and gave compensation to Attalos or he would be at war with Rome. To agree to what was in effect a Roman order would be to acknowledge Roman dominion, and Philip could not do that. Rome had staked its claim to a central place in Greek politics (Polyb. 16.25–7, 34; Derow 2003: 59). The war would be short in comparison with the wars against Carthage. In 197 Philip was defeated at Kynoskephalai in Thessaly and agreed to discuss peace terms; he was to become an ally of Rome, pay an indemnity of 1,000 talents, and withdraw from Greek cities he held both in Greece and Asia Minor. The settlement was relatively generous, a sign perhaps that Rome was thinking ahead to another eastern conflict.

Rome entered the war on behalf of the Greeks, a posture it maintained until its end. In early summer 196 at the Isthmian games, as the Aitolians in particular were beginning to question Roman motives and intentions, the Roman commander T. Quinctius Flamininus made a dramatic announcement to the Greeks assembled there. The Greeks were to be free. Those places previously subject to Philip would be left free, without garrisons, subject to no tribute and governed by their ancestral laws; importantly this meant that Rome would be evacuating the so-called 'fetters of Greece': Chalkis in Euboia, Demetrias in Thessaly and the Acrocorinth in the Peloponnese, where

Philip had kept his key garrisons. The Greek response was rapturous and Flamininus received honours throughout Greece (**Polybios J, p. 141; Plutarch A, p. 125; Inscription D, p. 106**). More than this Rome extended its role as defender of Greek freedom to Asia where Antiochos was steadily building up territory – or, as he preferred to say, reclaiming the kingdom of his ancestors. The scene was set for future conflict. As a political slogan 'The Freedom of the Greeks' had a long history of use among the kings of the Hellenistic world and here Rome is making it its own (Gruen 1984: 132–57; Dmitriev, forthcoming). That Rome was prepared to withdraw its garrisons probably impressed the Greeks (although it would be two years before they actually did so). It must, however, be remembered that Rome had already developed a complex system of rule in Italy and knew that it was possible to exert power even without garrisons.

By bestowing freedom Rome was setting itself up as the arbiter of the Greek world. This was freedom on Roman terms. There may have been no tribute or garrisons but governments would appear to have been those approved by Rome; thus Flamininus' liberation of Thessaly is followed by his reorganisation of the region, making it fit for freedom (**Livy D, p. 116**; cf. Livy 34.48, Briscoe 1967).

Even as the settlement with Philip was being negotiated, cities in Asia Minor were responding to Rome's new and self-assigned role as defender of the Greeks. Lampsakos and Smyrna, alarmed at Antiochos' growing power in the region, sought Roman protection. An important contemporary inscription records an embassy from Lampsakos (*SIG*^{3} 591, trans. in Bagnall and Derow 2004: no. 35), while Smyrna's concerns lay behind the establishment of a cult of the goddess Roma in 195 (**Tacitus A, p. 153**, see Chapter 4, section 3 below). By 191 Rome and Antiochos were at war. The first battle took place in mainland Greece, after Antiochos had crossed the Aegean to accept the city of Demetrias from the Aitolians, the last at Magnesia two years later, after the Scipio brothers had pursued Antiochos into Asia Minor. The war has been variously explained: Badian's 'Cold War' posturing expressed the fears of the 1950s (Badian 1959), Gruen saw reluctant superpowers drawn in by the intrigues of Greek states (1984: 456–80), Derow emphasised the pressure of continued Roman demands upon Antiochos (2003: 64–5), while Eckstein has interpreted it as a hegemonic war that brings to end what he sees as a 'power-transition crisis' that was set in motion by the weakening of the Ptolemaic kingdom almost two decades earlier (2008: 306–41). After a swift war the Roman settlement, agreed at Apamea, was severe; Antiochos had to pay 15,000 talents, well beyond the 10,000 paid by Carthage for their long war, and give up most of Asia Minor. Rome now reorganised Asia Minor and rewarded Pergamon and Rhodes, its chief allies in the region, with former Seleucid territories.

The defeat of these two powerful and wealthy kingdoms within the space of a few years dramatically transformed the politics of the eastern Mediterranean. Striking is the speed of their collapse, which contrasts sharply with the length of the wars against Carthage. Reasons can be proffered: the superiority of the Roman legion over the Macedonian phalanx (cf. **Polybios I, p. 137**), the greater effectiveness of the citizen soldier over the mercenary, the resilience of the city-state against the personal monarchy. The kingdoms survived (and maybe that was what was important) but in diminished form. Rome may have withdrawn its forces but by receiving embassies from the East and sending out investigating commissions it stayed aware of, and no doubt influenced, developments. When Philip's son and successor, Perseus, attempted to revive Macedon's fortunes, Rome intervened and after a short war defeated the king at Pydna in 168. Perseus was led as a captive in a triumphal procession through Rome and the kingdom of Macedon was terminated. In its place Rome created four separate, tribute-paying republics.

The disappearance of Macedon marked a change in Rome's treatment of Greece. There were no great claims of liberation this time. Instead there was an assertion of power on a massive scale; 150,000 were said to have been enslaved during the plundering of Epiros, a large number of the elite were massacred in Aitolia, 1,000 Achaians of questionable loyalty, including Polybios, were deported to Italy, pro-Roman governments were supported throughout Greece. The figures might be doubted but the impact is clear. Symbolic of this transformation is a monument that stood at Delphi. Near the temple of Apollo there was a marble pillar which was intended to support a statue of Perseus but when the Roman commander L. Aemilius Paullus saw it he ordered that it should be completed with his own statue; Roman dominance was further emphasised by the use of Latin on the statue base (**Plutarch B with Figs 5 and 6, p. 125**). Elsewhere in the East Rome expected to be obeyed. Steps were taken to reduce the power of its allies, Pergamon and Rhodes; in Egypt a single and abrupt instruction from the Roman legate, C. Popillius Laenas, was sufficient to force Antiochos IV to abandon his invasion of Ptolemaic territory. Polybios had begun his history asking 'how and by what sort of government in less than fifty-three years almost the whole inhabited world was subjugated and brought under the sole rule of Rome' (1.1.5). With the great kingdoms of Polybios' world either gone or acknowledging Roman authority it is no wonder that the historian dated the end of the fifty-three years to the fall of the Macedonian kingdom.

Evidence for Roman activity in the East now becomes much sketchier; Livy's surviving narrative runs out and Polybios' history is fragmentary. Only with the 140s and signs of resistance to Roman power does our information improve. In Macedon Andriskos, a pretender to the throne, inflicted a shock defeat on a Roman army before being defeated himself. In the Peloponnese Roman attempts to weaken the Achaian League led to war, the dismantling of the League and the sack of Corinth. The destruction of two great cities, Corinth and Carthage, in the same year was a forceful and vivid re-assertion of Roman authority in the Mediterranean, notwithstanding the likelihood that our sources have overstated the extent of the destruction (cf. Gebhard and Dickie 2003 on Corinth; for the Greek reaction, **Polybios N, p. 146**). The year 146 is thus often interpreted as a turning point, for the Greeks the end of their freedom (cf. Scullard 1980, Derow 1989). Macedon is usually understood to have become a Roman province at this point, signifying a more formal relationship between Rome and the Balkans, although it has also been suggested that the stationing of a commander in Macedon was aimed at defending the frontiers against Thracians rather than part of any regional reorganisation (Kallet-Marx 1995: 11–41).

Roman dominion in the East was further consolidated when in 133 Attalos III of Pergamon died leaving his kingdom to Rome in his will; since the terms of the will were no doubt publicized in advance, this act was probably more a precaution against assassination than one of eccentric benevolence. Rome could have used the occasion as an opportunity for the reorganisation of Asia Minor as it had done after the defeat of Antiochos the Great almost fifty years previously. In a sign of a changing approach, however, Rome becomes a more permanent presence and, after suppressing a claimant to the throne, takes control of this wealthy kingdom. There is, nonetheless, considerable modern disagreement over the speed and manner in which this occurred. While some believe that Rome turned the former Attalid territories into the Roman province of Asia fairly quickly (e.g. Harris 1979: 147–9), others stress the slow evolution of the Roman province (e.g. Kallet-Marx 1995: 97–122). The creation of a province may well not have been a single act but it should be noticed that it soon had a very real existence, visible to the native population. In both Macedon and Asia the Romans followed up with the infrastructure of control. The Via Egnatia which stretched from the Adriatic through Macedon and along the northern shore of the Aegean was very likely already under construction in the 130s, while the 120s saw extensive road-building in Asia Minor. In both cases Roman milestones, inscribed in Latin with Greek subtitles, acted as markers not only of distance but also of Roman power (Mitchell 1999; **Milestone A, p. 119**).

It would be a mistake to imagine that in the second century BC Rome's attention was directed solely towards the Greek East. The conflicts there are certainly the best documented, illuminated by the work of a contemporary observer, Polybios, and by epigraphic finds from numerous Greek cities, but the Roman legions were in action throughout the Mediterranean. A particular concern was the north of Italy where there was regular fighting against the Gauls and Ligurians, lasting until the late 170s and continuing sporadically afterwards. Roman control of the region was ruthlessly established with the imposition of colonies and the forced transfer of the native population to the south of Italy; figures suggest that around 50,000 were moved in this way (Harris 1989: 106–18). Spain, too, was the scene of frequent warfare for much of the century as the Romans encountered considerable resistance to any consolidation or extension of their rule; especially effective was the Lusitanian leader Viriathus in the 140s, who inflicted a number of defeats on Roman forces. Several wars were also fought here against the Celtiberians, culminating in 133 in the eight-month siege of the fortified town of Numantia and its subsequent destruction; the intensity of the siege is apparent from the network of camps and siegeworks that have been revealed by excavation (Richardson 1986 on Spanish wars; Dobson 2008 on Numantia). The Roman victory over Carthage in the 146 may have led to the small Roman province of Africa but it did not bring an end to conflict there. The closing years of the century would see prolonged campaigning by several Roman generals against the Numidian ruler Jugurtha, events recounted in Sallust's *Jugurthine War*.

4. Late Republic and Early Empire

By the end of the second century BC, therefore, Roman authority extended around the whole Mediterranean. It did not take the same form everywhere. In Italy there was an elaborate mix of colonies, alliances and classes of citizenship. Elsewhere direct rule was exercised through an emerging provincial system, as in Spain, Sicily, Asia and Africa. In other regions cities and kings acknowledged Roman power and for the most part obeyed Roman orders. Rome was the most powerful state in the Mediterranean but we should be careful not to exaggerate this; the conquest of Spain, for instance, was not complete until Augustus' victory over the Cantabrians in the wars of 26–19 BC.

The first century BC would see this whole complex structure severely shaken. Discontent among the Italian allies (*socii*) became so intense that in 91 many rebelled against Rome in what is known as the Social War. In one sense this was a civil war, a war between two parts of the highly-trained Roman army, and its impact would be far-reaching. So serious was the situation that it could only be brought under control by making concessions: citizenship was granted to all south of the Po. Where once taking Roman citizenship might have involved sacrificing independence and local identity, now it was preferable to subjection, an indication of how Rome's relationship with the rest of Italy had changed. The crisis, however, did not end here, it just changed its form. In 89 Mithridates VI of Pontos, a kingdom on the Black Sea, apparently provoked by Roman commanders in the region, took advantage of Rome's Italian difficulties to invade the Roman province of Asia and then mainland Greece itself. The invasion led to a widespread Greek uprising. Tens of thousands of Romans and Italians in Asia were said to have been massacred by the Greek inhabitants of the province, 'as much out of hatred of the Romans as fear of Mithridates' according to the Greek historian Appian (**Appian A, p. 91**). Mithridates was temporarily curbed by Sulla and finally defeated by Pompey over twenty years later. In the meantime the Roman elite had begun their late Republican pastime of civil war, which was to affect the empire from Spain to Syria. This combination of factors put Rome's *imperium* in Italy and beyond more at risk than at any time since Hannibal.

In his settlement at the conclusion of the Mithridatic Wars Pompey radically overhauled the shape of Roman power in the East; new provinces were created, kingdoms remodelled and in the case of the Seleucids deemed redundant. Shortly afterwards, the consul of 59, C. Iulius Caesar, embarked on a major expansionary campaign in Gaul, detailed and justified with care in his Gallic commentaries, a unique insight into a Roman commander's thinking. By the end of the decade he would have crossed the Rhine and the English Channel, conquered Gaul for Rome and gained glory and wealth for himself. Resistance, notably the revolt led by the Gallic chieftain Vercingetorix, was vigorously put down. There was now an increasing sense that Roman power was expressed by the imposition of direct rule. Many regions that had for a long time recognised Roman authority found themselves under Roman governors and paying tax to Rome. The growing Roman presence in the East from the time of the Mithridatic Wars led to the creation of several new provinces, thus Cyrene (75), Crete (66), Syria, Bithynia and Pontus (64–62) and the extension of Asia and Cilicia, the latter including Cyprus after its annexation in 58 until its return to the Ptolemaic kingdom in 48 (Lintott 1993: 22–7; Richardson 1994). Late Republican imperialism is sometimes seen as very different from that which preceded it, partly because of its more territorial character and partly because of the emergence of a class of super-generals whose wars seem to be almost independent of state institutions. Rather than a transformation, however, it may be preferable to see a development.

Amidst the successes of generals such as Marius, Lucullus, Pompey and Caesar there was one dramatic failure in the campaigns of the late Republic. East of Syria lay the Parthians whose empire encompassed much of the old Seleucid kingdom. When M. Licinius Crassus attempted to conquer them, he and his army met with a crushing defeat at Carrhae in 53, a major humiliation for Rome. This, however, pales in comparison with the self-inflicted devastation of the civil wars of the 40s and 30s. Out of these emerged the first emperor, Augustus, who oversaw an extraordinary extension of Roman power and territory, most importantly the creation of a series of new provinces reaching up to the Danube, those of Raetia, Noricum, Pannonia and Moesia. His campaigns have often been interpreted as defensive, an attempt to consolidate Rome's empire within easily defensible borders, but it is preferable to see him in the mould of the expansionary generals of the late Republic (Brunt 1963). Certainly that is how he saw himself (**Res Gestae C, p. 149**). Although the late Republic and the reign of Augustus witnessed the creation of many more provinces, this was not the only way in which Rome exercised control. Beyond the provinces were kings, who often owed their position to Rome and effectively exercised power on behalf of Rome, usually known as client or friendly kings, the scholarly equivalent of the more journalistic puppet rulers. These were men such as Herod the Great in Judaea, installed by Antony and kept in power by Augustus, and Juba II in Mauretania, a Numidian prince, brought up in Italy and made king of Mauretania in North Africa by Augustus (Braund 1984). In both cases their kingdoms would in time become Roman provinces, Judaea in AD 6 and Mauretania in AD 44 (for the empire in the mid-first century AD, see Map 2).

Augustus is said to have laid down that there should be no further expansion of Roman territory after his death (Tac. *Ann.* 1.11), advice sometimes explained as a reaction to the disastrous annihilation of the three legions of P. Quinctilius Varus in Germany in the last years of his reign. The Rome of the emperors does seem to have lost its expansionary momentum, though frontier warfare and the suppression of revolts continued (cf. Cornell 1993). There are exceptions – Claudius conquered much of Britain, Trajan annexed Dacia and campaigned against Parthia – but in general the boundaries of the empire are fairly settled. Where territory was brought under direct Roman control, it was more usually territory that was previously managed by a friendly king, and so marked a change of status rather than an extension of Roman power. In understanding why the expansionary momentum faltered, it may be necessary to understand the processes that drove Roman imperial expansion under the Republic.

CHAPTER 3

Explanations

And, as a matter of common sense and self-defense, America will act against such emerging threats before they are fully formed. We cannot defend America and our friends by hoping for the best.

George W. Bush, US President 2000–8

1. Ancient voices

That the rise of Rome demanded an explanation was evident already to Polybios in the second century BC. He had witnessed an extraordinary and unexpected transformation. The Greek world of the eastern Mediterranean, once shared and fought over by Greek kings and federations, was now dominated by Latin-speaking barbarians. This was the key question of his day. Its overriding importance is made clear in the very first chapter of the history: 'For who is so worthless or so indolent as not to wish to know how and by what sort of government in less than fifty-three years almost the whole inhabited world was subjugated and brought under one rule, that of the Romans'?' (Polyb. 1.1.5). For an explanation Polybios looks both to Roman motivation and to the character of Roman society. In this he foreshadows much modern scholarship.

For Polybios the Romans are essentially aggressive and expansionist. Several times he represents them as aiming for universal dominion; they wanted to rule the known world. Polybios sometimes writes as if this were a long-standing goal (cf. **Polybios A, p. 130**), although on one occasion he dates its formulation as late as the end of the Second Punic War (3.2.6), an inconsistency that has bothered scholars (Walbank 1963: 5–6; Derow 1979: 2–4; Gruen 1984: 345–6). He certainly did see the Second Punic War as a turning point (cf. 15.9–10), but preoccupation with inconsistencies should not distract from his main argument, that Rome had a desire to subjugate and rule others, a desire that drives its conquest first of Italy, then of the rest of the world. It was not uncommon to attribute universalist ambitions to major powers, but Polybios is unusually insistent in asserting this as a Roman goal (on the theme, J. Hornblower 1981: 166–71). As we will see in the next section, many scholars have been unhappy with this Polybian interpretation of Roman expansion, preferring to stress defensive thinking.

Rome may have aspired to world power but for Polybios it was the character of Roman society that allowed it to accomplish this goal and to overcome setbacks such as the defeat at Cannae. This is the subject of the sixth book of his history. Scholarly discussion has often focused on the analysis of the Roman constitution contained there. Rome, Polybios argues, has a constitution that combines kingship (consuls), aristocracy (Senate) and democracy (people), a combination that gives it a strength and resilience absent from the simpler constitutions of other states (6.18). But there is more to the sixth book than the Roman constitution. Polybios here seeks to explain Roman success by examining the nature and values of Roman society. The book contains the fullest account of the Republican Roman army, which is as much a portrait of the Romans as of their army; this is a war machine of relentless and highly-ordered efficiency. It is the very detail of Polybios' description that draws out the meticulous thoroughness of the Roman army, whether troops are being enrolled, a camp is being laid out, or a soldier is being clubbed to death by his comrades for falling asleep on watch (**Polybios D, p. 132, cf. also Polybios I, p. 137, on Roman legion v. Macedonian phalanx and Polybios G, p. 135, on the sack of New Carthage**). Underlying all this are customs that encourage self-sacrifice on behalf of the state, thus the funeral of an aristocrat becomes an inspirational pageant for young men as the deeds of their ancestors are publicly celebrated. So dedicated are Romans to their country that parents have been known to put sons to death in the interests of the state (**Polybios E, p. 132**).

Polybios, however, is Greek and his image of Rome is very much that of an outsider in awe of Rome. He has witnessed the Roman overthrow of his world and seeks to explain both Roman success and Greek failure. It would be good if there were contemporary Roman accounts to balance against Polybios but none survives. The senatorial decrees and letters of Roman magistrates found inscribed in the Greek cities of the second century BC may give glimpses but they are addressed to a Greek audience and directed towards particular problems; moreover, the surviving texts are written not in Latin but in Greek (cf. **Inscriptions C and E, p. 105–6**, and the collection of Sherk

1969 with many translated in Sherk 1984). To understand the mindset of the Roman elite we have to turn to the first century BC, the politician and writer Cicero, the historian Livy and importantly the victorious commander Caesar, but it is necessary to remember that they are writing in a developed empire and may not reflect the outlook of their predecessors.

Where Polybios saw the determined pursuit of an imperial dream, these writers present a Rome driven by goodwill and a need for security, its wars always fought in the defence of itself or its allies. This is put very neatly and somewhat paradoxically in a fragment of Cicero's *On the Republic:* 'Our people by defending its allies has become ruler of the whole world' (3.35, cf. **Cicero A, p. 96**). Elsewhere Cicero says that wars should be fought 'in order to live in peace without harm' (**Cicero C, p. 97**). This approach seems to go back at least as far as the lost history of the Roman senator Fabius Pictor, probably written around the end of the Second Punic War, and continues undiminished into the late Republic. Livy's history shows Rome handling one problem neighbour after another, while Caesar's commentaries on his Gallic War demonstrate how action was necessary to protect his Roman province and the Aedui, Rome's allies, from the threat posed by the Helvetii (**Caesar A, p. 94**, cf. 1.34–6). This, however, is the language of justification rather than explanation. Nevertheless, it is justification that could be reinforced by religious ritual in the hands of fetial priests as Cicero makes clear in his treatment of the just war in the *De Officiis* (*On Duties*) (**Cicero C, p. 97**; Brunt 1978, Riggsby 2006: 160–90; on fetial procedure, see next section). Roman views were complex and could come closer to Polybios than it at first sight appears. Cicero, for instance, may be an advocate of a just war but for him that does not exclude a war fought for supremacy, or *imperium* (on meaning of which, Chap. 1, section 2); *imperium* is itself a legitimate goal for Romans (Cic. *Off.* 1.38, *Rep.* 3.24). Pompey could boast that he had brought the boundaries of Roman rule to the limits of the earth (**Diodoros A, p. 103**, cf. Cic. *Cat.* 3.26, and on Caesar in Gaul, Cic. *Prov. cons.* 29 and 33; Brunt 1978; Nicolet 1991: 30–3).

In the first book of Vergil's *Aeneid*, written in the late first century BC, the god Jupiter grants to the Romans '*imperium* without end' (*Aen.* 1.278–9); *imperium* here is often translated as 'empire', but it is probably preferable to understand it in less formal terms as power exercised by Rome (contrast Gruen 1984: 274 with Richardson 2008: 132–5). The belief that divine favour lay behind Roman success was one that ran through much Roman thought. Nor was the goodwill of the gods arbitrary; it was consequent on Roman piety, as advertised by a Roman magistrate to the people of Teos in Asia Minor in the 190s BC, articulated by Cicero in speeches and evident in the epithet of pious Aeneas in the *Aeneid* (**Inscription E, p. 106, Cicero D, p. 98**, *Phil.* 6.19, Verg, *Aen.* 1.220; Brunt 1978). Such reasoning would not have impressed the pragmatic Polybios, for whom Roman religiosity brought not so much divine goodwill as social cohesion (6.56). Roman belief in divine favour persisted into late antiquity. Its force is evident in the Christian response to it; Tertullian, for instance, chose to ridicule it, while Eusebius turned it around and saw the guiding hand of the Christian god behind the Roman empire, creating a suitable environment for the spread of Christianity (**Tertullian A, p. 161, Eusebius A, p. 104**).

2. On the defensive

Although Polybios' narrative of Roman expansion has generally been accepted, his attribution of imperial ambition to Rome has often been rejected (as by Holleaux 1921, Walbank 1963; defended by Derow 1979). Instead many scholars have tended towards the defensive interpretation preferred by the Romans themselves, transforming it from a justificatory mantra into an explanatory theory, that of defensive imperialism. Rome, it is argued, fought its wars in pursuit not of empire but of security. Threats to itself, its possessions or its allies, whether these threats were real or imagined, prompted it to vigorous defensive action, the unintended result of which was increased power and territory. H. H. Scullard in a standard textbook, first published in 1935, can invoke defensive imperialism to explain both the First Punic War and the Second Macedonian War. Thus, at the outset of the First Punic War the Romans accepted the appeal of the Mamertines and intervened in Sicily because they were concerned for 'the safety of Italy', while crucial to the Roman decision to fight against Macedon in 200 was their fear of a coalition between Philip and Antiochos. In all this, far from being intent on world rule, the Romans were, rather revealingly, 'a people who, like the British, proverbially had a genius for muddling through' (Scullard 1980 (4th edn): 167, 249–51; for narrative of events, Chap. 2 above).

This enormously influential interpretation was first voiced by the German Theodor Mommsen in the mid-nineteenth century, and is found in more developed forms in the work of Maurice Holleaux and Tenney Frank, both writing in the early part of the twentieth century, the one in France, the other in America. None of the three used the oxymoron, defensive imperialism; Mommsen was writing before the word 'imperialism' became fashionable, while Holleaux questioned the application of both 'imperialism' and 'militarism' to Rome. There is a strong sense of identification with Rome in this defensive interpretation in its various forms (for a fascinating study of the intellectual context, Linderski 1984) and among those who subsequently adopted it. That this position won widespread acceptance in spite of its paradoxical character is a reflection of the scholarly environment of America and the leading European states in the early to mid-twentieth century, where international predominance could be taken for granted. Indeed in countries such as Britain and France identification with Rome was made that much easier by virtue of the possession of overseas territories of their own, which helped to encourage a positive view of Rome and its expansion. Directly or indirectly interpretations of contemporary imperialism came to influence the understanding of its Roman counterpart (and vice-versa, cf. Hingley 2000). Just as the extraordinary growth of British empire could improbably be considered an accident, acquired in a 'fit of absence of mind' as Sir John Seeley famously put it in his *Expansion of England* of 1883 (cf. Levine 2007: 82–3), so, following Holleaux and Frank, did the Romans become reluctant, even accidental, imperialists (Garnsey and Whittaker 1978: 1–3). The tenacious hold of the defensive interpretation on English-speaking scholarship in particular may also be in part a consequence of a World War which was seen as a necessary response to aggression. It would, however, be misleading to imply that defensive imperialism was ever universally accepted; in Italy, for example, it has never been the orthodoxy (cf. De Sanctis 1923 and 1964; Musti 1978).

Only in the 1970s did the anglophone fondness for defensive imperialism come under significant assault; by now the European powers had largely divested themselves of their empires and America was recovering from its controversial and unsuccessful intervention in Vietnam (the influence of the latter is noted by Saller 1998: 227). The most important and sustained attack was by W. V. Harris, whose *War and Imperialism in Republican Rome 327–70 BC* provoked considerable debate (1979, but cf. also Finley 1978, Hopkins 1978, Derow 1979, together suggesting that the late 70s was a time for reflecting on empire). The emphasis here is on the military ethos of Roman society, the pursuit of glory through war, and the potential economic benefits of expansion (see below). Nonetheless, while few now deny the aggressive and militaristic character of Rome, defence has not been completely ruled out, although its role is less overt. Roman behaviour has been seen as influenced by powerful, albeit often irrational, fears (Rich 1993) or by a tendency to equate safety and security with the maintenance of honour and status (Mattern 1999: 214–15). Most recently Arthur Eckstein has presented a scenario of international anarchy which compels all states to be both bellicose and therefore necessarily preoccupied with defence, an interpretation which might be seen as a response to an increasingly anarchic post-Soviet world (2006; 2008). Defensive imperialism has not gone away. In a new guise it has experienced something of a revival in modern political debate, especially in the wake of the attacks on the World Trade Center in New York and the subsequent invasions of Afghanistan and Iraq (Booth 2007: 296–7, noting Cooper 2002). Whether this will have any impact on the way Roman imperialism is studied remains to be seen.

The defensive imperialism case relies in part on the interpretation of individual wars, but that interpretation is shaped also by two other factors: the Romans' own belief that their wars were justified and an alleged reluctance to annex new territories.

Underlying the Roman belief in the rightness of their wars was a ritual procedure carried out by priests who were known as the *fetiales*. These priests oversaw the religious dimension of the transition from peace to war and in this capacity they were to ensure that the right conditions had been met: that the enemy had committed an offence against Rome or its allies, that a formal demand for satisfaction had been issued, and that in the event of non-compliance war was declared with the proper ritual, originally the casting of a spear into enemy territory. These would appear to be the essential elements, although they may represent an ideal rather than reality. Our sources are late Republican but they explain this procedure in the context of early Rome, which leaves considerable scope for imaginative reconstruction on their part. The fetial priests certainly seem to have been active throughout the Republic but the form this fetial procedure took must have changed with circumstances (**Livy A, p. 112, Cicero C, p. 97**; Rich 1976, Harris 1979: 163–75; North 1981: 1). That the enemy was in the wrong and had been given a chance to set matters right was felt by Romans to affirm the justness of their wars – and modern scholars have frequently agreed with them, notwithstanding disagreement over how often and in what form the procedure was actually used. But it is rare for a state to feel that its wars are unjustified and the Romans may have given their enemies the opportunity to make amends but their demands could be such that compliance could hardly have been expected. The fetial procedure's primary purpose was religious; it had the potential, if used in a conciliatory manner, to promote peace but it could also become the tool of self-righteous aggression.

The advocates of the defensive imperialist thesis want to show that the Romans were reluctant to annex territory and only did so when they had to; their opponents seek to argue the reverse position, that the Romans were eager to annex territory and only failed to do so when it was impractical. To some extent it is a matter of where the emphasis is placed. Does one stress the acquisition of Sicily, Spain and Sardinia after the First and Second Punic Wars or the withdrawal of Roman troops from the East after the wars against Macedon and Antiochos? Both positions, however, share a premise, which has its roots in nineteenth-century European imperialism: that empire is territorial. But it may be wrong to impose this conception on the Romans; they may not have realised that they needed to adopt a stance on annexation. When Polybios says that after the battle of Pydna in 168 BC Rome ruled almost the whole of the known world, he was describing a world where his Greek homeland was free of Roman governors and Roman troops; yet for him Greece was subject to Rome. What counted was obedience to Roman orders (Derow 1979), and this was something that could operate as easily outside a provincial structure as within it (succinctly expressed by Richardson 1986: 178–9, cf. the patron–client relationship or hegemonial imperialism of Badian 1958, 1968: 1–15). In the second century this conception of power was probably shared also by the Romans (Kallet-Marx 1995: 22–9; Richardson 2008: 61–2). That the empire of the Romans comes to be divided up into provinces signals a gradual shift in the way that power is represented, from orders to institutional structures.

Rome did acquire an empire. The thesis that this empire was as a consequence of a tendency towards self-defence which verged on the paranoid seems counter-intuitive, even paradoxical. Defence may explain some of Rome's wars and possibly also limited expansion, but Rome was repeatedly at war and the resulting empire embraced the whole Mediterranean and beyond.

3. War and glory

Critics of the defensive imperialism hypothesis have often preferred instead to stress the militaristic character of the Roman society. Militarism and defensive thinking need not be mutually exclusive but the regularity and frequency of Roman wars suggest that the impulse to war came from the Romans themselves. Republican Rome was a state geared for war in which scarcely a year would pass without a war being fought somewhere. According to Augustus the closure of the doors of the shrine of Janus, an act that symbolised peace, had happened only twice in recorded history (***Res Gestae* B, p. 149**, Cooley 2009: 156–61). Wars against major powers such as Carthage or the Hellenistic kings tend to dominate the narratives of modern textbooks, but fighting against less glamorous enemies such as Gauls in the North or native tribes in Spain occupies many of the intervening years (though see the cautionary remarks of Rich 1993). The military ethos can be seen to permeate all levels of the citizen body from the aristocracy to the soldiery (see in particular the fundamental discussion of Harris 1979: 9–53).

Warfare was an essential part of an aristocrat's life. According to Polybios (6.19) a young man had to serve ten military campaigns before he was eligible to stand for public office, a practice that presupposed not only that warfare in some form was frequent but also that it was the foundation of a political career. By the first century BC this custom appears no longer to have been strictly upheld, but the way of thinking that underpinned it had not significantly changed. Experience and achievement in war conferred status and this, some scholars believe, played a crucial role in the development of Roman imperialism.

Roman nobles were immersed in a constant struggle among themselves for prestige and pre-eminence within the state; Latin political vocabulary is full of abstract nouns that encapsulate this, words such as *auctoritas*, *dignitas*, *honor* and *gloria*, often translated by the English terms derived from them, authority, dignity, honour and glory. Such translations are convenient but they fail to convey adequately the complexity and subtlety of this vocabulary of honour (on their meaning, Lendon 1997: 272–6). This combination of aristocratic competition with a militaristic society, it is argued, drove Roman imperialism by requiring a constant supply of wars in which nobles could achieve distinction and glory. The situation was intensified by the Roman custom whereby magistracies were held only for a single year, thus increasing the pressure for annual warfare. A year without a war was an opportunity lost for an incumbent consul who had to compete not only with his peers but also with his ancestors. Polybios' depiction of a Roman aristocratic funeral with its invocation of the achievements of the family over generations vividly illustrates this (**Polybios E, p. 132**, cf. Flower 1996). These themes recur in the third and second century BC epitaphs from the Tomb of the Scipios in Rome; apart from the recording magistracies held and military successes the epitaphs display a preoccupation with maintaining and adding to the reputation of the family (**Tomb of the Scipios, p. 162**). The high value placed on attainment of glory is evident throughout Latin literature and the late Republican historian Sallust even goes so far as to attribute Rome's extraordinary success to an overwhelming desire for glory (**Sallust A, p. 151**, Harris 1979: 17–32).

The most striking visual manifestation of the role of warfare in Roman society was the triumph. This honour, awarded to a victorious commander, was one of the highest accolades a noble could attain, a very public display of glory achieved. It is estimated that in the second century BC approximately one in every four men who held the consulship would be awarded a triumph (Rich 1993: 49–54), making it an honour at once attainable but also exclusive. A procession would make its way through the streets of Rome to the temple of Jupiter on the Capitoline Hill. The general, usually escorted by his fellow senators, would be mounted on a four-horse chariot in dress that evoked the kings of old or even Jupiter himself. The Roman populace would watch a demonstration of their state's military might as the triumphant soldiers passed in front of them together with the prizes of war, booty exhibited, enemy prisoners humiliated, cities captured. Defeated rulers such as Perseus of Macedon or Jugurtha of Numidia would walk in chains, a walk that sometimes ended in their execution. The names of tribes, towns, rivers and mountains would be paraded on signs, sometimes accompanied by representations which would be carried in the procession, such as the 134 towns in L. Scipio's triumph over Antiochos III (**Livy D and E, pp. 116–18**; Mattern 1999: 164–8). At one time at least 5000 enemy dead were required to merit a triumph; this was not a culture of compromise in which wars were fought as a means to a negotiated settlement (**Valerius Maximus A, p. 163**, though Beard 2007: 209–10 suggests that the '5,000 rule' was produced by ancient scholars as they tried to systematise the vagaries of ancient triumphal practice). In the triumphal procession the whole state shares in a celebration of victory and war: the general, the senate, the army and the assembled citizens of Rome. More than this, it is a vigorous assertion of Roman power over others as the conquered world is presented to Rome. Some triumphs were no doubt more impressive than others and it tends to be the more spectacular ones, such as those of Aemilus Paullus over Perseus, Pompey after his eastern campaigns or Vespasian after suppressing the Jewish revolt, that have had the greater impact on the historical tradition (Plut. *Aem.* 32–4; App. *Mith.* 116–17, Plut. *Pomp.* 45; Jos. *Jewish War* 7.123–57, **Figs 1–3: Arch of Titus, with Josephus A, pp. 109–11**).

The greatest statement of this competitive militarism is probably the *Res Gestae* of Augustus which displays the same fetishistic delight in listing conquests so evident in the Roman triumph and boasts of world conquest: 'I extended the boundaries of all the provinces of the Roman people on which bordered peoples that were not subject to our *imperium*.' Yet, it also displays the complexity of Roman attitudes to war. Augustus, recalling Cicero in the *De Officiis*, represents himself as fighting his wars in the interests of peace: the enemies in Spain, Gaul and Germany are reduced to peace; against the Alpine tribes no war is waged unjustly (**Res Gestae B and C, esp. 27, p. 149**, Cooley 2009; Brunt 1963).

In spite of the extensive conquests of Augustus the Principate also brings an end to the expansionary momentum so familiar from the empire of the Republic. One way to explain this, and one which the proponents of defensive imperialism might prefer, would be to argue that the empire stabilised and warfare became more sporadic because there were no longer any powerful, threatening neighbours to deal with. Alternatively, one might argue that aristocratic competition in the military field was redundant once Augustus was emperor; the imperial system, in contrast to the senatorial Republic, could not allow competition of this form. Glory, and the triumph that symbolised it, became the prerogative of the imperial family alone (cf. Mattern 1999: 162–71, 194–202). With the absence of the driving force of competition imperial expansion largely ceased. Both positions may, however, be oversimplifications. Even before Augustus military campaigning came to be dominated by a few, very powerful individuals, generals such as Sulla, Pompey and Caesar, and wars were fought far from Rome by increasingly professional armies (cf. Cornell 1993). Nonetheless the ideology of competitive militarism persisted until Augustus proved in relentless detail on the bronze plaques of the *Res Gestae* outside his Mausoleum that the game was over – there was no one who could surpass him, whether that be in honours, benefactions or conquests (**Res Gestae, p. 148**).

4. Wealth acquisition

War could be expensive and destructive but a successful war could also be profitable, benefiting the state, aristocracy, troops and allies. Nonetheless, the part played by economic factors in the development of Roman imperialism has long been a matter of controversy. Although it is evident that Rome prospered as its empire grew, many

influential scholars have rejected the suggestion that Rome was moti-
vated by desire for economic gain. Three main forms of possible
economic benefit can be identified: profits that are an immediate consequence of a war, such as plunder and indemnities, revenue derived
from Roman occupation of territory, such as taxes and tribute, and
commerce. It is worth considering each of these in turn.

Victory in war brings opportunities for immediate enrichment,
notably by plundering the defeated and by the imposition of indemnities as part of the post-war settlement, ostensibly to reimburse the
cost of the war. While direct evidence that Romans initiated any war
with a view to economic gain of this form is slight, at the same time it
is clear that plunder was an essential feature of the Roman idea of war,
not some accidental by-product. In the Roman military ethos booty
was something to be prioritised and publicised, evidence of a mission
accomplished. Thus the display of booty was a distinctive part of the
Roman triumphal procession, its absence worthy of comment (e.g.
Livy 31.49, 40.59, 45.2). Furthermore, sources such as Livy repeatedly record the profits of war – one may question the figures (and
Beard 2007 does) but what is important is not so much their accuracy
as the Roman need to have figures to report in the first place; this is
what Romans expect to achieve from war. In 175 BC Ti. Sempronius
Gracchus in a thanksgiving dedication for victory in Sardinia briefly
outlined his achievements which included the huge quantity of booty
he brought home (**Livy F, p. 118**), Scipio before sailing for Africa
prayed not only for victory and a safe return but for plunder (Livy
29.27.2), and Plautus in his comedies regularly saw war as a means
of enrichment on both a public and a personal level (cf. *Epidicus*
158–60). The Roman concern with booty was observed by Polybios
who described at length the methodical way they went about sacking
a city and dividing up the spoils after its capture (**Polybios G, p. 135**,
allowing for a certain schematism, cf. Ziolkowski 1993). Not surprisingly there was among the soldiers an expectation of profit. It was the
prospect of plunder that was said to have encouraged the People to
vote for the war that became the First Punic War (**Polybios B, p. 130**).
Plunder features prominently in accounts of Rome's wars. Take some
moments from the narrative of the Third Macedonian War against
Perseus: men are eager to serve because they see that those who fought
on previous campaigns in the East have become rich; Roman commanders are accused before the Senate of plundering not only Rome's
enemies but her allies as well; Aemilius Paullus puts the riches of the
Macedonian kingdom on public view at Amphipolis before shipping

them back to Rome; he gives Epiros over to his soldiers to loot, resulting in the sacking of some seventy cities and enslavement of a reported
150,000 people; his triumph in Rome with its spectacular display of
plunder lasts three days; so great was the booty brought back the property tax was abolished for Roman citizens (Livy 42.32, 43.7–8, 45.33–4,
45.40, Plut. *Aem.* 32–4, 38, Cic. *Off.* 2.76). As the mass enslavements in
Epiros remind us, the defeated were as much spoils of war as their possessions were. Indeed there are those, especially though not exclusively
among Marxist historians, for whom the acquisition of slaves was one
of the driving forces of Roman imperialism, fundamental to the development and maintenance of the Italian 'slave economy' (Anderson
1974: 53–70, cf. North 1981: 4–5; Petit 1976: 248–9 for debate on 'slave
economy'; see further Chap. 5 section 4).

Where Rome left the defeated in power, it would benefit from substantial indemnities that were to be paid in instalments over a number
of years. Carthage had to come up with 3,200 talents over ten years after
the First Punic War and then, after the second war, 10,000 over fifty
years; Philip V had to pay 1,000 talents (an initial 500, then the remainder in ten annual instalments); Antiochos 15,000 talents (3,000 followed
by twelve annual instalments); and lesser players such as the Aitolians
and the Spartan king Nabis were also left with what for them would have
been hefty bills, 500 talents each, both to be paid in instalments. There
was a political component to this; paying by instalments made explicit
the continued subordination of the defeated to Rome, hence Carthage's
attempt to pay off its Second Punic War debt in a single instalment was
refused; equally political was the decision to let Philip V off his final
instalments in exchange for his support against Antiochos. That such
payments had political uses is not, however, to deny their economic significance. Romans would have been well aware of the sizeable quantities
of money flowing into Rome in this way and the benefits that resulted; it
was a matter of balancing political and economic benefits. War indemnities, however, were not a new phenomenon – Samos, for example,
paid the costs incurred by the Athenians after its failed revolt against
them in 440–439 (Thucydides 1.117) – but indemnity payments have a
prominence in accounts of Roman wars that they do not have in those
of earlier Greek wars. It might be argued that this tells us more about
the interests of the sources than of the Romans, but the degree of detail
given, both for indemnities and for booty brought to Rome, suggests
that this preoccupation originated with the Romans themselves, for
whom these figures were important and worth cataloguing. Economic
gain of this sort may not have been the principal motive for embarking

on any particular war but the high value the Romans clearly placed on it would have contributed in a more general way to creating an environment in which war was something worth pursuing.

In the early years of the second century BC, as Rome was receiving indemnity payments from the East and from the Carthaginians in North Africa, it was also experimenting with another form of income, the collecting of taxes in Spain and Sicily, territories acquired through the wars with Carthage. It is important not to draw too sharp a contrast at this early stage. Spain in the second century BC was a region where wars were still being fought, booty seized and triumphs won; this was a rather precarious context for a tax system to develop and it did so in a very piecemeal and ad hoc fashion (cf. Richardson 1976, Curchin 1991: 60–1). As Roman power became more formalised, especially from the first century BC onwards, shifting from indirect to direct rule with governors and troops stationed around the emerging territorial empire, so taxation became the primary method for extracting wealth from the subject areas. Booty and indemnities in turn became less significant forms of wealth acquisition in comparison, although plundering certainly did not come to an end, as Caesar demonstrated in Gaul, but the outcome in that case was direct Roman rule and taxation.

Rome did not impose a uniform system of taxation of its own across the empire; instead, as with many empires previously, it adopted and adapted existing practice, with the result that, even under the emperors, there could be considerable variety in the type of tax used and the way it was collected (Lintott 1993: 70–96; Rathbone 1996). The almost improvisational way in which Rome acquired territory and began to tax the inhabitants argues against treating this as an explanation for Rome's wars but once power was established the exploitation of subjects for the purpose of tax became a reason for maintaining and strengthening Roman authority. By the first century BC Cicero, writing in his *De Officiis*, can take it for granted that the aim of a good political leader is to do his best in war and peace to increase the state in power, in land and in revenue (2.85). This theoretical stance is put into practice when he speaks in support of giving the command against Mithridates to Pompey; here he stresses the vital importance of restoring the flow of revenue from the province of Asia which has been disrupted by Mithridates' invasion (**Cicero A, p. 96**). Cicero's concern with tax revenue reflects a change in the nature of Rome's empire as it becomes more territorial in character. Significantly too Strabo, writing a little later, could argue that one reason why the Romans did not occupy Britain was because it was not economically viable (**Strabo A, p. 152**).

Studies of imperialism in modern times have often looked to commerce and trade to explain the emergence of latter-day empires, emphasising the search for new markets and natural resources. Similarly, in the late nineteenth and early twentieth centuries mercantile interests were often adduced by ancient historians to explain Roman state policy; thus the destruction of Carthage and Corinth in the 140s could be put down to commercial rivalry. Such interpretations were subjected to a rigorous and influential critique by Tenney Frank (1914: 277–97); he pointed out that what little evidence there was for senatorial intervention in commercial matters made better sense when given a political explanation.

Nonetheless, traders and those involved in business did have an interest in Rome's wars and the resulting empire, even if they had no direct influence on state decision-making. As the empire expanded so businessmen moved with it to exploit the opportunities that arose (for the increasing presence of Romans and Italians around the empire, Purcell 2005). Under the Republic in particular there were those known as the *publicani* who contracted to perform services for the state, such as collecting taxes (salt taxes, harbour taxes, even in some cases provincial taxes as in Asia), running the highly lucrative gold and silver mines in Spain, arranging construction work in Rome or supplying the Roman army (Badian 1972; **Polybios C, p. 131, cf. *Digest* A, p. 101**, on the meaning of *publicani*). Romans also appear as moneylenders, a practice not unconnected with the process of empire-building. Loans are to be found being made to those newly incorporated, such as the Cypriot city of Salamis which borrowed at extortionate rates from an intermediary of the Roman noble M. Iunius Brutus shortly after the island became part of the province of Cilicia, or to those cities that had to borrow to pay their debts to Rome after a revolt, as was the case with the cities of Asia Minor which had supported Mithridates (Cic. *Att.* 6.1–2, Plut. *Luc.* 20).

Roman and also Italian traders tend not to feature prominently in the elite sources that survive but they do make their mark in other forms of evidence, showing up for example in the epigraphic evidence from Delos once it became a free port (i.e. without customs duties) in the 160s (cf. Rauh 1993 with the epigraphic text in Sherk 1984: no. 47; Paterson 1998 on trade and imperialism). They were also to be seen in the vicinity of military campaigns, ready to buy up and sell on any of the spoils that came their way, which could include large quantities of people for the slave market (Polyb. 14.7.2–3, Caes. *BG* 2.33). While scholars might often be reluctant to push the connection between commerce and imperialism too far, the subjects of Rome did not necessarily have such reservations. Businessmen and merchants were identified with Roman power and in times of revolt could expect to feel the full force of anti-Roman feeling, whether in Asia, Gaul or Pannonia (**Appian A, p. 91**, Caes. *BG* 7.3, Vell. Pat. 2.110.6; see further Chapter 4, section 4).

War brought Rome wealth, empire consolidated it. While this may not have been the primary explanation for Roman imperialism, it will have been an important part of the process. Certainly the economic impact of Rome was not lost on contemporaries, among whom Roman greed was a recurring theme, most vividly captured by Mithridates. In a symbolic gesture guaranteed to get attention in the Greek world he poured gold down the throat of the defeated Roman commander, Manius Aquillius (**Appian A, p. 91**, Erskine 1996).

5. Approaches

Discussion of Roman imperial expansion has tended to follow two overlapping lines of argument. Firstly, there is the debate over whether Rome is to be interpreted as defensive in outlook or aggressive. Defence is self-explanatory; the goal is security. To argue for an aggressive Rome, on the other hand, is not so much the conclusion of an argument as the opening of a whole new set of questions; wars can then be fought for power, glory, honour, wealth – and even security. Secondly, how much weight should modern interpreters of Roman imperialism give to conscious factors and how much to unconscious or structural factors? Harris, for example, although stressing the militaristic, competitive ethos of Roman society, devotes a considerable amount of attention to the decision-making process; thus he examines the causes of each war fought by Rome between the late third century and the early first century BC to prove that defence did not play a significant part in the Senate's thinking. Yet, as North argues (1981), to stress militarism, aristocratic competition, one-year consulships and the ready supply of troops from Italian allies is to point to structural aspects that may have driven Roman expansion quite independently of any Roman decision-making. Similarly, demonstrating (as Gruen 1984: 288–315 does) that economic motives do not figure prominently in our evidence for senatorial decisions does not mean that economic factors themselves are of little importance in explaining Roman imperialism. A senatorial decision is but one moment in a long process of imperial expansion that needs to be understood within a much broader context.

Theories of imperialism put forward by specialists in international relations can focus on the nature of the imperial power, on the influence of the periphery or on the international system itself – or on a combination (cf. Doyle 1986's review of these approaches). Such theories, even if we do not accept them, can offer useful ways of thinking about Roman imperialism. Much of the scholarship on the emergence of the Roman empire, from Polybios onwards, has focused on the first of these, looking to Rome itself for an explanation, its institutions, its character and its motivations (cf. for example Harris 1979). On the other hand, some scholars have chosen to place the emphasis not so much on the character of Rome as on the role of the periphery, on the states that Rome encountered and would ultimately make subject. One of the more influential historians here is Erich Gruen who concludes his study of Rome's conquest of the Greek East: 'Hellas ultimately fell under Roman authority not because Rome exported their structure to the East, but because Greeks persistently drew the westerner into their own structure – until it was theirs no longer' (1984: 730). Here Rome's empire happens almost despite itself. The third type of explanation, the systemic approach, has been less common among ancient historians but recently Eckstein, applying realist theories of international relations, has argued that scholars fail to understand Roman imperialism because they focus on factors internal to Roman society and not on the system of which Rome was a part; that system was an anarchic one in which all states were out for themselves and war was a necessary consequence (2006; 2008). Such a realist analysis may be overly reductionist but Eckstein is surely right to stress Rome's capacity to assimilate others as a significant factor in its success.

Rome's empire developed over centuries. Consequently different factors are likely to have been at work at different times; Rome itself was not static nor was the way it interacted with others. Fundamental was the military ethos that permeated Rome's social and institutional structures and which lay behind the almost constant warfare of the Republic, but that operated in conjunction with a competitive aristocracy and a ready supply of allied troops. The first century BC would see the transformation of the Italian allies into Roman citizens and the growing dominance of powerful individuals culminating in the arrival of the emperor. Together these two occurrences will have altered the dynamic of imperial expansion, ultimately having a restraining effect. Moreover, by the time of the great expansion of the first century BC under generals such as Pompey and Caesar the character of the empire had changed significantly. The informal ways of exercising power which are often to be observed in earlier years are now less in evidence. Increasingly direct control through permanent presence had become the norm and with this shift came a more territorial conception of empire. Nor can one ignore the likelihood that the pursuit of economic advantage would have given extra momentum to Roman expansion and may even have encouraged the development of these more formal imperial structures. Such structures could at the same time enable both political control and the economic exploitation of the subject peoples, the one reinforcing the other.

CHAPTER 4

The Subject

My heart rebels against any foreigner imposing on my country the peace which
is here called 'Pax Britannica'.

Mahatma Gandhi, 1925

Roman rule and its onset would have been experienced differently in
different parts of the empire and it would be foolhardy to try to encom-
pass all this in a single chapter. Nonetheless it is important to move
the focus away from Rome and onto the subject peoples. There is considerable research in this area with numerous specialist studies on the
regions and provinces of Rome's empire. Scholars have often thought
in terms of western and eastern provinces, the one more tribal and
known especially through material evidence, the other more urbanised
and with a long literary culture. The West accordingly has tended to
be studied by archaeologists in particular, amongst whom there has
recently been a vigorous debate about the nature of Roman imperialism and the validity of the concept of 'romanisation'. The Roman
East, on the other hand, has attracted ancient historians and classicists
whose interest has focused especially on what it was to be Greek in the
Roman empire. Dialogue between these two sides of Roman imperial
scholarship is not as common as it might be, though Greg Woolf is a
notable exception (1994; 1998).

1. Reflections on Roman power: the subject perspective

One means of understanding how Rome's subjects may have experienced Roman power would be to look at what they wrote about Rome.
Unfortunately there are severe limitations here. By the first century
AD the Roman empire may have contained some fifty or sixty million
people from a multiplicity of different religious, ethnic, linguistic and
social backgrounds, but direct comment on Rome largely emanates

from two groups, both in the East, the Greeks and the Jews. This section, therefore, will focus on their testimony in order to illuminate the subject's perspective on the Roman empire.

Of the two it is the Greeks who provide the most extensive comment; what survives, however, is representative not of all Greeks but rather of the urban elites. Nonetheless the texts written by Greeks, spanning the centuries from Rome's early involvement in the Greek mainland through to the late Empire, offer a valuable insight into the subject's changing encounter with Roman power and the very process of becoming a subject. From the beginning the Greek reaction to Rome was complex and varied. Rome was both demonised and glorified, a threat to Greek freedom and its saviour. Both these images are to be found in Polybios' history.

Writing in the mid-second century BC after the fall of Macedon, Polybios looks back to the early stages of the Roman intervention and reports several speeches warning against the 'cloud from the West'. In these speeches Rome is alien and threatening, a barbarian menace, cruel, plundering and lawless (**Polybios H, p. 136**, cf. 5.104, 9.39). The authenticity of these speeches has been questioned but what is clear is that someone was saying such things about Rome. Polybios himself reinforces this picture with his vivid description of the sack of New Carthage in Spain, which highlights Roman brutality and their methodical approach to plunder (**Polybios G, p. 135**). Anti-Roman oracular literature from the second and first centuries BC, some influenced by Jewish traditions, echoes this representation of Rome and calls for Rome to be repaid in kind; the vengeance takes the form of what the East itself had suffered at Rome's hands – destruction, enslavement and plunder (**Third Sibylline Oracle A, p. 162**, cf. also the very strange third marvel in Phlegon of Tralles, nicely translated in Hansen 1996). Already in the 190s an inscribed letter of the Roman commander T. Quinctius Flamininus shows that it was felt necessary to defend Romans against the charge of greed (**Inscription C, p. 105**).

Yet the early second century BC also reveals another image. Rome here is the liberator, feted at Corinth after the freedom proclamation of 196. Polybios' description of the joyous crowds clasping at their saviour Flamininus may be undercut by the historian's own knowledge of what was to come but epigraphic discoveries from throughout Greece confirm the widespread nature of this jubilation. Statues of Flamininus were erected and he was honoured as a saviour and benefactor; cult honours were paid to him and subsequently to various embodiments of Roman power (**Inscription D, p. 106, Plutarch A, p. 125**, see further section 3 below).

These two images represent extremes of animosity and adulation. For the most part cities and even monarchies were trying to find a place for themselves in this developing new world order. Polybios gives a sense of the tensions this created within the Achaian League, as politicians disagreed about the policy that should be adopted in dealings with Rome. The fact of Roman power was acknowledged but how readily should the Achaians accept Roman orders? Should these orders take precedence over Achaian laws? Some such as Kallikrates of Leontion advocated enthusiastic co-operation (**Polybios K, p. 143**), while others such as Philopoimen of Megalopolis, Polybios' own city, believed that to obey Roman orders regardless would only speed up the process of subjection: appeal to their laws and their alliance offered the Achaians some form of protection against a domineering Rome, one that should only be abandoned when there was no alternative (Polyb. 24.13). Second century BC inscriptions show how far-reaching this recognition of Roman power was. Eumenes II of Pergamon, when granting *polis* status to a community in Phrygia, affirms that his grant will be of lasting value because he himself has the backing of the Romans; later his brother Attalos II is reluctant to launch a war against the Asiatic Gauls without first consulting Rome; an alliance between Chersonesos and Pontos, both on the Black Sea, incorporates a clause requiring the parties to maintain good relations with Rome (Bagnall and Derow 2004: nos. 43, 50, **Inscription F, p. 107**).

Polybios' original intention had been to give an account of Rome's rise to world power over fifty-three years, but at some point he decided to extend the history beyond the end of the Macedonian kingdom in 167. His reason for doing this was that he felt it was also necessary to make some form of judgement about Rome rule. In this he seems to reflect contemporary debate about the nature of Roman dominion, one that revolves around questions of morality and justice. He himself can be very cynical, almost Thucydidean, in some of his remarks on the Romans in this period, representing them as pursuing self-interest in the guise of justice (**Polybios L and M, p. 145**). In the varied reactions of the Greeks to the Roman treatment of Carthage in the Third Punic War, reported by Polybios, we see the separation of self-interest and legality on the one hand and justice and morality on the other. The defenders of Rome emphasised the wisdom of eliminating Carthage and pointed out that Rome was legally in the right but others drew attention to Rome's craving for power and increasing disregard of accepted morality (**Polybios N, p. 146**). More bluntly the Academic philosopher Carneades is said to have argued that justice was incompatible with the acquisition of empire, a stance that may have led Greeks who were more well-disposed towards Rome to develop the influential counter-argument that empire could be in the interests of the subject (**Lactantius A, p. 111, Augustine A, p. 94**, often collected in Cic. *Rep.* 3; see also Chap. 5.1 below and Erskine 1990: 181–204).

Increasingly the Greek elite accepted the reality of Roman power in the East; Polybios himself is a notable second-century BC example, at one time a detainee in Rome, later instrumental in the reorganisation of Greece after Rome's destruction of Corinth in 146. At this stage allegiance to Rome was likely to have been as much the result of pragmatism as of conviction. The Greek reaction to Mithridates shows the fragility of loyalty to Rome, even in the early first century BC. Nonetheless, strong and sometimes longstanding ties develop between distinguished Greek families and the Roman aristocracy. First-century BC Mytilene alone can produce the relatively well-documented cases of Theophanes, friend of Pompey, and Potamon, friend of the Iulii (Robert 1969; Gold 1985; Parker 1991). Firm adherents included the historian Dionysios of Halikarnassos, a long-time resident of Rome, who argued at great length in his *Roman Antiquities* that Romans were really Greek by origin and that fellow Greeks who considered them to be barbarians were wrong. Yet, however much admiration Dionysios may have had for Rome and however much affinity he may have felt, Roman rule over the Greeks was only truly acceptable to him if the Romans themselves were in some sense Greek (Dion. Hal. *Ant. Rom.* 1.5.1).

Under the emperors a shift in Greek perception seems to have taken place. Members of the Greek elite, at least in their own eyes, became not so much subjects of Rome as participants in the Roman empire. Some acquired Roman citizenship and with it Roman names, others became senators and by the second century AD Greeks could even be found holding the consulship. An early entrant to the Senate was Q. Pompeius Macer, praetor in AD 15 and grandson of Theophanes of Mytilene, his name betraying the Pompeian origins of the family's Roman citizenship. It should be noted that the Greek elite were not unusual in this respect; by the end of the second century AD it is reckoned that roughly half of the Roman Senate came from outside Italy with most regions of the empire represented, a statistic that reveals much about the changing character of the Roman state and its empire (Hammond 1957; Hopkins 1983: 144–5).

There were also the Greeks, such as Appian of Alexandria in the second century AD and Dio Cassius in the third, who wrote histories of Rome. The fullest and most elaborate praise of Rome comes in Aelius Aristides' speech, *To Rome*. Here we see the Roman empire as a community and Rome as a bringer of prosperity, but it must be remembered that this was a speech delivered before the imperial family and Aristides' own view of Rome may have been more reserved (Aelius Aristides, *To Rome* 61–4, discussed in Swain 1996: 254–97). This acceptance of Rome, however, is often tinged with a sense of loss, even of resentment, which finds expression in the idealisation of the classical Greek past in the writers of what is known as the Second Sophistic, spanning the first three centuries AD. Plutarch of Chaironeia, for instance, wrote a series of biographies, known as the *Parallel Lives*, in which he paired a famous Greek with a Roman counterpart and thus made an implicit claim to equal status; some might even feel that the Greeks fare better. The past gave scope for Greek greatness but elsewhere Plutarch lamented the restrictions that Roman rule placed on the civic elites of his own day (**Plutarch E and F, p. 129**). A Greek who achieved high office in the empire was Arrian of Nikomedia, Roman consul and imperial legate in Cappadocia, but as a writer he too looked back to the past, modelling himself on Xenophon and choosing Alexander the Great as the subject of his historical work. Similarly Pausanias writes on the monuments of mainland Greece but his focus is almost exclusively on those that preceded Roman rule. It is as if the more Greeks became incorporated into the Roman power structure the more they needed to assert their Greek identity.

The only other group who have left a substantial and continuous literary record of their interaction with Rome are the Jews, whose situation was rather different from that of the Greeks. The evidence is written not only in Hebrew and Aramaic but also in Greek, reflecting the Greek domination of the eastern Mediterranean that followed the conquests of Alexander. Moreover, the Jewish diaspora resulted in Jews living scattered beyond their Palestinian homeland in cities such as Alexandria in Egypt. Consequently the Jewish and the Greek point of view can at times become blurred.

For the Jews of the second century BC, however, it was the Greeks, most recently in the form of the Seleucids, who were the oppressors. The story of their revolt against the Seleucids is narrated in the first book of *Maccabees*, written originally in Hebrew and translated into Greek. This also offers a fascinating account of Rome's rise from a very different perspective from the more familiar Greek and Roman ones.

The writer, who has only a hazy knowledge of the Roman state itself, is impressed by Roman power and greatly satisfied by their success against the Greeks. The Romans are characterised as strong and loyal to their allies but significantly they are also presented as destructive, given to enslavement and preoccupied with enriching themselves (**1 Maccabees A, p. 118**).

As Roman power came to be increasingly felt in Judaea itself, first with Pompey's capture of Jerusalem in 63 BC and then with the creation of the Roman province in AD 6, so Jewish attitudes to Rome became more complex. The centuries that followed would see repeated attempts at revolt, the failure of which was explained as God's punishment for the sins of his people. While some saw Rome as a protector saving the Jews from civil war and bringing harmony across the empire, others emphasised the hardship of Roman rule, especially the pressure of taxation. Among the Dead Sea Scrolls found near Qumran Rome is a 'devouring eagle', a theme found developed after the revolt of AD 66 (de Lange 1978; Hadas-Lebel 2006). The religious framework and imagery would perhaps have puzzled Polybios but the general sentiments are ones he would have recognised. He would have also had some understanding of the position of Yosef ben Mattityahu, a Jewish political leader who after the failed revolt became a Roman citizen and friend of the emperor Vespasian, and as Titus Flavius Josephus devoted his time to writing his *Jewish War* (for the comparison with Polybios, see Walbank 1995). Jewish identities in the Roman empire could indeed be multiple, especially in Alexandria. Here Philo, the first-century AD philosopher and leading figure in the Jewish community, could at the same time align with both a Jewish heritage and a Greek one while in his praise of Augustus show himself to be at one with the Roman imperial mission, in theory if not always in practice (contrast **Philo A** with **Philo B, p. 121**). His nephew, Tiberius Iulius Alexander, whose name signals a public identification with things both Greek and Roman, rose to be prefect of Egypt (Goodman 2007: 159–60). In contrast to the Greeks, however, members of the Jewish elite do not seem to have reached the higher echelons of Roman society to join the ranks of senators or consuls. This may to some extent be due to a reluctance to pursue public office, constrained by the requirements of Jewish cult and deterred by the religious ritual that was so much part of Roman aristocratic life. But there also appears to have been an unwillingness among the Romans themselves to treat the Jewish elite in the same way they treated similar groups elsewhere in the empire (Goodman 1987: 46–50).

Further West the native voice is less audible, at least until much later in the empire (cf. Woolf 1998: 1–7 on the late third-century Gallic orator Eumenius). A partial exception is the historian Pompeius Trogus, a third-generation Roman citizen from Gallia Narbonensis, writing around the time of Augustus. His family were from the Gallic tribe of the Vocontii and his grandfather had acquired citizenship through military service with Pompey in Spain, hence his name (**Pompeius Trogus C, p. 148**). His history, which focuses on the eastern Mediterranean rather than his native Gaul is preserved in an abridgement made by a certain Justin, probably in the second or third century AD. Significantly an important theme of the history is empire, beginning in the first book with the Assyrian Ninus, the first king with serious imperial ambitions and moving through the successive empires until Rome is reached. But, although Rome is in this sense central, it tends to enter the narrative as a player in other peoples' histories rather than being the force around which the narrative is shaped. We can take two examples from the abridgement of book 36. Here Trogus gives a brief history of the Jews and relates their rebellion against the Seleucids before concluding that they then 'sought the friendship of the Romans and were given their freedom, since the Romans found it easy to be generous with other people's property'; there is next a short account of the reign of Attalos III of Pergamon which ends with the Roman intervention that followed Rome being named as Attalos' heir, an intervention that is characterised in Trogus by the greed and petty rivalry of the Roman commanders. This way of structuring the narrative reflects a provincial rather than Roman perspective (Yarrow 2006: 148–9); Rome is something that happens to people. Some of Trogus' remarks, such as those in book 36, suggest a fairly jaundiced view of the Romans, not dissimilar to others encountered in this section, but attempts to see him as anti-Roman are probably misplaced; certainly there are very negative images of Rome in some of the speeches in his history (cf. that of Mithridates, 38.4–7, extract at **Pompeius Trogus A, p. 147**) but such speeches are not reliable evidence for his own position. What is interesting about Trogus is the way he seems to encapsulate a number of different identities, the Gallic provincial, the Roman citizen and the man of Greek culture. The provincial viewpoint has already been observed but it is expressed in Latin and the form, a history, is Greek. The end of the history (as it survives) implies a closer identification with Rome: here Augustus is represented as bringing law and civilised life to savage and barbarous Spaniards by organising them as a province, in other words by subjecting them to the Roman empire.

Yet, Trogus' presentation of the experience of his own people, the Gauls, is rather different; they lose their barbarous ways, not through the force of Roman arms, but through association with the Greeks of Massilia (Marseilles). This puts them on some form of equality with the Romans in spite of their subjection and allows Trogus to position himself with the civilised against the barbarous (cf. Yarrow 2006: 97–9; **Pompeius Trogus B, p. 148**). Trogus is not unique in this. Later, in the second century AD, the orator Favorinus of Arles who is also from southern Gaul shows himself to be acutely aware of all three identities in his own case (Wallace-Hadrill 2008: 1–8).

More often, however, what remains is a Roman construction. In AD 83 the Caledonian leader Calgacus, about to face a Roman army at Mons Graupius, utters a forceful condemnation of Roman imperialism that echoes some of the sentiments we have seen expressed by the Greeks and Jews. The speech, however, is in Latin and the words are those of the Roman historian Tacitus (**Tacitus D, p. 159**, cf. Iulius Civilis at Tac. *Hist.* 4.17). Calgacus' defeat shortly afterwards may have been seen as an appropriate retort to the hysterical rage of a barbarian (Veyne 1993: 362, though for an alternative interpretation, Clarke 2001). Similar sentiments are attributed to other resentful natives in other Roman historians, usually in speeches and usually not long before an unhappy end or at least a defeat. In North Africa Sallust portrays the Numidian king Jugurtha accusing the Romans of being 'unjust, intensely greedy and the common enemy of everyone' with a lust for ruling and a hatred of monarchies (*Iug.* 81). Caesar in his commentaries writes a long speech for Critognatus, a Gallic leader at Alesia, in which the Romans are contrasted unfavourably with the Cimbri and Teutones: those tribes may have ravaged the territory of the Gauls, says the speaker, but at least they left them with their rights, laws, lands and freedom, but the Romans take all these away and impose 'everlasting slavery' (Caes. *BG* 7.77). Rather than reflecting the real world of the Roman subject these speeches may be more influenced by the work of earlier historians; thus in Tacitus' *Annals* the British resistance fighter Caratacus encourages his men to recover their freedom or face 'everlasting slavery', calling to mind Caesar's use of the same phrase (12.34).

2. Cultural change: the problem of Romanisation

An Italian visiting Londinium (London) in the second century AD would have noticed that things were done differently from what he was used to back home, but in some ways he would not have been in unfamiliar surroundings, even though the region had only been under direct Roman rule since Claudius' invasion in AD 43. He could have asked directions to the forum, watched gladiatorial combat in a fair-sized amphitheatre, spent time at the baths, and dined with a wealthy friend in a house decorated with mosaics and heated by an under-floor hypocaust system. In this London was not unusual. Our visitor's experience here could be replicated with some variation throughout the empire. This striking uniformity has been commented on by ancients and moderns alike: cities with elaborate monumental centres; public sculpture and inscriptions; prominent altars or temples to the Roman imperial family; aqueducts supplying water for the baths and ornamental fountains; amphitheatres, some grander than others; the pervasive use of concrete as a basic building material. All these are identifiably Roman and they are the most tangible and obvious manifestations of Romanness to us now. Equally important, however, will have been ways of behaving, whether that be speaking and writing Latin, something especially common in the West, or elite sponsorship of civic amenities.

This phenomenon has led to considerable debate among scholars. It is evident that something has happened but what exactly and why? Scholars of the nineteenth and early twentieth century, under the influence of contemporary European imperialism, often saw the Romans as bringers of civilisation and Roman culture to backward peoples (cf. Mommsen 1887: 4–5; Haverfield 1905–6, on which Hingley 2000; Freeman 2007). Roman agency was captured in the terms used, 'to romanise' and 'romanisation'; this was something done by Romans to the conquered native population. The emphasis on backwardness tended to mean that this was applied to the peoples of the West rather than to the Greeks of the East. Support for such a position could be found in a much-cited chapter of Tacitus' *Agricola*, in which he describes how Agricola as governor of Britain introduced aspects of the Roman way of life to the uncivilised British; in Tacitus' cynical presentation such things were all features of their enslavement (**Tacitus C, p. 158**, cf. **Pliny the Elder A, 122**). Nonetheless, this one-way interpretation of the spread of Roman culture long ago lost favour among those studying the Roman empire, although echoes of it still run through the literature today.

Scholars, particularly since the influential work of Martin Millett on Britain (1990), have instead turned the indigenous population from passive recipient to active participant in the exchange. This has shifted the nature of the discussion and over the last twenty years or so the discussion has been vigorous, especially, though not exclusively, among archaeologists working in Britain. Consensus is yet to be achieved and questions proliferate: what was the role of the Romans themselves (e.g. pro-active or hands-off)? to what extent and in what way did Roman culture spread beyond the elite? what model best explains the culture change that takes place in the various regions of the Roman empire? do arguments about romanisation place too much stress on explaining homogeneity and insufficient on heterogeneity? Significantly a recent major study of Roman Britain dispenses with the idea of romanisation altogether as an unhelpful and outmoded concept, instead focusing on the variety of experiences and identities among the population (Mattingly 2006: 14–19). Studies of the empire as a whole will tend to approach the problem of the impact of Roman rule on the subject peoples in a different manner than studies of individual regions; they will highlight those features that are shared more from those that are distinctive but the very fact that there is diversity is itself important for understanding the Roman empire.

These recent developments in the study of cultural change in the provinces allow for a more nuanced examination of the relationship between ruler and subject, one that can explore regional differences within the Roman empire while also acknowledging what is shared. Provincials can both retain a local and ethnic identity while at the same time becoming part of the broader entity that is Rome. Whether in the West or the East, all are in some sense responding to Roman power but responding in their own way. The marked increase in urbanisation and the adoption of Latin in the West make change more obvious there, but the rest of the empire was not exempt. Although Greeks continued to speak Greek, live in cities and worship the same gods as before, their participation in the Roman empire went beyond merely paying taxes and recognising the Roman governor. The addition of aqueducts, public baths and fountains to the usual civic buildings (though rarely amphitheatres), the rise of Greeks to senatorial rank, and a change in the composition of city councils to something which was both more oligarchic and a more appropriate reflection of Roman political values were all elements of becoming Roman (Gleason 2006). Elsewhere indigenous and Roman practices can be seen side by side or amalgamated (cf. Woolf 1998: 206–37 on the development of Gallo-Roman religion). Similarly the public face of North African cities in the early Empire can appear very Roman, but the more private realm of funerary rites reveals the importance of an earlier pre-Roman identity (Fontana

2001). In Britain Roman-style housing in the form of villas may have been introduced but roundhouses, familiar from the late Iron Age, continue well into the Roman period (Mattingly 2006: 16, 353–78). Recent scholarship has tended to explore both the local variation and the common factors that enable the label 'Roman' to be applied (Woolf 1998; Hingley 2005).

The spread of Roman culture may not have been a deliberate policy on the part of the Romans but they certainly encouraged it indirectly by their actions. Roman goals were straightforward and pragmatic: the raising of tax and the maintenance of power. Crucial elements of the infrastructure that made these goals achievable were the long straight roads that crossed the landscape and the cities that they linked together. Administration and taxation could be conducted through these cities. The Romans gave support to developing native communities, they established colonies of their own citizens, often retired soldiers, and they upgraded native cities to the rank of *municipia*, modelled on political structures in Italy, thus setting in motion competition for status between cities (Edmondson 2006 on the western provinces). A number of municipal charters survive, the fullest being the *lex Irnitana* from the reign of Domitian which grants municipal status to the otherwise unknown town of Irni in southern Spain (González 1986; Fear 1996 131–69; **Lex Irnitana, p. 109**). In this way they not only promoted urbanisation, they also introduced a means through which Roman culture and Roman values could come that much more rapidly into the provinces and at all levels. The importance of cities in the spread of the Roman way of life was observed by the Greek geographer Strabo, for whom as a Greek the city was the cornerstone of civilised life (**Strabo B, p. 152**). Even the East, which was traditionally more urbanised, saw an extension of urbanisation under Roman rule (Woolf 1997).

Although the Romans may not have set out with the intention of converting their subjects into Romans, they did want to deal with a world that suited them and was familiar to them. Urbanisation and an elite that understood and accepted Roman values made ruling easier. This might be compared to what the political scientist, Joseph Nye, has called 'soft power', which 'co-opts people rather than coerces them' (Nye 2002: 8–12). For the local elites themselves Roman culture was, initially at least, a means of advertising their loyalty to Rome and also acquiring status for themselves as part of a bigger whole; it brought them closer to the centre of power and distinguished them from their compatriots. In a town that had been granted municipal status holding a magistracy was a route to Roman citizenship (**Lex Irnitana A, p. 109**). The preparedness of Rome to extend citizenship when necessary, which was observed in Chapter 2, meant that being Roman was not a matter of ethnicity but rather of sharing in a superior status. In that sense Romanness could be something to aspire to (cf. Woolf 1998). While it has become common to emphasise the active participation of the provincial elite in the process, it must not be forgotten that this was an unequal relationship. Power was in the hands of Rome. Where that participation was not forthcoming or not in the way that the Romans wanted it, Roman favour may have been withheld, as the case of the Jews suggests (cf. Goodman 1987: 46–50, section 1 above).

An important question has been avoided in the discussion above: what is meant by 'Roman'? If the adoption of a Roman way of life is the product of the interaction between subject and ruler rather than deliberately imposed, then the result may be something new. More than this, the transfer of cultural information may not take place merely between ruler and subject. Rather than simple imitation or even two-way traffic as subjects influence Rome in turn, it may be that influence goes in many different directions, following lines of communication between provinces and around the Mediterranean. In this we might see a parallel with the empire's road system, in which the roads, in contrast to many other empires, not only radiated out from the centre but also connected its various parts. Veteran soldiers settled in one province may have been recruited not in Rome or Italy but in another province; their presence helped spread Romanness beyond the elite, especially as on retirement from military service they would be rewarded with Roman citizenship (Wesch-Klein 2007). Revealing of the multi-cultural character of the empire and the level of mobility within it is a third-century AD tombstone found near Hadrian's Wall. It is set up in memory of Regina, a British woman, by her husband Barates, a legionary standard-maker, but the manner in which the woman is depicted can be compared to tombstones from the East, the text is in both Latin and Aramaic, and the husband is from Palmyra in Syria (**Fig. 7, p. 164**). The tombstone thus brings together two extremes of the Roman empire.

As a result of these networks of movement and exchange an increasingly homogeneous empire develops, but one which is Roman because everyone has some share of a common culture rather than because what is found is an image of the centre. Where yesterday's Roman empire may have been interpreted through nineteenth-century imperialism, today's may be being interpreted through contemporary globalisation (cf. Witcher 2000, Hingley 2005; Hitchner 2008). Positing a Roman culture that is taken up by the subject might, therefore, be a mistake; empire changed both subject and Rome. Everywhere local elites buy into an idea of what it is to be Roman and this is what makes it a success, but there may be no one place that is properly Roman, not even Rome itself (cf. Woolf 1998: 241). What being Roman meant will have differed from place to place, even though by AD 212, as a result of Caracalla's Antonine Constitution, all free inhabitants of the empire would have become Roman citizens (on which Hekster 2008 who notes the few exceptions). In considering Romanness it is important not to overstress homogeneity at the expense of the local.

The term 'romanisation' continues to be used to refer to, if not interpret, these processes, but it tends to be used out of convenience rather than because it is considered especially suitable. Nonetheless, it is a term that has proved very valuable at provoking fruitful debate. Some have been uncomfortable with its use and some have wished to reject it altogether, not merely because of the implication of Roman intention but also because it implies a one-way and rather simplistic transaction, whereas, as has been suggested above, what was happening was far more complex. Instead alternatives, such as 'acculturation', 'assimilation', or even 'creolisation' have been preferred, each drawing in different ways on more recent imperial or colonial experiences. Whatever vocabulary is used it is important that it helps rather than distracts from the complex problem of understanding the impact of Roman power on the conquered populations.

3. Worshipping Rome

A remarkable feature of the Roman empire is the worship of the ruler in some form or other. Throughout the empire altars, temples, priesthoods and festivals were set up with Roman power as their focus. Under the emperors this is often referred to as the imperial cult. This rather misleading phrase is another scholarly term of convenience, bringing together a wide range of activities under one heading. Rather than any unified, centrally-administered cult, however, what we are faced with is a collection of local cults, taking different forms in different places and originating in different circumstances. What they do have in common is that in each case Rome is given some form of religious identity. The merging of religion and politics was not uncommon in antiquity, the one serving to reinforce the authority of the other. This development is a potent reflection of the impact of Rome, while its continued existence over centuries is a sign of the extent to which the elite of the empire was implicated in Roman rule.

The evidence is varied and extensive. Literary sources, such Tacitus, Suetonius and Dio Cassius, tend to reflect the perspective of the centre, but epigraphic and archaeological evidence can show something different, namely the view from the provinces. Decrees regulating festivals, the tombstones of priests of the emperor and the remains of temples and altars all reveal the place of cults of Roman power in the communities of the empire. The earliest evidence comes from the East where Greek cities had given divine honours to rulers since at least the time of Alexander the Great in the fourth century BC. The phenomenon is sometimes explained as a means of coming to terms with the otherwise incomprehensible power of the Hellenistic monarchs (cf. Price 1984: 28–30). With their defeat of Philip V of Macedon the Romans too find themselves as the recipients of these honours. In the immediate aftermath of the victory and of the freedom proclamation of T. Quinctius Flamininus in 196 BC, honours are directed at both the successful commander and Rome itself; festivals are set up in Flamininus' honour and a temple to the goddess Roma is vowed at Smyrna in Asia Minor (**Plutarch A, p. 125 and Inscription D, p. 106, on Flamininus; Tacitus A (56), p. 154**). It should be stressed that the goddess Roma is no Roman god and she would not have been previously known in Rome (cf. Beard, North and Price 1998: I.158–60), although somewhat confusingly modern literature tends to latinise her name; rather, she is a Greek response to Roman power, a goddess who encapsulates that power and whose very name is identical with the Greek word for 'strength' (*rhome*, on which Erskine 1995). Over the next two centuries the cult of Roma appeared in Greek cities throughout the East, and prominent Roman commanders active in the region such as Sulla, Caesar, Pompey and Antony, were themselves given divine honours (**Inscriptions G and H, p. 107, Cicero G, p. 99**).

The emergence of Augustus as sole ruler, however, brought a significant shift. Not only was he more effusively praised than his predecessors but divine honours came to be more closely associated with Roman administrative structures than before. In addition to civic cults, there was now a sanctuary of Augustus and Roma at Pergamon, administered by the assembly (*koinon*) of the province of Asia, a grouping of the province's leading cities, and approved by Augustus (**Dio A, p. 102, Tacitus A (37), p. 153**). Acquiring a shrine with provincial status, as opposed to mere *polis* status, became a matter of fierce competition for these cities. When the assembly requested and was granted permission to set up a temple to Tiberius, Livia and the Senate, such was the prestige attached to the venture that eleven cities of Asia spent the next three years arguing their respective claims until the row was settled by the decision of the Roman Senate (**Tacitus A, p. 153**). Cults of the emperor continued to be a prominent presence in the cities. In Miletos those sitting in session in the Council House would hardly need reminding of the power of Rome; as they entered it, they would have passed the sizeable altar of Augustus located in the very courtyard of the Council House itself (Price 1984: 138).

Even more important, perhaps, are the changes that can be observed elsewhere in the empire under Augustus. For the first time cults of Roman power appear outside the Greek world, not in one province of the West but in several. As early as 26/25 BC the Spanish city of Tarraco (Tarragona) chose to honour Augustus with an altar, and on his death successfully petitioned for a temple to their late emperor (Fishwick 2004: 5–40). In 12 BC (or possibly 10 BC) an altar to Roma and Augustus was dedicated in the context of an elaborate sanctuary at Lugdunum (Lyons) in Gaul. As in Asia the overlap with administrative structures was unmistakable; Lugdunum was the meeting place of the annual assembly of the Tres Galliae, the three Gallic provinces of Aquitania, Belgica and Lugdunensis, attended by all the representatives of their component communities (*civitates*) (Fishwick 2004: 105–28). Both cults were of sufficient importance to be celebrated on local coinage (cf. **Fig. 13, p. 167**).

In explaining the Greek cults we can look to longstanding Greek practice, but the impetus for these western cults is more controversial. It has been suggested that here Roman initiative was very important. The establishment of the cult centre at Lugdunum, for example, occurred when Augustus' stepson, Nero Claudius Drusus, was based there and reorganising the administration of the region. While Roman encouragement is probable, indigenous input cannot be ignored and is crucial to the success of the cult over time. Just as the first priest of the Lugdunum altar was a Gallic aristocrat with Roman citizenship, C. Iulius Vercondaridubnus, so the sanctuary itself combines Roman architectural features with a rather more Gallic sacred grove (MacMullen 2000: 91–3). It may have been at roughly the same time that an altar was set up in the territory of the Ubii, a German tribe to the east of the Rhine, most likely with the aim of performing a similar function for the prospective province of Germania as the Lugdunum altar did for Gaul (Tac. *Ann.* 1.39.1; Fishwick 2002: 20–1). In Spain the spread of the cult of the emperor may have owed something to indigenous Spanish traditions that accorded leaders special reverence (Curchin 1991: 162). Even in the East there may have been a little Roman encouragement to shape the direction of these cult practices. When the assembly of the province of Asia offered a prize for the person who could come up with the best way of honouring 'the god', that is to say Augustus, it was won by the Roman governor who proposed beginning the year on Augustus' birthday. The governor thus promotes the cult worship of the emperor, while the assembly itself neatly manages to honour both the emperor and the governor (Price 1984: 54–5).

These cults have been dismissed as superficial, mere flattery of the ruling power, but such explanations, often heavily influenced by christianising assumptions about the nature of religion, leave much unanswered and fail to illuminate the important role that the cults play in the relationship between subject and ruler. In East and West these cults flourish and their longevity is striking. Even a figure such as Flamininus can still be found as the recipient of cult honours in the first century AD, some 200 years after the events that brought him this recognition, as a sacred law from Gytheion attests (Sherk 1988: no. 32, lines 11–12). The success of the various cults can be explained in part by the willingness of communities, especially the elites of those communities, to support and embrace them. Whether in Gaul, Spain, North Africa or the Greek East priesthoods of the emperor were highly prized and the object of competition among local aristocracies (cf. Drinkwater 1979: 94–6 on Gaul). The imperial cult was part of what it was to be Roman and the regular festivals that celebrated the emperor became occasions for practices perceived as Roman. Gladiatorial games, for instance, were features of festivals in honour of the emperor in both the western and the eastern provinces, paid for by the elite but enjoyed by all. Holding the priesthood was thus a costly business and so great was the pressure to excel that some aristocrats drove themselves almost to the point of bankruptcy (**Tacitus B (31)**, **p. 155**; Woolf 1998: 217).

These cults in their ritual, organisation and complexity served to highlight the power of Rome and the distance that divided the subject from the ruler. Yet at the same time paradoxically they brought subject and ruler together, in so far as the subject was now incorporated into the Roman empire as participant.

4. Revolt and resistance

Another response to Roman power was revolt. Revolts took place throughout the empire, in Spain, Britain, Gaul, Germany, North

Africa, Greece, Asia Minor, Judaea, often but not always in the earlier stages of Roman occupation (Dyson 1971; 1975). Some are better recorded than others, though rarely is the perspective of those opposed to Rome adequately represented. Appian gives a full account of the Greek rising against Rome prompted by Mithridates' invasion of the province of Asia in 89–88 BC (**Appian A, p. 91**); Caesar tells the story of Vercingetorix's revolt in Gaul in 52 BC from the point of view of the victorious Roman commander; Josephus writes seven books on the Jewish revolt of the AD 66–74, in which he himself was implicated; Tacitus in his *Annals* provides an extended treatment of Boudicca's revolt in Britain in AD 60–61 (**Tacitus B, p. 155**), while in the fourth book of his *Histories* he covers in detail the revolt of the Batavians along the Rhine in AD 69–70. Other revolts, however, such as that of the Nasamones in North Africa in the reign of Domitian, are given the briefest of notices, while some are simply unknown to us (**Dio B, p. 103**). Nor is identifying a revolt as straightforward as it might at first appear. The line between resistance to Rome and organised banditry can be a fine one, and the latter description might suit the Romans themselves best. Tacfarinas, for instance, although challenging the Roman army in Africa over some four years early in Tiberius' reign, appears to have been represented by the Roman authorities not as a rebel but as a bandit (Tac. *Ann.* 3.73).

With revolts ranging so widely across the empire, both in space and time, there will be no one universal explanation for their occurrence. They will need to be explained both by Roman actions and local circumstances, and the form each takes will vary accordingly. Many reasons for revolts have been canvassed: taxation, indebtedness, the expropriation of land for colonies, the loss of liberty, tension between old traditions and the new Roman ways, unwillingness to be recruited into the Roman army, Roman arrogance, religious interference and lower-class resentment against a local government backed by Rome. Accounts of revolts frequently highlight the killing of Romans and those associated with them, in particular merchants who had gravitated towards these new markets. At the time of Mithridates' invasion thousands of Italians resident in the province of Asia were said to have been massacred; sources give figures for the dead ranging from 80,000 to 150,000. The Gallic revolt against Caesar began with the killing of Roman traders at Cenabum (Orléans). Attacks on Camulodunum (Colchester), Verulamium (St Albans) and the commercial centre of Londinium claimed the lives of 70,000 Roman citizens and allies in the revolt of Boudicca, at least according to Tacitus while Dio reports the even higher figure of 80,000 dead. Such attacks are suggestive of the indigenous population's perception of Rome and what symbolised Rome, but the recurrence of this theme in accounts is equally revealing about how the Romans chose to represent these revolts. The emotive force of stories of the murder of civilians and fellow citizens when reported back home in Italy should not be underestimated – and doubtless the number of dead multiplied as indignation increased. We might compare this to the vivid stories told in England of the killing of Protestant settlers in the Irish Rebellion of 1641; several thousand dead escalated in the telling to hundred of thousands (Clifton 1999).

Other manifestations of Roman rule would also be targeted by rebels. Just as the development of cults of Roma and of the emperor reflected a recognition of Roman power and authority, so revolt could be expressed by the rejection of such cults. At the time of the successful German rising under Arminius in AD 9 a priest of the emperor at the altar of the Ubii was said to have thrown aside his official regalia and joined the revolt (Tac. *Ann.* 1.57.2); in Britain Boudicca's rebellion in the early 60s AD focused initially on the temple of Claudius at Camulodunum, a symbol of Roman despotism for the rebels and an imagined source of protection for the occupiers (**Tacitus B (31–2), p. 155**), while in Jerusalem the beginning of the Jewish revolt in AD 66 was marked by the abandonment of the daily sacrifices to the God of the Jews for the well-being of the emperor (Jos. *Jewish War*, 2.408–18). Statues too would feel the force of anti-Roman feeling. When Mithridates invaded Asia, for example, the Ephesians signalled their support for him by overthrowing the statues of Romans (**Appian A, p. 91**). A bronze head of a probable Claudius found in a river in Suffolk may come from an equestrian statue of the emperor mutilated during Boudicca's rebellion; a leg found in neighbouring Norfolk is likely to have come from the same statue (Hingley and Unwin 2005: 80–3 with illustration).

Revolts may vary but the Roman reaction is more uniform, a great and public show of force. The treatment of Jerusalem after the Jewish Revolt is characteristic. A five-month siege in 70 AD culminated in the destruction of much of the city and most importantly of the Temple itself. The Romans were clearly aware of the significance of the Temple; ritual objects from there, including the menorah, a distinctive seven-branched candelabrum, were prominent among the spoils carried in Vespasian and Titus' triumphal procession and the menorah in particular was made the centrepiece of Titus' triumphal arch that celebrated the victory (**Josephus A, Figs 1–3, pp. 109–11**). The ruthlessness with which the revolt was crushed sent a powerful message that no one rebels against Rome with impunity. That message had already been sent many times before. The Achaian revolt of the 140s BC was followed by the destruction of Corinth, one of the leading cities in mainland Greece; Athens' adherence to the cause of Mithridates led to its sacking by Sulla; the Gallic revolt of the 50s BC was repaid with massacres, including extensive slaughter at Avaricum (Caes. *BG* 7.28.5); some 80,000 Britons were said to have died in the final battle that ended Boudicca's rising (**Tacitus B (37), p. 158**). Defeat was then followed by reorganisation that reinforced subjection by allowing the Romans to redefine their relationship and tighten their grip, as happened for example in the East after Pompey's defeat of Mithridates. In some ways revolt might be seen as part of the process of subjugation. Rather than hindering the development of imperial structures, violent resistance could promote that development by creating opportunities for some of the native population to demonstrate their loyalty and so bond with the imperial power in a time of crisis, while the latter made clear the advantages of such a course of action (as Woolf 1998: 32–3 argues for Gaul).

To talk of 'revolt' assumes that those revolting had previously been acknowledged subjects of Rome but that is to approach the matter from the perspective of the imperial power for whom resistance may equate with rebellion. In practice what is termed 'revolt' may reflect native unwillingness to accept the Roman view of the situation. It is noticeable that the Gallic revolt, described and suppressed by Caesar, involved tribes that had not previously fought against him and so were Roman subjects by default rather than defeat (Woolf 1998: 30–1). Similarly when the Achaian League fought against Rome in the 140s BC after the Romans had effectively ordered the break-up of the league, it was the first time they had come into armed conflict with Rome. Modern scholarly literature knows the events both as the 'Achaian War' and as the 'Achaian Revolt', the former suggesting that this should be seen as Achaia's assertion of its independence, the latter as an attempt to reclaim what had already been lost. The uncertainty of the nomenclature shows how it is not so easy to determine at what point Rome becomes the ruler, and that whether a conflict is considered war, resistance or revolt may depend on perspective. In this case the Romans expected to be obeyed but the Achaians had not yet got to the point where they took their own obedience to Roman orders for granted.

Some revolts have a higher profile in the historical record than others. The creation of a narrative can make them self-contained, chronologically-defined stories that distract from the low-level disruption that was more continuous and more widespread than at first appears. In Spain there was on-going resistance over some 200 years linked to the gradual extension of Roman power across the peninsula in the second and first centuries BC. In Gaul, where Caesar had crushed the revolt of Vercingetorix in the 50s BC, trouble persisted nonetheless into the first century AD. Then there are the bandits. Although these may have included some who deliberately resisted Roman rule, there were others who did not necessarily reject Roman power but they were not incorporated into the structure of the empire either. Instead they inhabited a liminal position in regions beyond the limits of Roman authority, yet within the territory of the empire, such as the rugged mountains of Isauria and Cilicia in southern Turkey (Shaw 1984; 1990). Their equivalents can be found at sea. Piracy is presented by our sources as a major problem of the mid-first century BC, one infused with contempt for Rome and brought to an abrupt end by the brilliance of Pompey (**Plutarch D, p. 128**). This image of the piracy and its rise and fall is partly due to the demands of narrative and Pompey's career. Like the mountains the sea was an area where Rome's authority did not always hold sway, even in the heyday of the *pax Romana* (Braund 1993; de Souza 1999).

There may have been resistance to Roman rule and even revolts, but notwithstanding such dissent the empire was remarkable for the length of time it lasted. This longevity has prompted Clifford Ando (2000) to argue that there was a developing consensus among its subjects that the empire was beneficial; in this they were endorsing, and even contributing to, imperial ideology. In effect, therefore, the subjects acquiesced in their own subjugation because of the advantages it brought them. While there is something in this and the emerging idea of Romanness can be adduced in support of it, we need to avoid going too far in imagining that the Roman empire changed from one based on coercion to one based on goodwill. In reality there was always a combination of these two elements. The Roman authorities never lost their appreciation of the value of terror. Whatever rules a provincial governor may have been bound by, he was still a figure of unpredictable and arbitrary power in the eyes of his subjects. Terror as much as loyalty kept them in their place, which from the governor's point of view might have been construed as the deference that was his due (cf. Lendon 1997: 201–9). State-sponsored violence is rarely far from the surface in the Roman world, a truth evident to all ages and all levels of society.

Chance preserves a late antique schoolbook that treats typical experiences in the daily life of young boy; included among such mundane events as getting up in the morning, going to school and having lunch is watching the governor presiding over the public torture and execution of a bandit (**Schoolbook, p. 151**). The public character of this is important; it provides everyone with a vivid, immediate, and no doubt recurring, lesson in Roman power. It is no coincidence that Rome's contribution to the public entertainment of the provinces was the brutality of the amphitheatre. Here the public torture and execution of the socially marginalised, whether through crime, war, poverty or religion, would have had the effect of reinforcing the existing Roman social and political order, both in the provinces and at Rome itself. The games may have been fun but they were also a warning of what it meant not to be Roman.

CHAPTER 5

The Ruler

The British Empire is greatest secular agency for good ever known to mankind.
Lord Rosebery, British Prime Minster, 1894–95

1. Ruling an empire

Polybios saw the Romans as rulers of the world after the battle of Pydna brought an end to the kingdom of Macedon in 168 BC. It is less easy to identify when the Romans first formed this conception of themselves – or indeed at what point they conceived of themselves as an imperial power at all. Polybios treats world rule as a Roman aspiration from as early as the mid-third century, one expressed by the Romans themselves; thus, before the battle of Zama in 202 Scipio Africanus could tell his soldiers that victory would not only make them masters of Africa but it would also gain them and their country 'undisputed leadership and power over the rest of the world' (15.10.2). Nonetheless, however close Polybios may have been to the Roman elite, he was still an outsider interpreting what he saw from a Greek perspective rather than speaking with an authentically Roman voice. What we lack is sufficient contemporary Roman evidence prior to the first century BC to allow us to determine how the Romans themselves viewed their increasing dominion. The limited material that is available to us suggests that a Roman senator of the second century BC thought in terms of power exercised rather than territory ruled (Richardson 2008: 191–3), but where they imagined the limits of Roman power to be is less clear.

By the time that evidence from Roman sources is more plentiful, imperial power has become something to be celebrated in Rome; it is a recurring theme, widely found in public speeches, literature and art. From the 70s BC the globe, which is best interpreted as symbolising universal rule, features on Roman coins, sometimes under the foot of the *genius populi Romani*, the personification of the Roman People,

or later under that of Roma, Venus or Victory. The earliest example
appears on a coin minted by the moneyer Cn. Lentulus in 76–75 BC;
on one side there is the head of the *genius populi Romani* (marked
with the initials GPR), on the other a globe between a sceptre and a
ship's rudder, plausibly interpreted as representing control over land
and sea (**Fig. 11, p. 166**, Nicolet 1991: 36-7, Crawford 1974: no. 393,
cf. **Fig. 12**). Cicero in his speeches repeatedly praises Rome's imperial
success. He considers extending the boundaries of the empire to be
one of the goals of a Roman general and applauds Pompey and Caesar
for bringing Roman power to the limits of the world (Brunt 1978). At
times, however, such praise may have been intended to deflect attention away from the uncomfortable fact that the leading generals of the
late Republic had so often gained their victories not against external
enemies but against each other. Not only did the Romans of the late
Republic equate their rule with the known world, some at least saw
this as divinely-ordained (Verg. *Aen.* 1.277–9, Cic. *Phil.* 6.19, Livy
1.16.6–8). Roman claims to universal rule are also evident in the map
of the world that decorated the Porticus Vipsaniae, a project initiated
by Augustus' right-hand man, M. Vipsanius Agrippa, and completed
by the emperor himself (Pliny, *NH* 3.16–17, though Brodersen 1995:
275–86 questions whether it is a map to which Pliny refers). It was
only natural too that Rome and Italy should have been considered the
centre of the world (Pliny, *NH* 37.201–5, cf. Vitruvius 6.1.11).

Many of these themes come together in the celebrations that followed Pompey's campaigns in the East in the 60s BC. These campaigns
involved not only victories over the pirates and Mithridates but also a
radical re-organisation of the eastern Mediterranean bringing much of
it firmly under Roman control. Diodoros records an inscription that
Pompey had set up which listed his achievements and all the peoples
he had made subject to the Romans. In this he claims that he had made
the limits of Roman rule identical with those of the earth (**Diodoros
A, p. 103**, cf. Cic. *Pro Sestio* 67). This claim was brought vividly before
the public through the scale and magnificence of his triumph and displayed for posterity in the enormous theatre complex that he built in
Rome with the profits of his campaigns. Here amid reminders of the
peoples and places he had conquered was a colossal statue of Pompey
himself holding a globe in his hand; that at any rate is the most likely
identification of a statue discovered in the sixteenth century (Beard
2007: 7–41; Plut. *Pomp.* 45).

Empire might seem essentially self-interested, but Rome, like
many imperial powers since, dressed its power in the language of

benevolence; Roman rule was, or at least should be, in the interests of the subject. When his brother Quintus takes up the governorship of Asia, Cicero writes him a long letter to advise him how to conduct himself in his new position. He stresses the interests of the provincials writing: 'I think that in all matters those in power must adhere to the following principle, that their subjects be as happy as possible' (**Cicero H (24), p. 100**, cf. 27). This is put on a more theoretical footing in the third book of his *On the Republic*, much of which is now lost although a summary of its arguments survive in Augustine's *City of God* (**Augustine A, p. 94**). This conception of Roman rule is not restricted to Cicero. Pliny the Elder, for example, in the first century AD can see Italy, and Rome in particular, as divinely chosen to unite the peoples of the world and bring civilisation to them (**Pliny the Elder A, p. 122**). It can also be seen in the epic poetry of Vergil, where the capacity to rule is one of Rome's essential features. When Aeneas visits the underworld to meet his father Anchises, he witnesses a parade of great Romans yet to be born and is told something of Rome's destiny: 'Remember, Roman, to rule nations with authority – these will be your skills – to establish the habits of peace, to spare the subjugated and to crush the proud in war' (*Aen.* 6. 851–3), though the violence of the closing words is not to be ignored.

Such statements of concern about their subjects were, however, rather undercut by continued and thorough exploitation. The city of Rome was itself a striking testament to the efficiency with which wealth was extracted from the provinces (see next section). Cicero was aware of this dichotomy; in his *De Officiis*, written shortly after the assassination of Caesar, he contrasts the protective character of Roman rule in the past with the oppression of his own time. The latter he blames on the failure of the Republic when not even Rome's own citizens are safe (2.26–7). This may be an idealisation of the past, a not uncommon tendency in Roman literature, but it also reflects a view of how things should be, even if reality might fall short. There is certainly considerable evidence that both as public officials and in a more private role as businessmen and moneylenders Romans sought to get as much out of the empire as possible. During the Republic a particular problem for subjects in the provinces was the collaboration that is known to have taken place between the provincial governor and the *publicani*, private groups independent of the state who would bid for the right to collect taxes (***Digest* A, p. 101, Polybios C, p. 131**). What scholars euphemistically term 'maladministration' could have a major impact on Rome's provincial subjects, as a reading of Cicero's *Verrines* demonstrates.

These prosecution speeches which Cicero prepared for the trial of Gaius Verres, the former governor of Sicily, offer a case study in how not to be a governor. No doubt they are exaggerated but nonetheless they constitute the most detailed and sustained indictment of a Roman governor to survive (**Cicero B, p. 97**).

Prosecutions such as these would have taken place before the *quaestio de repetundis*, a standing court set up in 149 BC to try instances where a magistrate was accused of profiting illegally from his time in a province; the name of the tribunal derived from the phrase, *pecuniae repetundae*, meaning 'money to be recovered'. By the time of Caesar's *lex Iulia de repetundis* in 59 BC legislation defining what magistrates could and could not do in a province had become increasingly complex and wide-ranging and moved beyond simple cases of extortion (Lintott 1993: 99–107). This type of legislation has often been taken as evidence that the Romans were not indifferent to the welfare of their subjects. Nonetheless, it is important not to over-emphasise this aspect; other factors come into play, in particular the need to restrain aristocrats away from home whose behaviour may conflict not only with the interests of the empire but also with those of their fellow aristocrats. In a system where the governor changed frequently but Roman power was constant it was important that a governor did not carry his enthusiasm for profit so far that he undermined the stability of the province. Furthermore, the competitive character of the Roman aristocracy will have pushed in two directions: on the one hand senators will have looked to a provincial governorship as a way of increasing their own wealth and status; on the other they will have been keen to impose some constraint on their rivals. In practice neither legislation nor the fall of the Republic put an end to corruption in the provinces. Thus well into the Principate Tacitus can praise his father-in-law Agricola for cracking down on corruption in Britain and so reducing the causes of native resentment against Rome (**Tacitus C, p. 158**, cf. Brunt 1961).

Although the Romans may have presented themselves as looking out for the interests of their subjects, this was very much conditional on obedience. Cicero in *On the Republic* proposed several analogies for Rome's relationship with its subjects, one of which was revealingly that between master and slave: for some men, we are told, 'slavery is useful'. The alternative to submitting to these benevolent Roman masters is starkly presented in the passage of the *Aeneid* quoted above, annihilation. Nor was this a hypothetical alternative: Augustus in the *Res Gestae* (3) prides himself on preferring to preserve foreign peoples where possible rather than destroying them, while Germanicus was said to have boasted of the total destruction of the Germans (Tac. *Ann.* 1.21–2). The Roman treatment of rebels shows what little sympathy they had with the disobedient (see Chapter 4, section 4 above; on Roman mass slaughter, Isaac 2004: 215–24).

Rome may have conquered a vast empire and brought many peoples under its control but it ruled with a surprisingly small number of administrators; even the term 'administrator' might suggest a greater degree of organisation and professionalism than was the case. At the empire's height in the first two centuries AD it is estimated that a mere 160 or so elite officials were appointed to govern a subject population of forty-five to fifty-five million; Keith Hopkins contrasts these figures with some 4,000 high status officials who catered for a similar-sized population in southern China in the twelfth century (Hopkins 1983: 186). The figures may be rough and the comparison loose but they point up the rudimentary character of Roman imperial administration. Furthermore, Roman officials, such as provincial governors, would be accompanied only by a small staff, whose experience of provincial administration could often be fairly limited. Rome was able to rule this empire with so little bureaucracy because, although authority lay in the hands of Roman officials, much of the routine administration was carried out by the subjects themselves. Crucial here was the role of cities. Rome looked to these and the local elites that ran them to see that affairs ran smoothly, not intervening itself unless there were obvious problems as when Pliny was sent to Bithynia and Pontus (Garnsey and Saller 1987: 20–40, Lintott 1993, Ando 2006; for Pliny, see below). The provincial elites were thus co-opted as partners in Roman rule. In most provinces as the governor's military role receded with time, so other aspects of administration came to the fore, in particular his role in matters of jurisdiction (see, for example, the stress on it in Cicero's letter to Quintus, **Cicero H, p. 99**, Lintott 1993: 54–69).

Important evidence for provincial administration under the Republic comes from the correspondence of Cicero, who served as governor of Cilicia in 51–50 BC when it was still a relatively new province; it included parts of southern Asia Minor and from 58 the island of Cyprus which had been annexed by Cato. In this correspondence which consists mostly of private letters to his friend Atticus Cicero presents himself as a good governor, fair to the provincials and putting the interests of the state rather than himself first, in marked contrast to the archetypal bad governor Verres or indeed his predecessor in Cilicia, Appius Claudius Pulcher (**Cicero G, p. 99**). The letters reveal much about the day-to-day life of a governor, but also something of the

pressures that could be put on the governor by his peers as they sought
to persuade him to use his influence on their behalf in the province.
One friend, M. Caelius Rufus, repeatedly asks Cicero to supply pan-
thers for the games which he plans to give as aedile in Rome (Cic. *Fam.*
8.9). Another, the senator M. Iunius Brutus, not coincidentally the
nephew of the same Cato who annexed the island, had loaned money
through his agents to the Cypriot city of Salamis at the excessive rate of
4 per cent per month, effectively 48 per cent per year, and now sought
repayment. Appius had thrown the weight of the governor behind
these demands and provided armed support for the moneylenders
which allowed them to besiege the Council House resulting in the
deaths of five of its members from starvation. Cicero was under considerable pressure to continue these efforts to enforce payment (Cic.
Att. 5.21.10–13, 6.2.7–9). Nor did such financial practices end with
the Republic – one of the explanations given for the revolt of Boudicca
in Britain was Seneca's decision to call in loans he had made to the
Britons and to do so with force (Dio 62.2.1).

A second glimpse at a governor in action comes from another set
of correspondence but on this occasion it is a governor operating in a
very different world, some 150 years after Cicero; Roman rule, far from
being a novelty, is now long-established and at the centre of power
there is the emperor. Unlike the private letters of Cicero this is a dossier
of official correspondence, between the emperor Trajan and Pliny, his
trouble-shooting governor in Bithynia and Pontus. It contains reports
and problems raised by Pliny and importantly the emperor's replies.
This province was usually administered by the Senate but a number
of high-profile corruption cases had led the emperor to intervene
and appoint Pliny as his own representative. As such Pliny was not a
typical governor, but many of the problems he is addressing will have
been common elsewhere. He shows himself concerned with the living
conditions of his subjects: that they have an adequate water supply,
that they should not have to live with the stench of an open sewer
running down the main street. In particular, however, his mission is
to bring order to civic finances and to ensure that no seditious groups
are allowed to develop. Both these objectives are fundamental to the
maintenance and stability of Roman order, the one tackling the causes
of resentment by making the payment of taxes less oppressive, the
other removing a vehicle for the expression of resentment (**Pliny the
Younger A and B, p. 123**). Noticeably both Cicero and Pliny present
themselves as model governors; bad governing may be common but it
is something done by others.

2. Building an imperial city

Ruling an empire changed Rome itself. It became the largest city yet known, with a huge population, impressive buildings and spectacular games, all of which were funded by the wealth of empire, extracted from its subjects and from the defeated. No other city could compare; it inspired awe in those who saw it. The poet Vergil, who was himself from northern Italy, depicts a peasant who has visited Rome describing the city to a friend on his return:

> The city they call Rome, in my ignorance, I thought was like this town of ours, to which we shepherds are often accustomed to drive our young sheep: so too I knew that puppies are like dogs, and kids their mother-goats; in this way I was used to comparing great things with small; but this city raises her head as far above all other cities as the cypress towers above the wayfaring tree. (*Eclogues* 1.19–25).

In the second century AD the Greek rhetorician Aelius Aristides could envisage Rome as a mighty city carrying other cities one on top of the other, so many and so extensive that if laid out on the ground they would stretch to the Ionian Sea (*To Rome* 8).

Rome was not merely bigger and more populous than other cities, it also had a monumental centre that befitted its role as the ruling city of an empire; here there were the imperial fora with their porticoes and temples, the Colosseum and Circus Maximus, those two great centres of Roman entertainment, the various triumphal arches celebrating military victory and everywhere statues. Repeatedly the buildings and sculptures carried clear messages of Roman superiority. Trajan's Forum, constructed in the early second century AD with the proceeds of his successful campaign against the Dacians, was heavy with military imagery and decorated with statues of defeated Dacians. Its centre-piece was the famous column which in its spiralling relief-sculpture told the story of the campaign; here the enemy could be seen, subjugated, decapitated and in chains (Packer 2001**; Figs 8 and 9, p. 165**). Not far away was the Colosseum in which Rome's power over life and death was graphically displayed; its association with war is clear in the recently-recovered dedicatory inscription that stood over the entrance: 'Emperor Titus Caesar Vespasianus Augustus ordered the new amphitheatre to be built from the spoils of war' (**Fig. 10, p. 166**). The war in question was the crushing of the Jewish revolt of AD 66–70, referred to explicitly on a no longer extant triumphal arch at the Circus Maximus erected in honour of Titus (Coleman 2000, **Inscription I, p. 108**; note that this is distinct from the Arch of Titus that is still to be seen on the Via Sacra near the Forum).

But this was the Rome of the emperors; its monuments necessarily made a statement not only about the power of Rome but also about the power of the emperor. What is in some ways surprising is how long it took Rome to reach this position. By the early second century BC Rome was a major Mediterranean power, which had defeated Carthage, Philip V of Macedon and Antiochos III. Yet, the city itself failed to impress; Livy tells how its rather restrained appearance was the object of some ridicule at the Macedonian court (Livy 40.5.7). This was no doubt in part because it was not the centre of a Hellenistic kingdom and so did not come with the great palaces and the creations of royal patronage. Nor did second-century BC Rome have the theatres and gymnasia of the Greek *polis*, institutions that embodied the communality and exclusiveness of the citizenry. Instead Rome reflected its own political context.

The shape and appearance of Republican Rome owed much to its competitive aristocracy and their shared military ethos (cf. Cornell 2000: 53–4). The city's many temples, for example, may have been a sign of Roman religiosity but in their inception, construction and location they were often the products of war. They would have been vowed by a general during a campaign and dedicated after its successful completion. These temples, frequently decorated with booty, became monuments commemorating the achievement of the victorious general. They were often placed along or near the traditional route of the triumphal procession, further emphasising the dedicator's military success and acting as a permanent reminder to be seen by every future *triumphator* as he passed (Hölkeskamp 2006: 483–6, though note Beard 2007: 104–5's scepticism that there was a traditional triumphal route). The gods and goddesses honoured here could evoke war and victory by their very names: Venus Victrix, Hercules Victor, Mars, Virtus, Fortuna (Cornell 2000: 48 with n. 39). Such temple construction was most pronounced in the third century BC, although the resulting temples may have been comparatively small-scale and made of tufa and traventine rather than the marble that began to be used from the mid-second century BC onwards. The four republican temples excavated side by side in Largo Argentina offer striking testimony to the concentration of victory temples in the city of Rome (**Figs 14–15, p. 168;** Claridge 1998: 215–19, Torelli 2006: 92–3).

The profits of war financed the construction of these temples, although scholars disagree over whether this was done directly by the general out of the spoils of his campaign (Ziolkowski 1992) or with senatorial intervention (Orlin 1997). Nonetheless, by the third century BC Rome was a city where the prizes of war were increasingly in evidence. Some 2,000 statues were said to have been seized when the Romans captured Etruscan Volsinii in 264 (Pliny *NH* 34.34); the number may be exaggerated but the remains of a dedicatory inscription confirm that some were indeed exhibited in Rome (Gruen 1992: 87). Once Rome's victories extended to the Greek world, works of Greek art came to be part of the visual make-up of the city. Thus Q. Metellus Macedonicus followed up his suppression of the Macedonian revolt of the 140s by bringing back to Rome a statue group that showed Alexander and his companions, a creation of the great sculptor Lysippos, which he displayed in his newly-built portico, the Porticus Metelli (Gruen 1992: 115–16). Booty in various forms could also be seen fixed to the outside of the houses of aristocrats who had been awarded a triumph, a symbol of their achievement which could outlast even their ownership of the house (Rawson 1990, **Pliny the Elder B, p. 122**). The huge quantity of plunder that was taken from Syracuse after Marcellus' sack of the city in 212 prompted critical comments from Polybios and for some was seen as the beginning of the moral decline of Rome (**Polybios F, p. 134**, Lintott 1972). Of course as Rome and the Roman elite became richer they could also buy what they had not plundered; Cicero was not alone in using his wealth to buy up high prestige art from the Greek world and slaves from the West (**Cicero E, F, I, p. 98, 101**).

In the erection of commemorative temples, arches and porticoes aristocrats competed with each other and so left their mark upon the rambling urban landscape of Rome. Other public buildings, such as bridges, aqueducts and market-halls, were often functional and their construction for the most part overseen by magistrates. Although they may not have had an explicit connection to war, the money to fund them would have come from Rome's military campaigns. Aqueducts were particularly expensive to build; the Aqua Anio Vetus (272 BC) was paid for by booty captured from Pyrrhos (Frontinus, *On Aqueducts* 6) while the impressive Aqua Marcia, constructed in the late 140s BC, is believed to have been financed by plunder seized from the cities of Corinth and Carthage, both recently sacked by Rome (Dodge 2000: 172–4). Even here the Roman aristocratic preoccupation with perpetuating the family name is evident; buildings were given the name of the magistrate responsible, a practice that may have limited more grandiose and ostentatious building projects (so the Aqua Marcia after the praetor Q. Marcius Rex).

The first century BC sees the emergence of powerful figures such as Pompey and Caesar and with them a change in the way that the city develops but it is still the resources of war and empire that fund it. As a means of commemorating a successful military campaign Pompey's theatre dwarfed anything that had gone before. This huge complex in the Campus Martius was paid for out of the tremendous wealth that Pompey had acquired through his campaigns in the East. Dedicated to Venus Victrix, it was adorned with fourteen sculptures representing the nations he had conquered and significantly, as was observed in the previous section, one of himself holding a globe (Welch 2006: 512, Nicolet 1991: 37–41). Now it is no longer simply conquest that is being celebrated but worldwide rule. The scale of the building projects undertaken by Pompey, Caesar and the emperors that followed served to emphasise the superiority of Rome to its subjects but also to any Roman nobles who still thought it worth competing. Augustus drew attention to his transformation of Rome with the claim attributed to him that he found Rome in bricks and left it in marble (Suet. *Aug.* 28). Vitruvius captures the mood when he opens his *On Architecture* with praise of Augustus not only for increasing the territory of Rome but also for ensuring that 'the majesty of empire was expressed through the grandeur of the public buildings' (Preface 2).

3. Inhabiting Rome

The physical transformation of Rome may be clear enough, but other aspects are more controversial. Our understanding of the impact of empire on Rome, and on Italy as well, is very much caught up with questions of numbers; statistics that differ from scholar to scholar and model to model. Varying estimates are proposed for the population of Rome, of Italy and of rural Italy, for the number of slaves, of small holders and of large estates, for urban and rural mortality and for death-rates in war, each estimate having some impact on the other estimates.

Rome's gradual evolution from an Italian to a Mediterranean power brought about a substantial change in its population, even if there is disagreement about how substantial. Estimates commonly put the number of inhabitants at the beginning of the second century BC at more than 200,000. By the time of Augustus Rome had become a vast cosmopolitan city of around 750,000 to one million people, far surpassing any other ancient city. In spite of the debate that frequently surrounds attempts to estimate ancient population sizes these figures have found general though not universal acceptance (Morley 1996: 33–9, but Storey 1997 doubts that Rome ever exceeded half a million). They suggest not only the extraordinary growth of the city but also something easily overlooked; it was already of a significant size in the second century BC as it was coming into its Mediterranean empire. Indeed, even by the mid-fourth century BC it had a not inconsiderable wall, the so-called 'Servian' wall, which enclosed over 420 hectares of land, making it comparable in extent to some of the larger cities in the western Mediterranean (Cornell 2000: 45–6). By the late first century BC the walls were all but invisible in the urban sprawl and it was hard to tell where the city began and the country ended, so observed Dionysios of Halikarnassos (*Ant. Rom.* 4.13).

This growth can be attributed to Rome's imperial expansion. As Rome became the focus of wealth and power in the Mediterranean, so it drew people towards it, no doubt first those of Latium and surrounding parts of Italy but later from further afield. Some came voluntarily, attracted by the prospects the city offered, whether that be construction work, aristocratic patronage or, as the more cynical preferred to claim, the grain dole, all financed by the profits of empire. The visits of others were less voluntary; some came as slaves, captured in Rome's wars, others such as the Achaian historian Polybios were effectively hostages for the good behaviour of their hometowns. The practice of freeing or manumitting slaves meant that their descendants could come to merge with the rest of city population. The involuntary may also have included those who for one reason or another had lost their land and had nowhere else to go (see next section). To these can be added the temporary residents, coming to and from Rome as traders, or present on embassies to make representations on behalf of their community, some kept waiting so long in Rome that they died there (Noy 2000).

Once the population had reached its height, it remained stable for several centuries. This might suggest that, with the great expansion of the empire over, immigration to the city largely ceased but recent research has suggested that Rome's death-rate was far in excess of its birth-rate. The effect of this was that without a constant supply of new blood Rome's population would have gone into decline; there must therefore have been a continuing and substantial migration into the city. The bulk of the inhabitants lived and died in over-crowded, unsanitary, multi-storey dwellings and, however much free or subsidised grain there may have been, was probably malnourished as well

(Scobie 1986, Shaw 1996). In spite of these conditions Rome continued to attract. Indeed it might be said that everything came to Rome,
so much so that by the first and second centuries AD it became hard
to distinguish Rome from the rest of the world (Edwards and Woolf
2003: 1–7). Athenaeus puts it very neatly when he says that 'Rome is
an epitome of the world', because every city seems to be present there
(1.20b–c). In Rome could be found every people, every kind of produce
and every kind of art (Aelius Aristides, *To Rome*, 10, 13). But as that
alarming death rate suggests, this was not all that came to Rome. Here
were also to be found the diseases of the empire (Scheidel 2003). For
Rome in a very real sense embodied its empire.

Such a flow of new people into the city was not always easily tolerated
by those already there. As so often migrants were met with prejudice.
Gauls, increasingly in evidence in late republican Rome, were mocked
for their hair and their clothes, in particular their habit of wearing
trousers (Sherwin-White 1967: 59–60, Suet. *Caes.* 80). Greeks too were
a regular target for Roman hostility (Petrochilos 1974), whether in the
second century BC letter of Cato the Elder to his son which warned of
the dangers of using Greek doctors (Pliny *NH* 29.7, Plut. *Cato Mai.*
23) or, much later, in Juvenal's xenophobic third satire. Significantly
this satire, written in the second century AD, presents a Rome that has
virtually ceased to be Roman; its main character Umbricius is aban-
doning the city, because he feels 'there is no place for any Roman in it'
(Juvenal 3.119). Attitudes to foreigners in Rome are likely to have been
complex, shaped by many factors, among which would have been the
fact that slaves made up a sizeable proportion of the foreigners within
the city (Noy 2000: 35).

4. The Italian countryside

War and empire brought evident material change to the city of Rome
but their impact in the countryside is more elusive and more controversial. Working the land was fundamental to the Roman self-image;
its empire and success was based on the hardy, virtuous Roman
peasant, the mainstay of the Roman army. Even the aristocracy are
represented as working the land in person; back in the fifth century BC
Lucius Quinctius Cincinnatus was famously recalled from the fields
to take up the dictatorship and defend Rome against the Aequi, only
to resign the position and return to his farm once the task was complete. By the Augustan era this story was so much part of the collective
memory that Romans could identify the place where he had had his

small farm, the so-called Quinctian Meadows on the banks of the Tiber (Livy 3.26.8). Yet scholars have often seen a paradox here; alongside the myth of the Roman peasant who created an empire is, they suggest, the reality of a peasantry displaced by slaves imported from the lands that had been conquered. This was a transformation that affected not only the countryside of Latium and the areas close to Rome but most of Italy as well.

This position can be found in its most developed form in the arguments of Peter Brunt and Keith Hopkins. Here it is proposed that in the second century BC there was a decline in the peasantry in Italy and a concomitant rise in rural slavery, both a consequence of Rome's wars. When in the earlier years of the Republic peasants fought in the army during the summer fighting-season and then returned home to work their farms, there was no problem, but everything became much more difficult for the peasant-soldier from around the time of the Second Punic War when Rome's armies began fighting overseas on extended campaigns that might last several years. Now the soldiers, both Romans and Italian allies, were no longer able to return at the end of the summer to maintain their farms, a circumstance that led to the impoverishment of themselves and their families and to the loss of the farm that was their livelihood. What put additional pressure on these small farmers was the existence of an elite that was growing increasingly rich through these very same wars and who wished to invest their new wealth in land. After buying up or otherwise acquiring land in the Italian countryside, they evicted the peasant farmers who had previously worked that land and replaced them with slaves, which Roman victories had so conveniently made available in large numbers. The result was the emergence of large slave estates as a feature of Italian agriculture and the migration of dispossessed peasants to the towns and cities, in particular to Rome where the tension between rich and poor that began in the countryside would find expression in the political conflicts of the late Republic, beginning with the agrarian reforms of Tiberius Gracchus in 133. War and empire were fundamental to this transformation. As Hopkins succinctly put it, 'Roman peasant soldiers were fighting for their own displacement' (1978: 30).

This account of the impact of Roman imperialism on the countryside and by extension upon Rome itself has been very influential. A number of factors can be adduced in support of it. First, there is the literary evidence which presents a very similar scenario, notably in the works of Appian and Plutarch, both of whom are seeking to explain the events of the tribunate of Tiberius Gracchus (**Appian B,**

p. 92, Plutarch C, p. 127). In doing so they stress the way that slave labour was ousting the peasant farmer from the countryside; they are, however, both Greeks writing in the first and second centuries AD, so in a very different social and political context. Secondly, the account outlined takes what limited population data there is to suggest that the free population of Italy remained roughly stable at around 4 million between the late third and late first century BC while at the same time the population of the towns and cities rose substantially, leading to the conclusion that the free population of the countryside was in decline. A third factor introduced in support is a change in army recruitment from the late third century onwards; on the one hand there was a reduction in the property qualification for the army, on the other there was an increasing reluctance to serve; taken together these could suggest a decline in the number of *assidui*, that is to say those with sufficient property to make them eligible to serve in the army. Again this appears to confirm a shift in the patterns of rural landholding. It might seem that disruption of the war with Hannibal would explain these changes (as Toynbee 1965), but its demographic impact may well have been short-term rather than long-term (Brunt 1971b: 269–77, in turn criticised by Cornell 1996).

More recently this thesis has been called into question or at least modified from a number of angles. Particularly important was the development of survey archaeology from the 1950s onwards which introduced a new form of evidence for the countryside; this type of archaeology involved not excavation but field-walkers carefully recording surface finds. By examining, for example, the density of finds it is possible to learn something of rural settlement patterns, both where people lived and change over time. Initially it was thought that the results of these surveys revealed an Italy very much at odds with the picture drawn by the literary sources of an agrarian crisis in the second century BC (cf. the landmark paper of Frederiksen 1970–71). Now, survey archaeology tends to be seen as adding another dimension to our understanding of what was happening in the countryside during Rome's imperial expansion, one very decidedly rural in contrast to the urban perspective of the literary sources. Yet it is not without its own problems of interpretation, especially with regard to what the material signifies and how readily it can be dated; it tends to be indicative of broad trends rather than revealing of a particular moment. But whereas the literary sources had led scholars to make rather generalised claims about Italy, the combined results of various surveys are contributing to our appreciation of the diversity of the Italian countryside, as different regions are affected in different ways by the Roman imperial enter-prise. Survey, for example, reveals the high level of occupation around Rome, as population and agricultural activity are drawn towards the growing Roman market (Morley 1996, Witcher 2005).

Recent scholarship has also challenged some of the assumptions that underpinned the traditional position as outlined by Brunt and Hopkins, notably on the population data, the place of slavery in the countryside, and the relationship between war and agriculture. Elio Lo Cascio in an important series of articles (for instance 1994, 1999, 2001 and 2009) has argued strongly for a free Italian population of something over 10 million by the time of Augustus, a huge rise on Brunt's proposed 4 million; an effect of this calculation is to produce a very different Italian countryside, one well-stocked with both free and slaves but with the slaves making up a much smaller proportion of the population. In this case imperial success leads not to the decline of the peasantry but rather generates such prosperity that the countryside is almost overpopulated. It should be noted, however, that Lo Cascio's figures have not won universal acceptance but they have nonetheless caused scholars to think again about alternative models (cf. the imagi-native essay of Morley 2001). Longstanding ideas about the emergence of rural slavery have also been subject to revision. Rather than slave estates forcing out peasant farms wholesale, the two forms of farming may well have co-existed in a relationship of mutual dependence; estates, for example, will have needed to supplement their labour force at certain times of the year (Rathbone 1981). Another key element of the traditional picture of the decline of the peasantry is the small farmer's inability to cope with the demands of extended campaigning seasons but in a detailed study Rosenstein has argued that Rome may well have resolved this problem long before the Second Punic War (2004).

Such uncertainties mean that scholarship on the character of the Italian countryside often talks in terms of hypotheses. Nonetheless, it is evident that the countryside was reshaped as a result of Rome's imperial expansion. The mega-city of Rome drew people and produce towards it, slaves became a more significant part of the agricultural workforce, villas appeared in the landscape, a reflection of increased security as much as changed farming practices, Roman roads linked one end of the peninsula to the other, land was confiscated and sys-tematically divided up for Roman colonies. Debate, however, con-tinues about the precise nature and the relative importance of these developments.

5. From republic to emperor

During the time when Rome was acquiring much of its empire, it was a dynamic and aggressive city-state with a republican constitution, but as the empire developed so the character of the Roman state changed. By the first century AD it was neither a city-state nor a republic. Attention has often focused on the emergence of the emperor and the fall/collapse/end of the Republic, a process rather less abrupt than these terms imply (cf. Morstein-Marx and Rosenstein 2006). It is this turning point that has shaped historical narratives, both ancient and modern, but in some ways the more profound change had happened already, the granting of Roman citizenship to the free population of Italy in the aftermath of the Social War early in the first century BC. Romans had always been more open with their citizenship than their more exclusive Greek neighbours, albeit often with reluctance, but on this occasion by the wholesale integration of the communities of Italy into the Roman state they were changing the very nature of that state. Aggression and success in war may have been fundamental to the creation of the empire but it is this capacity to incorporate others, even those from outside Italy, that gave it its longevity. Whether retired auxiliary soldier or member of the provincial elite, there were opportunities to join the Roman citizen body and so share in what it was to be Roman.

In the long run these two developments, the extension of citizenship and the emergence of a form of government that was monarchic in all but name, contributed to a redefining of the empire. It was not merely that one changed the composition of the state and the other its top tier; together they changed the relationship between subject and ruler. The emperor broke the boundaries of Rome. Rather than being the leading citizen in a state that ruled an empire, he became the ruler of the whole empire and was perceived as such by those in the provinces, hence, for example, the proliferation of cults of the emperor and his family. Parallel to this development was the transformation of the Senate from a civic to an imperial body with a significant proportion of its membership coming from the provinces. Eventually the empire would catch up with the emperor and with the Antonine Constitution in AD 212 all free inhabitants of the empire became Roman citizens.

When the empire came to be ruled not by the city of Rome and its institutions but by the emperor, then if the emperor left Rome so the centre of power moved with him. Of the Year of the Four Emperors, AD 69, Tacitus said that it revealed 'the secret that emperors could be created elsewhere than at Rome' (*Hist.* 1.4). Indeed the emperor did not even need to come from Rome; Vespasian was from the Sabine town of Reate in Italy and Trajan and Hadrian were from Spain, but all three were Roman citizens. After the demise of the Julio-Claudian dynasty many emperors would spend a significant amount of time away from Rome with the army, seeing to the security not only of the empire but also of themselves; Hadrian, for instance, visited almost every part of the empire before finally settling down in Rome. By the late third century AD emperors were a rare sight in Rome (Barnes 1975).

With citizenship more widely-diffused and a ruler who reached beyond the city, Rome itself took on an increasingly symbolic role, ultimately becoming an abstract concept as much as a city. We might say that Rome became so successful that it lost control of its own product. In the first century BC Rome had been the centre of the world where Gauls in trousers were an object of derision but by late antiquity trousers had become commonplace (James 2001: 202) and the emperor, now resident in the north Italian town of Ravenna, on being told that Rome had perished could mistakenly assume that it was his pet cock of the same name that had died (Procopius 3.2.25–6). This story of Honorius' reaction to Alaric's sack of Rome is no doubt apocryphal but it nonetheless neatly captures the way Rome became sidelined in its own empire.

Part II

Documents

Documents

Appian

Appian was a Greek historian from Alexandria in Egypt, writing in the second century AD; he was the author of a history of Rome.

A (Mithridatic Wars 21–3) The beginning of the First Mithridatic War
21. Not long afterwards Mithridates captured Manius Aquillius [the Roman commander], the man chiefly responsible for this embassy and this war. He led him round, bound, riding on an ass and announcing to onlookers that he was Manius. Finally, at Pergamon he poured gold down Manius' throat, thus reproaching the Romans for their bribe-taking. After setting in place satraps over the various peoples, he went on to Magnesia, Ephesos and Mytilene, where everyone readily received him, the Ephesians even tearing down the statues of Romans in their city, for which they were punished not much later . . .

22. This was the situation with Mithridates. As soon as the Romans learned of his first assault and invasion of Asia, they voted to send an army against him, although they were occupied with unending civil conflict and a difficult war at home, since almost the whole of Italy had revolted in turn. When the consuls cast lots, Cornelius Sulla won the task of governing Asia and fighting Mithridates. As they had no money to cover his expenses, they voted to sell all those things that King Numa Pompilius had set aside for sacrifices to the gods. So great was their lack of everything and so great their ambition for everything. Some of this was sold hurriedly and brought in gold to the weight of 9,000 pounds, which was all they had to spend on such a major war.

The civil wars detained Sulla for a long time as I wrote in *The Civil Wars*. Meanwhile Mithridates constructed a good many ships to launch an assault on the Rhodians and wrote secretly to all the satraps and city governors, that they should wait until the thirtieth day and then all together attack the Romans and Italians living among them, not only the men but also their wives and children and any freedmen of Italian birth; after killing them they were to throw them out unburied and divide their possessions with King Mithridates. He proclaimed that there would be punishment for those who buried the victims or kept them hidden and rewards for those who acted as informers or who did away with those in hiding; slaves who took action against their masters would get freedom, debtors who did likewise against their creditors would get remission of half the debt. Mithridates sent these orders secretly to all at once and when the day arrived every sort of misfortune occurred across Asia, of which the following are examples.

23. Those who had fled for sanctuary to the temple of Artemis and were clinging to the statues of the goddess, the Ephesians dragged away and killed. The Pergamenes shot arrows at those who had taken refuge in the Asklepeion while they were still clinging to statues there. The Adramyttians went into the sea after those who tried to escape by swimming; they killed them and drowned their children. The Kaunians, who became subject to the Rhodians after the war against Antiochos, had been set free by the Romans not long before this; yet, after dragging away those who had taken refuge with the statue of Vesta in the council house, they first killed the children in front of the eyes of their mothers, then the mothers themselves and finally the men. The people of Tralles, in order to avoid actually committing the crime themselves, hired Theophilos, a savage from Paphlagonia, to do the job for them. Leading them to the temple of Homonoia [Concord], he slaughtered them there and when some clung to the statues of the gods he chopped off their hands. Such was the fate met by the Italians and Romans in Asia, men, children and women as well as their freedmen and slaves of Italian birth. Consequently it became extremely clear that the people of Asia acted against them in this way as much out of hatred of the Romans as out of fear of Mithridates. But they were punished twice over, first when Mithridates treacherously mistreated them not long afterwards, and then by Cornelius Sulla.

B *(Civil Wars 1. 7–9) Agriculture and the growth of slavery in Italy*
7. When the Romans were subduing Italy in war, one part of it after another, they used to confiscate part of the land and build cities or they selected colonists from their own people to go to existing cities. They had in mind to use these instead of garrisons, but in the case of the land that they had gained in war on each occasion, they assigned the cultivated part straightaway to the settlers or sold it or leased it. As they did not have the time to allot the land that was uncultivated as a result of war, which was a substantial amount, they announced that in the meantime those who wanted to work it might do so in exchange for a tax on their annual produce, one tenth of the grain and one fifth of the fruit. Similarly for those farming pastureland taxes of larger and smaller animals were set. They did these things to increase the Italian population, thinking them especially tough, so that they had allies near at hand.

But the opposite happened. For the rich gained possession of the majority of the undistributed land and in time grew confident that they would never be dispossessed. They added neighbouring land and smallholdings belonging to the poor, some purchased by persuasion, some seized by force. In this way they came to farm vast plains instead of single farms, using slaves as farmers and herdsmen in order to avoid the free men being drafted from agriculture into the army. At the same time this ownership of slaves brought them much profit because the slaves had many children and increased in number without risk because there was no military service. As a result the powerful became extremely rich and the race of slaves increased across the land but the Italians suffered from a declining population and lack of manpower, worn down as they were by poverty, taxes and military service. If they had any rest from these things, they spent their time doing nothing, because the land was occupied by the rich who used slaves as farmers instead of free men.

8. Consequently the Roman people became concerned that they would no longer have sufficient allies from Italy and that their supremacy might be at risk on account of this huge number of slaves. They did not devise any reform since it was not easy nor altogether just to deprive so many men of so much property that they had held for so long, including their own trees, buildings and equipment. With difficulty a law was passed on the proposal of the tribunes that no one should hold more than 500 iugera [approximately 125 hectares or 310 acres] of this land nor pasture on it more than 100 larger animals or 500 smaller ones. In addition it was prescribed that there be a set number of free men who would watch and report on what was happening. Once they had embodied these things in law they swore an oath on the law and fixed the penalties, thinking that the remaining land would soon be sold off to the poor in small parcels. But no notice was taken of either the law or the oath. Some who seemed to take note of it distributed the land to their relatives by fraudulent transactions, but the majority treated it with complete contempt.

9. Finally Tiberius Sempronius Gracchus, a distinguished man, eager for glory and a very powerful speaker and for all these reasons very well-known to everyone, became tribune and made an impressive speech about the Italian race, saying that they were excellent warriors and kin to the Romans, but little by little they were declining into poverty and lack of manpower with no hope of rectifying it. He angrily criticised the whole slave body as of no value for the army and never loyal to their masters and cited the disaster that the masters had recently suffered in Sicily at the hands of their slaves, where the

number of slaves had been increased by their use in farming; he also drew attention to the war the Romans had fought against them, which was neither easy nor short but dragged on for a long time with all sorts of dangerous and unexpected changes. After speaking in this way he sought to renew the law that limited holdings to 500 iugera.

Augustine

Augustine (AD 354–430) was a Christian writer and bishop from North Africa; he wrote in Latin. Cicero's *De Republica* survives only in a fragmentary state; for those fragments relevant to this argument see the translation of the surviving parts of book 3 in Zetzel 1999.

A (City of God, 19.21) The justice of empire
In this same book, *De Republica* [Cicero's *On the Republic*], there is a very vigorous and forceful argument against injustice on behalf of justice. First, the case for injustice against justice was laid out and it was said that without injustice a state could neither exist nor be governed [or possibly 'be increased']. The key argument put forward here was that it is unjust that some men should serve others who are their masters, but if an imperial state, the head of a great commonwealth, did not adopt injustice of this sort, then it could not rule its provinces. It was replied on behalf of justice that ruling provinces is just because servitude is useful for such men and it is done for their own good, when it is done properly, that is to say when the licence to do harm is taken away from wrongdoers; furthermore those who are made subject will be better off since, before they were made subject, they were worse off. To support this line of argument, a notable example taken from nature is introduced: 'Why,' it is asked, 'does god rule man, the soul rule the body and reason rule desires and the other vicious parts of the soul?' This example leaves no doubt that servitude is useful for some men and, indeed, to serve god is useful for all.

Caesar

C. Iulius Caesar (100–44 BC) was a Roman politician and military commander. In addition to his account of the conquest of Gaul he wrote several books on the civil wars. He speaks of himself in the third person.

A (Gallic War 1.10–11) The beginning of Caesar's campaigns in Gaul
10. It was reported to Caesar that the Helevetii planned to march through

the land of the Sequani and Aedui into the territory of the Santones, which is not far from the territory of the Tolosates, a state which is in the province. If that happened, he realised that it would put the province in serious danger to have warlike men, who were hostile to the Roman people, close to vulnerable and important corn-producing regions. For these reasons he put Titus Labienus his legate in charge of the fortifications he had built; he himself pressed on to Italy by forced marches and enlisted two legions there and mobilised three that had been in winter quarters around Aquileia. With these five legions he pressed on by the closest route across the Alps into Further Gaul. There the Centrones, the Graioceli and the Caturiges who had occupied the higher ground tried to obstruct the army's progress. After he had defeated these in several battles he arrived in the territory of the Vocontii in the further province seven days after leaving Ocelum which is the most remote town in the nearer province. From there he led his army into the territory of the Allobroges and from the Allobroges to the Segusiani. These are the first people outside the province on the far side of the Rhone.

11. The Helvetii had by now led their forces through the narrow pass and territory of the Sequani and had arrived in the territory of the Aedui and were plundering their lands. The Aedui, since they were unable to defend themselves and their property from the Helvetii, sent ambassadors to Caesar to ask for help; they said that they had at all times deserved well of the Roman people so that almost in sight of our army their lands ought not to be devastated, their children taken into slavery and their towns stormed. At the same time the Ambarri, who are related to the Aedui, informed Caesar that with their lands ravaged they could not easily hold back the force of the enemy from their towns. Similarly the Allobroges, who had villages and possessions across the Rhone, fled to Caesar and pointed out to him that they no longer had anything but the soil of their fields. For these reasons Caesar decided that he should not wait until all the property of our allies had been destroyed and the Helvetii had reached the Santoni.

B (Gallic War 8.44) *Caesar punishes the rebels at Uxellodunum, 51 BC*
Caesar was aware that his leniency was known to all men and he had no fear that harsher action would be interpreted as innate cruelty; he also realised that his plans would not succeed if more of the enemy in different districts embarked on this sort of action. Therefore he decided to inflict a punishment that would act as a deterrent to the rest. So he cut off the hands of all who had borne arms but granted them their life, so that the punishment for wrongdoers might be broadcast widely.

Cicero

Marcus Tullius Cicero (106–43 BC) was a Roman politician, orator and writer, many of whose speeches, treatises and letters survive.

A (On the Command of Gnaeus Pompey or For the Manilian Law 6.14–16) *Speech to the People advocating Pompey be given the command against Mithridates, 66 BC*

14. Our ancestors waged war against Antiochos, Philip, the Aitolians and the Carthaginians for the sake of our allies, in spite of not having suffered injury themselves. Therefore, how great should your eagerness be to defend both the safety of your allies and the dignity of your own rule, when you actually have been provoked by injuries, especially when it is a question of your most substantial revenues? For the revenues of our other provinces, citizens, are such that it is hardly worth our while protecting those provinces, but Asia is so rich and fertile that it is easily superior to all other lands in the productiveness of its fields, the variety of its crops, the size of its pasturage and the quantity of its exports. And so, citizens, if you want to keep a hold on what is useful in time of war and confers prestige in time of peace, this province must be defended not only from disaster but from fear of disaster.

15. For in other matters, it is when disaster strikes that loss occurs, but in the case of revenues it is not only the arrival of something bad but the very fear of it that brings disaster. For when the forces of the enemy are not far away, even though no invasion has taken place, livestock is still abandoned, fields cease to be cultivated and merchants stop sailing the seas. As a result there is no longer revenue to be gathered from harbour taxes, or from tithes, or from taxes on pasturage. Often, therefore, a single rumour of danger or a single war scare can mean the loss of an entire year's income.

16. What, then, do you think is the state of mind of those who pay us taxes or those who collect them when two kings with massive armies are close at hand? and when a single cavalry attack can carry away a whole year's revenue in a moment? and when the *publicani* think that only at great risk do they maintain the substantial staffs that they have at the saltworks, in the fields, and in the ports and guardposts? Do you imagine that you can enjoy these things if you do not protect those men who get them for you, not only from disaster, as I said before, but also from the fear of disaster?

B (II Verrines *5.117–19) The governorship of C. Verres in Sicily*
The condemned captains were confined in the prison. Sentence was passed on them but it was also imposed on their poor parents. They were prohibited from visiting their sons; they were prohibited from providing their own children with food and clothes. These very fathers that you see before you lay in the doorway. The distraught mothers spent all night at the entrance to the prison, denied a final sight of their children; all they asked for was to be allowed to feel their sons' final breath on their face. The prison guard was there, the governor's executioner, the incarnation of death and terror for both allies and Roman citizens alike; this man was the lictor Sextius, for whom there was a set amount of profit to be made from every groan and every agony. 'In order to visit him you will have to pay so much, in order that you might be allowed to bring food in, so much.' No one refused. 'What will you pay me to put your son to death with a single blow of the axe? so that he is not tortured for too long, so that he is not struck too many times, so that his spirit departs without feeling pain?' Even for this reason money was given to the lictor. O what great and unbearable pain! O what terrible and bitter ill fortune! Parents were forced to purchase not the life of their children but the swiftness of their death. And even the young men themselves spoke with Sextius about the execution and that single blow and they begged one final thing from their parents, that they pay the lictor to lessen their agony.

C (De officiis 1.34–6) On making war
34. In state policy justice in warfare must be strictly observed. For since there are two ways of fighting something out, one through discussion, the other through force, and since the former is what is appropriate to men and the latter to beasts, we must resort to force only when it is not possible to use discussion.

35. Wars, therefore, should be undertaken for this reason, that we may live in peace without harm; and once victory has been achieved those whose behaviour in the war has not been cruel and savage should be spared. Thus our ancestors even accepted into citizenship the Tusculani, the Aequi, the Volsci, the Sabines and the Hernici but they completely destroyed Carthage and Numantia. I would rather they had not destroyed Corinth, but I believe they had some objective, principally related to the advantages of its position, that the location itself might not some day be an encouragement to war. In my opinion we should always strive to secure a peace in which treachery will have no part. If any notice had been taken of my advice, we would still

have, if not the best, at least some form of republic, where now we have nothing. While you should show consideration to those you have conquered by force, you should also receive into your protection those who have put down their arms and taken refuge in the good faith of the generals, even though the battering ram has pounded their walls. In this justice has been observed to such an extent among our countrymen that those who receive into their good faith states and nations defeated in war become their patrons in accordance with the custom of our ancestors.

36. Fairness in warfare has been put into writing in the fetial code of the Roman people in full conformity with religious scruple. From this it can be understood that no war is just unless it is waged after a demand for satisfaction has been made or unless a warning has been given beforehand and the war has formally been declared.

D (On the Responses of the Haruspices *19*) *Religion and empire*
For who is so senseless that, when he has looked at the heavens, he does not feel that there are gods and actually thinks that those things happen by chance which are done by such a great intelligence that hardly anyone however skilled can fully explain their order? Or who is so senseless that, when he has understood that there are gods, he fails to understand that this mighty empire was created, increased and preserved by their divine power? However fond we are of ourselves, conscript fathers, we do not surpass the Spaniards in number or the Gauls in strength or the Carthaginians in shrewdness or the Greeks in the arts or finally the Italians and Latins in that way of thinking native to the people of this land, but in piety and in religion and in the special wisdom of perceiving that everything is ruled and steered by the power of the gods, in these we have surpassed all peoples and nations.

E (Letters to Atticus *1.8.2*) *Cicero seeks art from Greece, 67 BC*
I have paid L. Cincius the 20,400 sesterces for the statues of Megaric marble in accordance with your letter to me. As to your Herms of Pentelic marble with bronze heads, about which you wrote to me, I have fallen in love with them on the spot. So please send both them and the statues, and anything else that may appear to you to suit the place in question, my passion and your taste – as many and as soon as possible. Above all, anything you think appropriate to a gymnasium and colonnade. I have such a passion for things of this sort that while I expect assistance from you, I must expect something like rebuke from others. If Lentulus has no ship there, put them on board any one you please.

F (Letters to Atticus 1.9) 67 BC

I am waiting impatiently for the Megaric statues and the Herms, which you mentioned in your letters. Anything you have of the same kind which may strike you as worthy of my 'Academy', do not hesitate to send, and have complete confidence in my money-chest. My present delight is to pick up anything particularly suitable for a gymnasium. Lentulus promises the use of his ships. I beg you to be zealous in these matters.

G (Letters to Atticus 5.21.7) Writing from his province, 13 February 50 BC

I myself started for Asia from Tarsos on 5 January – and by Hercules it is hard to describe the admiration shown by the cities of Cilicia and especially by the people of Tarsos. After I had crossed the Tauros range I found an extraordinary sense of expectation among the districts of Asia, which in the six months of my administration had not received a single letter of instruction from me nor had they had a single official to entertain. Now before my time that particular period each year had been devoted to profiteering: the richer cities would pay large sums of money to be exempted from furnishing the soldiers with winter quarters. The Cypriots used to pay 200 Attic talents, from which island – and this is no exaggeration but the simple truth – not a single penny will be exacted under my administration. For these benefits, which they regard with speechless astonishment, I allow no honours, apart from verbal ones, to be decreed to me: I forbid statues, temples, chariots; nor do I cause trouble for the cities in any other way, although perhaps I do to you by thus blowing my own trumpet. But, if you love me, put up with it! It was you who wished me to act in this way.

H (Letters to his brother Quintus 1.1.20–5) Advice on provincial administration; Cicero's brother Quintus is governor of Asia, late 60 or early 59 BC

20. It will not be easy for us to justify these and similar instances of strict decisions in your province unless they are accompanied by the highest integrity. So let there be the utmost strictness in your administration of justice, provided that it is never varied due to favour but is maintained impartially. But there is little point you administering justice impartially and carefully if those you have entrusted with any element of this task do not do the same. Certainly in my view there is no very great variety of business in the government of Asia, rather it all mostly revolves around the administration of justice. The actual

knowledge this requires, especially in relation to the provinces, is straightforward; one must exercise sufficient consistency and firmness, not only to resist favouritism but even the suspicion of it.

21. To this must be added readiness to listen, mildness in pronouncing a decision and diligence in answering complaints and in argument. It is by such habits that Gaius Octavius has recently made himself very popular, in whose court the first lictor had nothing to do, the attendant had nothing to say, while everyone spoke as often and for as long as he wished. In which conduct Octavius might perhaps be thought too mild, if that mildness had not enabled him to maintain his rigour: Sulla's men were forced to restore what they had taken by violence and fear; those who had given unjust rulings while in office now as private citizens had to submit to the principles they had established. This rigour of his would have seemed harsh, if it had not been made palatable by a generous sprinkling of humanity.

22. But if this mildness is welcome at Rome, where there is such great arrogance, such unrestrained freedom, such unlimited licence, and finally so many magistrates, so many sources of assistance, such great power in the hands of the people, such authority in the Senate, how welcome then must the courtesy of a governor be in Asia? That is a place where there is such a vast crowd of citizens and allies, so many cities, so many communities, and they are all hanging on the nod of one man – there is no source of assistance, no one to whom to make a complaint, no Senate, no popular assembly. So it requires a really great man, not only moderate by nature but also educated by instruction and study in the liberal arts, so as to conduct himself while in possession of such immense power in such a way that those over whom he rules do not feel the need for any other power than his.

23. Take the case of that famous Cyrus, portrayed by Xenophon, not as a historical character but as a model of just government, the great dignity of whose character is represented by that philosopher as combined with a singular courtesy. Indeed it is not without reason that our own Africanus was accustomed always to have that book in his hands. For there is no duty relevant to the careful and moderate exercise of power which is not to be found in it. If Cyrus, a man who was destined never to be a private citizen, cultivated these qualities, how carefully ought they to be maintained by those to whom power is given on the understanding that it must be surrendered and given by laws to which they must eventually return?

24. I think that in all matters those in power must adhere to the

following principle, that their subjects be as happy as possible. That this is your prime consideration, and has been so since you first landed in Asia, has become widely known through the stories that are constantly circulating and the talk of all. It is, let me add, not only the duty of one who has command over citizens and allies but also of one who has command over slaves and dumb animals to serve the interests and advantages of those under him.

25. On this point I notice that everyone agrees that you take the greatest pains; no new debt is being contracted by the communities, while many have been relieved by you of heavy and longstanding debts; several cities that had become dilapidated and almost deserted were restored by you, including Samos and Halikarnassos, one the most famous state of Ionia, the other of Caria; there is no rioting or civil conflict in the towns; you take care that the government of the communities is administered by the best class of citizen; banditry has been done away with in Mysia and murder kept in check in many districts; peace has been established throughout the province; not only has robbery been driven from the roads and countryside but also, on a much greater scale, from the towns and temples; the reputations, possessions and peace of mind of the rich have been relieved of that most oppressive accessory of a governor's greed, the false accusation; the expenses and tribute of the communities are made to fall equally on all who live in the territories of those communities; access to you is as easy as possible and your ears are open to the complaints of all; no man's want of means or want of friends prevents him from approaching you, not only in public and on the tribunal but even in your home and chamber. In a word, your exercise of power is completely free from harshness or cruelty; instead every aspect of it is full of clemency, gentleness and humanity.

I (Letters to his brother Quintus 3.9.4) Quintus Cicero is on campaign with Caesar in Britain, 54 BC
I am exceedingly obliged for your promises as to slaves, and I am indeed, as you say, shorthanded both at Rome and on my estates. But pray, do nothing for my convenience unless, my dear brother, it entirely suits your own and your means.

Digest

The *Digest* was a selection of legal texts by prominent jurists, compiled under the authority of the emperor Justinian and published in AD 533.

The two extracts that follow come from Ulpian, a third-century AD Roman lawyer.

A (39.4.1.1)

Publicani are those who handle public property (hence their name), whether they pay revenue to the treasury or collect tribute.

B (49.15.24)

Enemies are those on whom the Roman people have publicly declared war, or who have themselves declared war on the Roman people; others are called bandits and robbers. Therefore, anyone who is captured by bandits, is not the slave of bandits and does not have any need of the right of *postliminium* [by which previous status or situation is restored]. But someone who has been captured by enemies, for instance, by the Germans or Parthians, is the slave of enemies and recovers his former status by the right of *postliminium*.

Dio Cassius

Dio Cassius (c. 164–after 229 AD), also known as Cassius Dio, was a Greek historian and Roman senator from Nikaia in Bithynia. He wrote a history of Rome in eighty books; only books 36–60 survive, covering the years 69 BC–AD 46; the rest is known from excerpts or epitomes of the missing books.

A (51.20.6–9) Cults of Roman power in Asia and Bithynia, 29 BC

Meanwhile, Caesar [soon to be Augustus], in addition to dealing with general business, allowed sacred precincts to be dedicated in Ephesos and Nikaia to Roma and his father Caesar, naming him the deified Iulius. For at that time these cities were the most important in Asia and Bithynia respectively. He instructed the Romans living there to do honour to them. He also gave permission to the non-Romans, or Greeks as he called them, to consecrate precincts to himself, the inhabitants of Asia doing this in Pergamon and those of Bithynia in Nikomedia. This practice, which began here, continued under subsequent emperors not only among the Greek peoples but also among others, as many as are subject to the Romans. For in the capital itself and in the rest of Italy no emperor has dared to do this, however worthy of renown he may have been. Nonetheless, even there, once they have died, the emperors who have ruled well become the recipients of other divine honours and shrines are even built for them.

B *(67.5.6) The revolt of the Nasamones,* AD 85–86

Many of those who paid tax to the Romans revolted when payment was exacted forcibly, as in the case of the Nasamones. They massacred the tax-collectors and when Flaccus the governor of Numidia marched against them they defeated him so effectively that they even plundered his camp. But, finding the wine and other supplies there, they took their fill and fell asleep. Flaccus, when he heard of this, attacked them, wiped them all out and even destroyed all those who did not fight. Domitian was delighted with this and said to the Senate, 'I veto the existence of the Nasamones.'

Diodoros of Sicily (Diodorus Siculus)

Diodoros was a Sicilian Greek historian of the first century BC. He wrote a history of the world ('universal history') in forty books, of which fifteen survive complete and the rest only in fragments. It began in mythological times and continued to 60 BC.

A (40.4) Pompey's inscription

Pompey inscribed his achievements in Asia and set them up as a dedication, of which the following is a transcription: 'Pompey, son of Gnaeus, the Great, Imperator, having freed the coast of the inhabited world and all the islands on this side of the Ocean from the pirate war; being the man who rescued from siege the kingdom of Ariobarzanes, Galatia and the lands and provinces that lie beyond it, Asia, and Bithynia; having acted as protector to Paphlagonia and Pontus, Armenia and Achaia, and to Iberia, Colchis, Mesopotamia, Sophene, and Gordyene; having made subject Darius king of the Medes, Artoles king of the Iberians, Aristobulus king of the Jews, Aretas king of the Nabataean Arabs, and Syria that lies by Cilicia, Judaea, Arabia, the province of Cyrenaica, the Achaians, the Iozygi, the Soani, the Heniochi and the rest of the tribes that occupy the coast between Colchis and the Maeotic Lake, and their kings, nine in number, and all the peoples that live between the Pontic and the Red Seas; and having brought the boundaries of Roman rule to the limits of the earth; and having secured and increased the revenues of the Romans; and having seized the statues and the images set up to the gods and other treasures from the enemy, he has dedicated to the goddess twelve thousand and sixty talents of gold and three hundred and seven of silver.'

Eusebius

Eusebius of Caesarea (c. 260–339 AD) was a Christian writer and bishop, author of many works in Greek.

*A (*Demonstratio Evangelica or Proof of the Gospel *3.7.30–3)*
And yet all must wonder, if they consider and reflect, that it was not man's doing that most of the peoples of the world came under the single rule of the Romans at no other date apart from the time of Jesus. For his unexpected residency among men and the peak of Roman power occurred simultaneously, just when Augustus first became supreme ruler over most peoples, in whose time after the capture of Cleopatra the dynasty of the Ptolemies came to an end in Egypt. From that time to the present the kingdom of Egypt, which had lasted so to speak from the beginning of humanity, was expunged. Since that time also the Jewish people have become subject to the Romans, and so too have the Syrians, the Cappadocians, the Macedonians, the Bithynians and the Greeks and to put it briefly all the other peoples who are now under the rule of the Romans. That all this could not have been synchronised with the teaching about our Saviour without the intervention of God, no one would disagree if he did but consider the difficulty of the disciples travelling in foreign lands, when the peoples are at odds with each other and there are no mutual dealings because of the many national governments. But when these were done away with, the disciples could then achieve their objective without fear and in safety, since the supreme God had prepared the way for them in advance and restrained the spirits of the superstitious in the various cities with the fear of a greater power.

Inscriptions

A (SIG³ 543, lines 26–39)
This letter of the Macedonian king Philip V, written in Greek, is part of a long inscription from Larisa in Thessaly, 215 BC; for the whole inscription, Austin 2006: no. 77 and Bagnall and Derow 2004: no. 33.
King Philip to the chief magistrates and the city of the Larisaeans, greetings. I hear that those who were enrolled as citizens in accordance with the letter I sent and your decree and whose names were inscribed on the *stelai* have been removed. If this has happened, those who advised you have failed to act in the interests of your country and in accordance with my decision. The best situation of all is that with as

many as possible sharing in citizenship the city grow in strength and the land is not left to lie shamefully deserted as now is the case. This is something I believe none of you would disagree with and it is possible to see others who adopt similar practices in the enrolment of citizens. Among these are the Romans, who receive into their citizen body even slaves when they have freed them and give them a share in the magistracies. In this way they have not only expanded their own state but they have sent out colonies to around seventy places. Yet, even now I call you to take steps in this matter without rivalry and to restore to their citizenship those who were chosen by the citizens, but if any of them has done anything unpardonable against the monarchy or the city or for any other reason is not worthy of being part of this *stele*, postpone consideration of these until I hear the cases on my return from campaigning. But warn those intending to bring accusations against these men that they should not appear to be doing this out of rivalry. Year seven, thirty-first day of Gorpaios.

B *(Moretti ISE II. 87)*

Remains of the Greek text of the treaty between Rome and Aitolia, 212 or 211 BC, see also **Livy C** *below. Text in square brackets is an epigraphic convention signifying that words are missing or uncertain.*

. . . If the Romans take by force any cities of these peoples, let it be permitted for the Aitolians to have these cities and these lands, as far as the Roman people is concerned; whatever the Romans take apart from the city and land, let the Romans have. If Romans and Aitolians in combined operations take any of these cities, let it be permitted for the Aitolians to have these cities and lands as far as the Roman people are concerned; whatever they take apart from the city, let it belong to both jointly. If any of these cities joins or goes over to the Romans or to the Aitolians, [let it be permitted, as far as concerns the] Roman people, for the Aitolians to take these people and the cities and the lands [into their] League . . .

C *(RDGE 33, SIG³ 593)*

Letter of T. Quinctius Flamininus to the city of Chyretiai in northern Thessaly, between 197 and 194 BC; inscribed text in Greek.

Titus Quinctius, consul of the Romans, to the chief magistrates and the city of the Chyretians, greetings. Since in all other matters we have made quite clear the policy of ourselves and of the Roman people towards you, we have wished also, in those that follow, to show ourselves in every part to be the champions of what is honourable, so that in these matters too those who are not in the habit of acting from the best motives are not able to slander us. As many of your possessions in land and houses as remain in the hands of the Roman state, we will grant them all to your city, in order that in these matters too you may learn our nobility and that in no way at all have we wanted to be money-loving, putting instead the highest value on goodwill and love of reputation. But whoever has not recovered what belongs to them, if they make their case to you and appear to speak reasonably, so long as you proceed in accordance with my written decisions, I judge that it is just that their property is restored to them. Farewell.

D (SIG³ 592)

Inscribed base of statue of T. Quinctius Flamininus from Gytheion in the Peloponnese, shortly after 196 BC, written in Greek. The phrase given in the second set of brackets would have been understood by the observer and did not appear in the stone itself (cf. also **Inscriptions H and I** *below).*

The People (*demos*) of the Gytheates (dedicate this statue of) Titus Quinctius, son of Titus, consul of the Romans, its saviour.

E (RDGE 34, SIG³ 601)

Letter of M. Valerius Messala to the city of Teos, 193 BC; inscribed text in Greek.

From the Romans. Marcus Valerius, son of Marcus, praetor and the tribunes of the plebs and the Senate to the council and people of the Teans, greetings. Menippos, the ambassador who was sent to us by King Antiochos and also chosen by you as ambassador for your city, gave us the decree and himself spoke in accordance with it with every enthusiasm. We received the man in a friendly way both because of his previous reputation and because of his innate nobility and we listened with goodwill to the requests he made. And that we continue always to place the highest value on piety towards the gods, one can best deduce from the favour that we have for these reasons received from the divine power. From many other things besides we are persuaded that the high honour in which we hold the divine is clear to all. And so for these reasons and because of our goodwill towards you and because of the esteemed ambassador, we judge your city and land to be sacred, as it is even now, and inviolable and free from taxation by the Roman people, and as regards honours for the god and privileges for you we shall try to assist in increasing them, so long as you maintain in the future your goodwill towards us. Farewell.

F (IOSPE I² 402)

End of treaty between the city of Chersonesos and Pharnakes I of Pontos, written in Greek, 155 BC; for translation of the whole inscription, Sherk 1984: no. 30.

. . . nor will I do anything with respect to Chersonesitans which is likely to harm the *demos* of the Chersonesitans, but I will join in protecting the democracy as much as I can, so long as they continue in friendship with me and have sworn the same oath and preserve their friendship with the Romans and do nothing to oppose them. May it turn out well for me swearing a true oath, and turn out badly for swearing falsely . . .

G (Milet. *I.7*)

Remains of a decree of the Greek city of Miletos in Asia Minor, establishing regulations for the cult of the Demos (People) of the Romans and of Roma, probably around 130 BC. The demos *here is thus personified and made the object of worship. The text includes references to various local magistracies and officials, not all of which are fully understood,* basileus *(pl.* basileis*),* stephanophoros *(the eponymous magistrate),* gymnasiarch *(responsible for gymnasium),* paidonomoi *(in charge of education),* prytany treasurer, aisymnetes, prosetairoi *and* archons. *Ephebes are young men in their teens going through a period of training.*

a) With good fortune. The man who buys the priesthood of the Demos of the Romans and of Roma will register straightaway a priest with the treasurers and the *basileis*; this man should be not younger than twenty years old. The man registered will act as priest for three years and eight months, starting in the month of Metageitnion when Kratinos is *stephanophoros*, or he will put forward another man who will act as priest instead of himself for the same period of time, once he has been consecrated to Zeus Telesiourgos, and each year on the first day of the month of Taureon he will get sixty drachmas from the treasurer and on the first day of the month of Taureon he will sacrifice a fully-grown animal to the Demos of the Romans and to Roma. On the eleventh day of the same month let those gymnasiarchs who are entering office, together with the ephebes sacrifice a fully-grown animal to the Demos of the Romans and to Roma. Similarly, when they leave office, let the gymnasiarchs together with those completing their time as ephebes sacrifice a fully-grown animal and let each give to [the priest] the prescribed perquisites (i.e. the share due the priest).

b) . . .] and for the other athletic events distributing to each the appropriate prizes and setting up prizes for dedication, namely the arms of a warrior, no fewer than three sets, with the contest inscribed on them, and making the most glorious effort concerning these in accordance with our people's respect for the divine and gratitude towards the Romans. And, together with the priest, the gymnasiarchs of the young men are to share the responsibility and organisation so that the contests might be as impressive as possible. On the eighth day at the close of the same month let him hold a contest in the children's palaestra, including the torch race and the other athletic events, and conduct it in the proper manner. And, together with him, the *paidonomoi* are to share the responsibility and organisation. There is to be a dedication of the arms that were set up in the Roman games, for the present taking place in the gymnasium of the young men but later, when the temple of Roma is finished, in the Romaion. Let the priest sacrifice, on the first day of each month, a fully-grown animal to the Demos of the Romans and Roma, having been given by the prytany treasurer ten drachmas for the sacrifice. On the seventh day of the month of Thargelion let the *aisymnetes* sacrifice a fully-grown ox and let him give the priest the perquisites that have been laid down; and let him sacrifice on the twelfth day of the month of Metageitnion in the same way and give the perquisites. If, however, the god buys the position of *aisymnetes*, then let the *prosetairoi* of the god sacrifice a fully-grown animal on both days and let them give the priest the perquisites as arranged. On the eighteenth day of the month of Boiedromion let the fifty archons sacrifice a fully-grown pig and give the perquisites to . . .

H (SIG³ 760)

Inscribed base of statue of Caesar from the Greek city of Ephesos in Asia Minor, c. 48 BC, written in Greek.

The cities of Asia and the peoples and the tribes (dedicate this statue of) Gaius Iulius Caesar, son of Gaius, pontifex maximus and imperator and consul for the second time, descended from Ares and Aphrodite, god manifest and common saviour of human life.

I (ILS 264)

Dedicatory Latin inscription from an arch in the Circus Maximus, Rome, AD 80–81, now lost.

The Senate and the Roman People (dedicate this) to Imperator Titus Caesar Vespasianus Augustus, son of the deified Vespasian, pontifex maximus, ten times holder of tribunician power, seventeen times imperator, eight times consul, father of the country, their own leader, because following the instructions and plans of his father and under his auspices he subdued the Jewish people and destroyed the city of Jerusalem, a city that had been besieged in vain by previous generals, kings and peoples or left altogether unattempted.

Lex Irnitana

This is part of the text of a lengthy municipal constitution granted to the Spanish town of Irni by the Flavians (full text, translation and commentary in González 1986), preserved on bronze tablets found in 1981 by a group with metal detectors searching for ancient coins.

A (Section 21)

Rubric: In what manner they may obtain Roman citizenship in that *municipium*.

Those of the senators, decurions and conscripti [i.e. local councillors] of the Municipium of Flavian Irni who have been or will be appointed magistrates as understood by this law, once their term of office is over, are to become Roman citizens, together with their parents, their wives and those children who have been born in lawful marriage and have been in the power of the parents, similarly grandsons and granddaughters who have been born from a son and who have been in the power of the parents, provided that no more become Roman citizens than the number of magistrates proper to be appointed under this law.

Josephus

Flavius Josephus was a Jewish political leader and historian, born in AD 37. His *Jewish War* and *Jewish Antiquities* were written in Greek.

A (Jewish War 7.148–52) Vespasian's triumph in Rome

The spoils in general were carried in disorderly heaps but more conspicuous than the rest were those captured in the temple of Jerusalem, a golden table, many talents in weight, a golden lampstand also made of gold but constructed in a different way from those we customarily use. For fixed to the base was a central shaft, from which slender branches extended with an arrangement like the shape of a trident, a wrought lamp attached to the end of each. There are seven of these, signifying the honour paid to this number among the Jews. Next the law of the Jews was carried, the last of the spoils. Then many men followed carrying images of Nike [goddess of Victory], all constructed out of

Fig. 1 Arch of Titus, Rome (photo: author)

Fig. 2 Relief from Arch of Titus: menorah in triumphal procession; see **Josephus A**; note also the placards (photo: author)

Fig. 3 Relief from Arch of Titus showing Titus riding in a chariot in the triumphal procession (photo: author)

ivory and gold. After these rode Vespasian with Titus following, while Domitian rode alongside, magnificently dressed and his horse too a wonderful sight.

Lactantius

Lactantius (c. 240–c. 320 AD) was a Christian apologist from North Africa. His major work, *The Divine Institutes*, written in Latin, was a response to the critics of Christianity.

A (Divine Institutes 5.16.2–4)

Since the arguments of the philosophers [defending justice] were weak, Carneades undertook the audacious task of refuting them, because he realised that they could be refuted. The substance of his argument was this: that men have enacted laws for themselves with their own advantage in mind, varying certainly according to their ways of life and even among the same people they often change with the times; that there is, however, no natural law; both men and animals alike go for what is useful for them as their nature directs; therefore there is no justice

or, if there is any, it is the height of stupidity, because it harms itself
by looking to the interests of others. And Carneades brought forward
these further arguments: that if all the nations which prospered as a
result of empire, including the Romans themselves who controlled the
whole world, wanted to be just, that is if they returned what belonged
to others, they would have to return to living in huts and lie around in
want and misery.

Livy

The Roman historian Titus Livius (59 BC–AD 17) came from Patavium
(Padua) in the north of Italy. His history of Rome from its foundation
(*ab urbe condita*) until his own day was an enormous work in 142
books, of which only books 1–10 and 21–45 survive, the latter group
stretching from the outbreak of the Second Punic War to 167 BC; the
rest are known from summaries.

*A (1.32.5–10) Introduction of the fetial rites for declaring war by Ancus
   Marcius, traditionally fourth king of Rome, later seventh century BC*
Since Numa had established religious practices for peacetime, Ancus
Marcus would hand down ceremonies appropriate to war. In order,
therefore, that wars might be not only fought but also declared with
some ritual, he wrote down the law as taken from the ancient tribe
of the Aequiculi under which the fetial priests act to this day when
seeking restitution for some wrong.

When the envoy has reached the frontiers of those from whom
satisfaction is demanded, with his head bound in a woollen fillet he
says, 'Hear me, Jupiter, hear me, frontiers of (here he names which-
ever people it is), let divine law listen, I am the official messenger of
the Roman people. Rightly and duly authorised do I come; let faith be
placed in my words.' Next he recites the demands. Then he calls Jupiter
to witness, 'If I am demanding the surrender of those men or those
goods contrary to justice and religion, may you never allow me to enjoy
my native land again.' This he recites, with some slight changes in the
wording of the formula and oath, as he crosses the frontier, then again
to whoever happens to be the first person he meets, again on entering
the gates and again after he has entered the forum. If what he demands
is not surrendered once thirty-three days have passed – for that is the
period of grace – then he declares war in the following words, 'Hear
me, Jupiter and you also, Janus Quirinus, and all the heavenly gods,
and those of the earth and those of the underworld, hear me; I call you

to witness that this people (he names whoever it is) is unjust and has not made proper restitution. But about these matters we must consult the elders in our country as to how we may obtain what is rightfully ours.'

B (8.13.10–14.12) Rome restructures its relations with the Latin cities, 338 BC

13. Before the consular elections for the following year took place, Camillus brought the matter of the Latin peoples before the Senate and spoke as follows, 'Conscript fathers, our military operations in Latium have now come to a conclusion thanks to the favour of the gods and the bravery of our soldiers. The armies of the enemy were cut to pieces at Pedum and Astura. All the Latin towns and Antium in the land of the Volsci have either been taken by force or have surrendered and are now held by your garrisons. Since they harass us so often with their renewal of hostilities, it remains for us to deliberate about how we can keep them quiet and permanently at peace. The immortal gods have given you such complete control of the situation that they have put it into your hands to decide whether or not Latium continues to exist in the future. As far as the Latins are concerned, therefore, you can obtain a lasting peace for yourselves either by violence or by forgiveness. Do you wish to adopt cruel measures against a people that have surrendered and been defeated? You are free to destroy the whole of Latium and create vast deserts of the very place that so often supplied you with a splendid army of allies to use in many a great war. Or do you wish to follow the example of our ancestors and increase the Roman state by accepting the defeated into citizenship? The material for growth is here in abundance and with it the utmost glory. Certainly the strongest form of government by far is that which subjects take pleasure in obeying. But whatever decision you reach, you must make haste about it. You are keeping so many people in a state of suspense between hope and fear. And so you have to free yourself from your worries about them as soon as possible and pre-emptively strike their minds with punishment or benevolence while they are still stupefied with expectation. It has been our task to put you in a position to deliberate about the whole matter, it is yours to decide what is best for yourselves and for the republic.'

14. The leading men in the Senate praised the way the consul had reported on the substance of the matter but they said that since the cases of the various Latins differed so widely, his advice would best be carried out if proposals were introduced about each individual people

by name so that each case might be decided on merit. Therefore proposals and decisions were made about each individually. The Lanuvini
received citizenship and their temples were restored to them, on the
understanding that the temple and grove of Juno Sospita should belong
in common to the Roman people and the citizens of Lanuvium. The
Arici, Nomentani and Pedani were accepted into citizenship on the
same terms as the Lanuvini. The Tusculani retained the citizenship
which they had had before and the charge of renewing the war was
attached to a few individuals without any detriment to the community
as a whole. The Veliterni as longstanding Roman citizens were dealt
with severely because of their many revolts; their walls were torn down,
their senate deported and ordered to live on the other side of the Tiber;
if any of them was caught on this side of the river, his ransom was to
be a thousand pounds of bronze and the man who caught him was
not to release him from captivity until the money was paid. Colonists
were sent onto the senators' land and when they were enrolled Velitrae
looked as populous as it had before. A new colony was also sent to
Antium, on the understanding that the people of Antium were permitted to enrol themselves as colonists if they wished. Their warships were
taken away and the sea was forbidden to them; they were admitted to
citizenship. The peoples of Tibur and Praeneste had land confiscated,
not only because of the new charge of rebellion that they shared with
the rest of Latium, but also because, unable to stand Roman power,
they had once joined arms with the Gauls, that savage race. The rest
of the Latin cities were deprived of the rights of intermarriage, trade
with each other and common councils with each other. Citizenship
without the vote (*civitas sine suffragio*) was given to the Campanians,
as a reward for the refusal of its aristocracy to join the Latins, and also
to the Fundani and Formiani, because they had always allowed a safe
and peaceful passage through their territory. It was decided that the
people of Cumae and Suessula should enjoy the same rights as Capua.
Some of the ships of Antium were taken into the Roman dockyards,
while others were burnt and it was decided to use their prows (*rostra*)
to decorate a platform erected in the Forum and this sacred place was
called the Rostra.

C (26.24) Rome allies with the Aitolians, 212 or 211 BC
For the epigraphic remains of this agreement, see **Inscription B** *above*
Around the same time M. Valerius Laevinius, who had earlier sounded
out the leading Aitolians in private interviews, arrived with a fleet
of swift ships at the council of the Aitolians which had already been

called for that very purpose. He drew their attention to the capture of
Syracuse and Capua as instances of Roman success in Italy and Sicily
and then added that it was the practice of the Romans, handed down
from their ancestors, to look after their allies. Some of their allies, he
explained, they had received into citizenship on the same footing as
themselves, others they had allowed to remain under such favourable conditions that they preferred to be allies than citizens. The
Aitolians, he continued, would be held in greater honour as the first
of all overseas peoples to enter into friendship with them. Philip and
the Macedonians were troublesome neighbours, whose strength and
aggressiveness he himself had already weakened and would reduce still
further to the point that they would not only abandon those cities that
they had seized from the Aitolians but they would find Macedon itself
threatened. As for the Akarnanians, whose forcible removal from the
league was a cause of much resentment among the Aitolians, he would
bring them back to the old terms under which they would be subject to
Aitolian control.

These then were the statements and promises of the Roman commander. Skopas, the chief magistrate of the Aitolians at the time, and
Dorimachos, one of their leading men, both supported them with
their own authority and praised the power and majesty of the Roman
people, their lack of reserve making them all the more persuasive. It
was, however, the hope of becoming masters of Akarnania that had the
most influence.

The terms on which they were to become friends and allies of the
Roman people were put in writing, with the following additional
clauses:

1. if it pleases them and they so wish, the Eleans, the Lakedaimonians,
    Attalos, Pleuratos and Scerdilaidas should have the same rights
    of friendship (Attalos being king of Asia, the latter two of the
    Thracians and Illyrians respectively);
2. the Aitolians should straightaway make war on Philip by land;
    the Romans should assist them with no fewer than twenty-five
    quinqueremes;
3. of the cities between Aitolia and Corcyra, the soil, buildings and
    walls together with their farmland should belong to the Aitolians,
    all the remaining booty should belong to the Roman people,
    and the Romans should ensure that Aitolians take possession of
    Akarnania;
4. if the Aitolians make peace with Philip, they should add to their

treaty that the peace would be valid only if Philip abstained from making war on the Romans and their allies and those subject to them; similarly if the Roman people make a treaty with the king, they should take care that he should not be permitted to wage war against the Aitolians and their allies.

These were the terms they agreed and two years later the text of them was deposited at Olympia by the Aitolians and on the Capitol by the Romans, so that the sacred monuments might bear witness to them. The reason for this delay was because the Aitolian envoys were detained in Rome for quite some time, although this was no obstacle to getting the campaign under way. The Aitolians immediately began hostilities against Philip, as did Laevinius against Zakynthos, a small island near Aitolia which has a single city of the same name. He captured it by force with the exception of the citadel. He also captured Oiniadai and Nasos which belonged to the Akarnanians and gave them to the Aitolians. Then feeling satisfied that Philip was now sufficiently involved in a war with his neighbours not to be able to give thought to Italy or the Carthaginians or agreements with Hannibal, he withdrew to Corcyra.

D (34.51–2) *T. Quinctius Flamininus re-organises Greece after his victory in the Second Macedonian War and returns to triumph in Rome, 194 BC*

51. Flamininus set off for Chalkis, where, once he had withdrawn the garrison not only from there but also Oreos and Eretria, he held a conference of all the cities in Euboia. After he had reminded them in what condition he had found them and in what state he was now leaving them, he sent them away. Next he went on to Demetrias where he removed the garrison and with everyone accompanying as had happened at Corinth and Chalkis he continued on his way to Thessaly. There the cities had not only to be liberated but also brought back to some tolerable order out of complete confusion and chaos. The disorder of the Thessalians was not only due to the problems of the time and the violence and lawlessness of the king but also the result of the restless character of the people who throughout their history have never been able to carry out elections, assemblies or council meetings without riot and disturbance. Flamininus chose the senate and judges mainly on the basis of a property qualification and placed power in the hands of that part of the state that would benefit most from general security and peace.

52. After this thorough reorganisation of Thessaly, he went through Epiros to Orikos, from where he intended to cross to Italy. From Orikos all his forces were carried across to Brundisium; from there they went through the whole of Italy to the city almost as if they were in a triumphal procession with the column of captured booty no less a size than the army itself. On their arrival in Rome a meeting of the Senate was held outside the city to allow Flamininus to make his report and the senators gladly awarded him a well-deserved triumph. His triumph lasted three days. On the first day the procession carried the arms and weapons and the bronze and marble statues, most taken from Philip rather than captured from the cities. On the second day all the gold and silver, wrought, unwrought and coined, was carried in the procession. The unwrought silver came to 18,270 pounds in weight, while the wrought silver included vessels of every sort, most embossed, some works of outstanding craftsmanship; there were also many made of bronze and ten silver shields as well. Of the silver coinage there were 84,000 Attic pieces, known as tetradrachms, with a weight in silver roughly equivalent to three denarii. There was gold to the weight of 3,714 pounds, a shield made entirely of gold, and 14,514 gold Philippics. On the third day 114 gold crowns, the gifts of Greek cities, were carried in the procession. Animals were led to be sacrificed and before the triumphal chariot went many noble prisoners and hostages, among whom were Demetrios, son of king Philip, and the Spartan Armenes, son of the tyrant Nabis. Next Flamininus himself entered the city. Following his chariot was a tremendous crowd of soldiers, as the whole army had been brought back from the province. The sum of 250 asses was distributed to each infantryman, twice that to the centurions and three times to the cavalry. A distinctive feature of the triumph was the sight of men who had been freed from slavery following with their heads shaved.

E (37.59) The triumph of Lucius Scipio, 189 BC

Rightly, therefore, was the greatest possible honour paid to the immortal gods for having made a remarkable victory also an easy one and a triumph was decreed for the general, Lucius Scipio. He triumphed in the intercalary month on the day preceding 1 March. His triumph was more spectacular than that of his brother Africanus but if one recalls what was achieved or evaluates the danger and struggle involved it no more merits comparison than if the two generals are compared with each other or Antiochos as leader is compared with Hannibal. In the triumphal procession he displayed 224 military standards, 134 representations of towns, 1,231 ivory tusks, 234 gold crowns, 137,420 pounds

of silver, 224,000 Attic tetradrachms, 321,070 cistophori, 140,000 gold
Philippics, 1,423 silver vessels, all embossed, 1,023 pounds of gold ones,
and thirty-two of the king's officers, both military men and courtiers,
were led before the general's chariot. The sum of twenty-five denarii
was given to each soldier, twice that to the centurions and three times
to the cavalry and after the triumph they were given twice their pay and
corn allowance. He had already given double after the battle in Asia. He
celebrated his triumph around a year after he left the consulship.

> *F (41.28) Gracchus celebrates his victory in Sardinia, 174 BC*
In the same year a tablet was placed in the temple of Mater Matuta
with the following inscription: 'Under the command and auspices of
the consul Tiberius Sempronius Gracchus a legion and an army of the
Roman people subjugated Sardinia. In that province more than 80,000
of the enemy were killed or taken prisoner. With his public duty successfully accomplished, the allies liberated and revenues restored, he
brought his army home, safe, sound and thoroughly laden with booty.
Celebrating a triumph for the second time, he entered the city of Rome.
For this reason he has given this tablet as an offering to Jupiter.' There
was a representation of the island of Sardinia and images of the battles
depicted on the tablet.

1 *Maccabees*

1 *Maccabees* is believed to have been written in Hebrew around 100 BC
by an unknown author and subsequently translated into Greek; it is the
Greek text that survives.

> *A (1 Maccabees 8)*
Judas heard of the reputation of the Romans, that they were very strong
and they were well-disposed to all who took their side, and they would
establish friendship with all who came to them and that they were very
strong. He was told also of their wars and the bravery that they had displayed among the Gauls and how they had conquered them and made
them subject to tribute. He was told of all the things that they had done
in the land of Spain to seize control of the silver and gold mines there
and how they conquered the whole place by their planning and their
persistence, even though the place is very far from them. He was told of
the kings who came against them from the edges of the earth, until the
Romans had crushed them and dealt them a great blow and the rest gave
tribute to them every year. And they crushed in battle and conquered

Philip and Perseus king of the Kitians [i.e. Macedonians] and the others who rose up against them. And Antiochos the Great, king of Asia, who marched against them in war with 120 elephants and cavalry and chariots and a very large army was also crushed by them and they took him alive and made him and those who ruled after him pay a great tribute and give hostages and surrender Indian, Median and Lydian lands which were among his best lands and taking them from him they gave them to King Eumenes. And that men from Greece had planned to go and get rid of them, but this became known to them and they [the Romans] sent a single general against the Greeks and made war on them, inflicting many casualities, and they took their women and children captive and plundered them and conquered the land and tore down their fortresses and enslaved them to this day. The remaining kingdoms and islands, as many as ever opposed them, they destroyed and enslaved, but with their friends and those who relied on them they maintained friendship. They conquered kings near and far, and whoever heard their name was afraid of them. And whoever they want to help and to be kings, they make kings, and whoever they want to depose, they depose. And they have been greatly exalted. And in all this none of them put on a diadem nor wore purple in order to show his power by it. They have created a council house for themselves and every day 320 deliberate constantly about the multitude that they might live in an orderly way. And they trust one man each year to rule them and govern their whole land, and all obey the one man, and there is no envy nor jealousy among them.

And Judas selected Eupolemos son of John, son of Accos, and Jason, son of Eleazar, and sent them to Rome to secure friendship and alliance and to take the yoke from them because they saw the kingdom of the Greeks was enslaving Israel.

Milestones

These were usually cylindrical blocks of stone roughly 2m. in height, inscribed with details of the magistrate responsible for building or repairing the road or, under the empire, with the name of the reigning emperor.

A (CIL 3.7205) Asia Minor, near Ephesos, 129–126 BC
Bilingual text (ordinary print = Latin, italic = Greek). Illustrated, Fig. 4.
  Manius Aquillius, son of Manius, consul. Mile 5
  Manius Aquillius, son of Manius, consul of the Romans. Mile 5

Fig. 4 **Milestone A** from near Ephesos (photo: Peter Thonemann)

B *(ILLRP 461) Late 2nd Century* BC *Spain, in Latin*
Quintus Fabius Labeo, son of Quintus, proconsul. Mile 92.

C *(ILS 5863) Danube region, reign of Trajan, in Latin*
Emperor Caesar Nerva Trajan Augustus Germanicus, son of the deified
Nerva, pontifex maximus, in his fourth year of tribunician power,

father of his country, consul for the third time, mountains having been cut through and the bends removed, constructed this road.

Philo of Alexandria

Philo was a leading Jewish philosopher and writer from Alexandria in Egypt, whose extensive surviving writings were written in Greek. As an old man in AD 39/40 he led the embassy of the Alexandrian Jews to the emperor Gaius Caligula.

A *(Embassy to Gaius 146–7) On Augustus*

This is the man [Augustus] who emptied the sea of pirate ships and filled it with merchant ships. This is the one who gave freedom to every city, who turned disorder into order, who brought civilisation and harmony to all unsociable and brutish peoples, who increased Greece with many Greeces and who brought Greekness to the barbarian world in its most important regions. He was the guardian of peace, the distributor of what was due to each, the one who was liberal with his favours in the public arena, and who in his whole life kept nothing good or fine concealed.

B *(The Special Laws 3.159–62) Tax-collecting*

Recently, when some men who apparently owed tax due to poverty took flight in fear of the most cruel punishments, a certain collector of taxes who had been appointed in our area seized their wives, children, parents and the rest of the family by force. He beat them, abused them and inflicted every form of suffering on them, in order to make them either give information about the fugitive or to pay what he owed, but they could do neither, the one because they did not know, the other because they were as badly off as the man who had fled. The tax collector did not release them until tormenting their bodies with racks and instruments of torture he killed them with newly-devised forms of death. He fastened a basket full of sand with ropes and suspended this very weight from their necks, then he stood them in the open air. The results were twofold. On the one hand, they themselves sank under the cruel pressure of all these punishments at once, the wind and the sun, the shame in the face of passers-by and the heavy weight hanging from them; on the other hand, those watching these people's punishment suffered in anticipation. Some of these spectators, seeing more clearly with their souls than their eyes, as if they themselves were being mistreated in the bodies of others, committed suicide by swords or poison or hanging, because in their terrible circumstances they thought that death without torture was great good fortune. But those who did not kill themselves in advance were led away in the kind of order that is found in legal actions over inheritances: first it was the closest relatives that were led away, after them those who were second and third in line and finally the distant relatives. Then when there were no relatives left, this evil moved on to their neighbours and sometimes to whole villages or cities, which quickly became abandoned and empty of inhabitants, who left their homes and dispersed to wherever they thought they would escape notice.

Pliny the Elder

Gaius Plinius Secundus (AD 23/4–79) wrote *The Natural History*, a wide-ranging 37-book encyclopaedia in Latin. He was the uncle of Pliny the Younger and died at the eruption of Vesuvius.

A (Natural History 3.38–9) Italy selected by providence
Next comes Italy, first the Ligurians, then Etruria, Umbria and Latium, where one finds the mouth of the Tiber and Rome capital of the world, sixteen miles from the sea. Afterwards comes the coast of the Volsci and of Campania, [there follows a list of regions and peoples of Italy] I am not unaware that people could rightly think me ungrateful and lazy if I describe in such a brief and cursory manner the land which is both foster child and parent of all lands. For it is a land selected by the providence of the gods to make heaven itself more glorious, to bring together scattered empires, to make customs and manners more gentle, to unite in dialogue through community of language the discordant and wild ways of speaking of so many peoples, to give civilisation to men and in short to become a single fatherland for all the races in the whole world.

B (Natural History 35.6–7) Memorials of Roman ancestors
Among our ancestors it was different; in their halls there were portraits to be looked at, not statues made by foreign sculptors, nor works in bronze or marble; faces modelled in wax were arranged in separate cabinets so that they might be ancestor portraits to accompany funerals in the family. And whenever someone died, every member of his family that had ever lived would always be present. In fact the family trees traced their lines to painted portraits. The archive rooms were filled with books and records of deeds done while holding office. Outside the house and around the entrance there were other portraits of those

mighty spirits with spoils taken from the enemy attached which not even the buyer of the property was allowed to remove and so houses forever celebrated a triumph even though the owners changed. This was an enormous stimulus, when every day the walls reproached an unwarlike owner for intruding on the triumph of another.

Pliny the Younger

Gaius Plinius Caecilius Secundus (c. AD 61–c. 112) was a Roman senator, who served as governor of the province of Bithynia-Pontus in around 110. He published ten books of letters, the last of which contains his correspondence with the Emperor Trajan. He was the nephew of Pliny the Elder.

A (Letters *10.33–4*)

33. Pliny to the Emperor Trajan

As I was making my way round a different part of the province, a tremendous fire at Nikomedia destroyed many private houses and two public buildings, the Gerousia and the temple of Isis, even though they were on opposite sides of the street. It spread fairly widely, partly because of the force of the wind, partly because of the inertia of the people, who, it is clear, stood there throughout as idle and unmoving spectators of this great disaster. Besides the city was furnished with no fire pump, no fire bucket, nor any equipment for putting out fires. These things will be made ready for the future, as I have now given instructions. You, my lord, must consider whether you think that a company of firemen should be set up, consisting of not more than 150 men. I will see to it that only firemen are enrolled and that privileges which are granted them are not used for any other purpose. It will not be difficult to keep a watch on so small a number.

34. Trajan to Pliny

It occurs to you that following a number of precedents elsewhere a company of firemen could be set up in Nikomedia. But we are to remember that this province and especially these cities have suffered from disturbances caused by groups of this sort. Whatever title we have given them and for whatever reason, those groups that have formed for a common purpose will nonetheless become political clubs and it doesn't take long for that to happen. So it may be better to provide whatever equipment is of assistance in putting out fires and to advise property-owners to take action themselves and, if the situation demands it, make use of the crowd that gathers round.

B (Letters *10.39–40*)

39. Pliny to the Emperor Trajan

The theatre at Nikaia, my lord, is now for the most part constructed, although still unfinished; it has, however, exhausted more than ten million sesterces, or so, at least, I hear – the accounts have not yet been prepared. All I fear in vain. For it is sinking and displaying enormous cracks, whether because of the damp and soft soil or because the stone itself is poor and crumbling. It is certainly a matter for consideration whether it should be completed or left as it stands or even pulled down. For the buttresses and substructure by which it is supported look to me to be more expensive than solid. Many additional elements have been promised for the theatre by private individuals and are still due, for example the adjacent basilicas and the colonnade above the auditiorium. But all this is now postponed, since the work that must be completed first has now come to a halt. The Nikaians have also begun to rebuild the gymnasium which was destroyed in a fire before my arrival. The new one is on a far more ambitious and extensive scale than the old one and they have already spent a fair sum. There is a risk that it has all been wasted; for it is badly-planned and too scattered. In addition to this an architect, admittedly a rival of the one whose work is in progress, claims that the walls although twenty-two feet thick are unable to sustain the weight put on them as their core is rubble and they are not faced with brick.

Also the inhabitants of Claudiopolis are excavating, rather than building, a huge public bath complex in a hollow at the foot of a mountain. It is being financed by the money which those who joined the council by your favour either have already paid in return for their admission or will pay when I ask them. I am afraid that in the one place public money is being misused and in the other something that is more valuable than any money, your generosity, is abused. Consequently I am compelled to ask you to send out an architect to inspect the theatre and baths to determine whether it is better, after all the expense which has been laid out, to finish them on the present plan or to make the improvements and changes that seem necessary. For otherwise in wanting to save what is already spent we might end up employing any additional sums badly.

40. Trajan to Pliny

Since you are on the spot, you are in the best position to deliberate and decide about what needs to be done about the theatre that the Nikaians are currently constructing. It is sufficient for me if you let me know your decision. But, once the theatre is finished, see that the private individuals carry out the work that they promised. These little Greeks do love a gymnasium; so perhaps the people of Nikaia have been rather too ambitious in planning one, but they must be satisfied with one that suits their needs. What advice should be given to the people of Claudiopolis about the baths which, as you write, have been begun on an unsuitable site, you will decide. Architects cannot be in short supply where you are. No province is without men of skill and talent. You should not imagine that it is quicker for them to be sent from Rome when they usually even come to us from Greece.

Plutarch

Plutarch of Chaironeia in Boiotia (mid first century AD until some time after AD 120) was a Greek writer whose literary output and range was quite extraordinary. His many essays, often philosophical in character, are collected as the *Moralia*. More widely read today are his *Parallel Lives*, a series of biographies that pair famous Greeks with Roman counterparts.

A (Flamininus 16–17) Cult honours for T. Quinctius Flamininus
16. The Chalkidians, after being saved in this way, dedicated to Titus [Quinctius Flamininus] the most beautiful and largest votive offerings they had. The inscriptions on these are still visible today and run as follows: 'The people dedicate this gymnasium to Titus and to Herakles', and then in another place, 'The people dedicate the Delphinion to Titus and Apollo'. Even in our time, a priest of Titus is formally elected and declared; after sacrificing and pouring libations in his honour, they sing a set hymn, much of which I will omit because of its length and only quote the concluding verses of the song:

> The faith of the Romans we revere,
> Which we have solemnly sworn to cherish.
> With singing and dancing, maidens, celebrate
> Great Zeus and Roma and Titus and the faith of the Romans as well
> Hail, hail, O Titus our saviour.

17. He also received fitting honours from the rest of the Greeks and what made all these honours genuine was the extraordinary goodwill that resulted from his fairness of character.

B (Aemilius Paullus 28) Aemilius Paullus tours Greece
Then, Paullus gave his army a rest while he devoted himself to seeing Greece and spending his time in pursuits that were reputable and

Fig. 5 Relief sculpture of battle from top of pillar of Aemilius Paullus, Delphi; see **Plutarch B** (photo: Shane Wallace)

Fig. 6 Inscription from base of pillar of Aemilius Paullus, Delphi. It reads in Latin: L. AIMILIUS L. F. INPERATOR DE REGE PERSE MACEDONIQUE CEPET, which translates as 'Lucius Aemilius, son of Lucius, imperator, took this from King Perseus and the Macedonians' (*ILS* 8884; photo: Shane Wallace)

humane. As he went on this way, he restored democratic governments and established constitutions; he also gave gifts to cities, grain from the king's store to some, oil to others. For they say that the stockpiles that were found were so great that the people taking them and putting in requests for them ran out before the great quantity of material they had found was exhausted. At Delphi when he saw a great square pillar made of blocks of white marble on which a golden statue of Perseus was to have been placed, he ordered that a statue of himself be placed there instead. For it was right, he said, that the conquered should make way for the victors. At Olympia he is said to have made that well-known statement that Pheidias had crafted the Zeus of Homer.

C (Tiberius Gracchus 8.1–4, 8.7, 9.4–5) Italian agriculture before Tiberius Gracchus

8. Of the land that the Romans took from their neighbours through war, some they sold, some they made public land and assigned in exchange of a small rent to those citizens who were poor and in need. But when the wealthy began to offer higher rents and drove the poor out, a law was passed that forbade anyone from holding more then 500 iugera of land. For a short time this law restrained their greed and helped the poor, who stayed on the land they had rented, each occupying the portion he held from the beginning. Later the rich men of the neighbourhood using fictitious names transferred the tenancies to themselves and in the end openly held most of the land in their own name. The poor, driven out in this way, no longer presented themselves with enthusiasm for military service and took no care in the bringing up of their children, so that in no time at all the whole of Italy noticed the shortage of free men and it became filled with barbarian slave gangs, which the rich used to farm their estates now that they had driven away the citizens. Gaius Laelius, a close friend of Scipio, tried to correct this but in the face of opposition from the powerful and fearful of unrest he brought a stop to his attempt and earned the name Wise or Prudent; for the Latin 'sapiens' can mean either. But Tiberius, as soon as he was elected tribune, immediately took the matter in hand . . . His brother Gaius in a certain small book describes Tiberius travelling to Numantia through Etruria and observing the depopulation of the countryside and that those working the land or pasturing were imported barbarian slaves. It was then, he says, that Tiberius first came up with the policy that would be the cause of so many troubles for the two of them . . .

9. Tiberius was fighting for an honourable and just cause with an eloquence that had the power to enhance even less worthy matters. He was formidable and unchallengeable whenever he mounted rostra with the people crowding round and spoke about the poor: 'the wild beasts that inhabit Italy have, each one of them, their cave or lair for protection, but those who fight and die for Italy have a share of the air and

the light but nothing else. Without a house or a home they wander with their children and wives, while generals lie to their soldiers in battle, encouraging them to defend tombs and shrines from the enemy. For none of these men has an ancestral altar, none of these many Romans has a tomb of their forebears, but they fight and die on behalf of the luxury and wealth of others. They may be called the masters of the world but they do not have one single piece of turf as their own.

D (Pompey 24) The rise of piracy

The power of the pirates was initially based in Cilicia and to begin with was reckless and elusive but it gained confidence and daring during the Mithridatic war when it was in the service of the king. Then while the Romans were struggling with each other in the civil wars at the gates of Rome, the sea, now without protection, became increasingly attractive to the pirates, who no longer limited their attacks to shipping but also laid waste islands and coastal cities. Now men of wealth, noble birth and intelligence embarked on pirate ships and shared in the enterprise as one that brought a certain fame and distinction. In many places there were pirate harbours and fortified stations for fire signals and the fleets that landed were not only well fitted out for their particular task with good crews, skilled helmsmen and fast, light ships. Formidable though they were, however, it was their odious arrogance that caused the greater indignation, their gilded sails, purple awnings and silvered oars, as if they luxuriated in their wrong-doing and prided themselves on it. Their flutes, stringed instruments, drunken parties along every coast, their kidnapping of leading figures and their ransoming of captured cities, all these were an insult to Roman supremacy. The ships of the pirates numbered in excess of a thousand and the cities captured by them four hundred. They also attacked and plundered sanctuaries that were previously inviolable and untouched, Klaros, Didyma, Samothrace, the temple of Chthonia at Hermione, the temple of Asklepios in Epidauros and the temples of Poseidon at the Isthmos, at Tainaron and at Kalauria, the temples of Apollo at Aktion and at Leukas and the temples of Hera at Samos, Argos and Lakinion. They themselves also offered strange sacrifices at Olympos and performed certain secret rites including those of Mithras, which were first introduced by the pirates and are still celebrated today.

But it was against the Romans that their insolence was directed most of all, even following their roads inland from the sea and plundering there and sacking the nearby villas. Once they kidnapped two praetors, Sextilius and Bellinus, in their purple-edged robes and carried them off along with their servants and lictors. They also captured a daughter of Antonius, a man who had had the honour of a triumph, while she was on her way to the country, and obtained a substantial ransom for her. But the summit of their insolence was this. Whenever anyone who was captured cried out that he was a Roman and said his name, the pirates would pretend to be panic-stricken and terrified. They would strike their thighs and fall at his feet begging forgiveness. Seeing them abject and pleading, the captive would believe them. Then some would put Roman boots on him, while others dressed him in a toga, all, so they said, to prevent the mistake being made again. After making fun of the man for a long time in this way and getting a good bit of amusement out of him, they would finally let down a ladder in the middle of the sea and tell him to disembark and wish him a pleasant journey. If he was not willing to go, they would push him overboard themselves and drown him.

E (Precepts of Statecraft 10 = Moralia 805A–B)

Now, therefore, since the affairs of the cities no longer involve the leadership of wars nor the toppling of tyrannies nor the business of alliance, what should anyone do to begin a distinguished and splendid public career? There remain the public law courts and embassies to the emperor, which require a man who is fiery in character while at the same time having courage and good sense. There are also many noble practices in the cities that are neglected which a man can revive and many others that have crept in due to bad habits, much to the disgrace or damage of the city, that he can change and so turn to account for himself.

F (Precepts of Statecraft 18 = Moralia 814C–D)

Not only must the statesman show himself and his own state blameless in respect of the ruling power, but he must also always have someone from among its most powerful members as a friend, to serve as a secure support for the government. For the Romans themselves are very keen when it comes to promoting the political interests of their friends. It is right that those who profit from friendship with the rulers should do so for the public good as Polybios and Panaitios did as a result of Scipio's goodwill to them, conferring great benefits on their own states.

Polybios (Polybius)

Polybios of Megalopolis (c. 200–c. 118 BC) was a Greek historian, who wrote an account of Rome's rise to power in the Mediterranean. Rome's victory over Macedon in 168 put an end to a promising political career in the Achaian League and he was taken to Rome as a detainee where he was to remain until the late 150s. His *Histories* were written in forty books, of which the first five survive intact, the sixth in moderate condition, and the remainder are known only through excerpts and references in later writers.

A (1.3.1–6) Polybios' history

My history begins in the 140th Olympiad [220–216 BC]. The events from which it starts are these: in Greece the war known as the Social War, which was the first to be waged by Philip, son of Demetrios and father of Perseus, in league with the Achaians against the Aitolians; in Asia the war for the possession of Coele Syria which Antiochos and Ptolemy Philopator fought against each other; in Italy, Libya and neighbouring regions the conflict between Rome and Carthage, which most people call the Hannibalic War. My work thus begins where that of Aratos of Sikyon leaves off. In earlier times the affairs of the inhabited world had been, so to speak, scattered, on account of their being separated by origins, results and place. From this point onwards, however, history becomes an organic whole and Italian and Libyan affairs are interlinked with Asian and Greek affairs, all leading up to one end. This is why I have fixed upon this era as the starting point of my work. For having defeated the Carthaginians in this war and thinking that they had accomplished the most difficult and most important step towards their goal of universal dominion, thus and at that point were the Romans for the first time emboldened to reach out their hands for the rest and to cross with an army into Greece and Asia.

B (1.10.1–11.3) The beginnings of the First Punic War (264–241 BC)

10. Thus were the Mamertines first deprived of support from Rhegion and then subjected, from causes which I have just stated, to a complete defeat on their own account. Thereupon some of them turned to the Carthaginians for protection and were for putting themselves and the citadel into their hands, while others set about sending an embassy to the Romans to offer to surrender the city and to beg assistance on the grounds of the ties of race which united them. The Romans were long in doubt. The inconsistency of sending such aid seemed clear. A little while before they had put some of their own citizens to death, with the most extreme penalties of the law, for having broken faith with the people of Rhegion. If now so soon afterwards they were to assist the Mamertines, who had done precisely the same thing not only

at Messene but also at Rhegion, it would be an act of injustice that would be very hard to defend. But while certainly not unaware of any of these points, the Romans saw that the Carthaginians had not only made Libya subject but also many districts in Spain and that they were in possession of all the islands in the Sardinian and Tyrrhenian seas. The Romans, therefore, were beginning to be exceedingly anxious lest, if the Carthaginians became masters of Sicily also, they would be very dangerous and formidable neighbours, surrounding the Romans as they would on every side and occupying a position that commanded all the coasts of Italy. Now it was clear that if the Mamertines did not obtain the assistance they requested, the Carthaginians would very soon reduce Sicily. For if they became masters of Messene once it was handed over to them, they were certain before long to crush Syracuse as well, since they already controlled nearly the whole of the rest of Sicily. The Romans saw all this, and felt that it was absolutely necessary not to let Messene slip or to allow the Carthaginians to secure what would be like a bridge to enable them to cross to Italy.

11. In spite of protracted deliberations the Senate did not approve the proposal, on account of the reasons just given; for the inconsistency involved in supporting the Mamertines appeared to them to be evenly balanced by the advantages to be gained from doing so. The people, however, although they had suffered much in the previous wars and were also in need of all-round recovery, did vote in favour of giving aid. They did so when the consuls, in addition to what was said earlier about the war being in the national interest, pointed out the great gains in terms of plunder that would clearly be available to each individually. The decree having thus been passed by the people, they elected one of the consuls, Appius Claudius, to the command and sent him out with instructions to provide assistance and cross to Messene.

C (6.17) Government contracts in Rome

Similarly the people (*demos*) for its part is far from being independent of the Senate and is bound to take its wishes into account both collectively and individually. Contracts, too numerous for anyone to count, are given out by the censors in all parts of Italy for the repair and construction of public buildings; there is also the collection of revenue from many rivers, harbours, gardens, mines and lands, in fact everything that comes under the control of the Roman government. In all these the people at large are engaged so there is scarcely a man, so to speak, who does not have some interest in the contracts and the profits from them. Some purchase the contracts from the censors for themselves, some go partners with them, some act as security for these contractors, and others pledge their property to the treasury for them. Over all these transactions the Senate has absolute control. It can grant an extension of time and in case of unforeseen accident can relieve the contractors from a portion of their obligation or release them from it altogether if they are absolutely unable to fulfil it. And there are many respects in which the Senate can impose great hardship on those who manage public property or alternatively ease their burden; for in every case the appeal is to it.

D (6.37.1–6) Military discipline

The military tribunes immediately hold a court-martial and if the man is found guilty he is punished by the *fustuarium*, the nature of which is as follows. The tribune takes a cudgel and merely touches the condemned man, whereupon all the soldiers fall upon him with cudgels and stones. Generally speaking men punished in this way are killed in the camp itself, but if by any chance they escape they do not find safety as a result. For how could they? It is not possible for them to return to their home nor would anyone of their relatives dare to receive such a man into his house. Therefore those who have once fallen into this misfortune are utterly ruined. The same fate awaits the leader of the squadron as well as his rear-rank man if they fail to give the necessary order at the proper time, the latter to the patrols and the former to the leader of the next squadron. The result of the severity and inevitability of this punishment is that in the Roman army the night watches are faultlessly kept.

E (6.53–5) The Roman funeral

53. Whenever one of their distinguished men dies, in the course of the funeral procession he is carried with every kind of honour into the forum to what is known as the rostra; usually he is conspicuous in an upright position, only rarely is he lying down. Then with all the people standing round, his son, if he has left an adult son who happens to be present, or, failing him, one of his relatives mounts the rostra and delivers a speech about the virtues of the deceased and the successes he achieved during his lifetime. By these means the people are reminded of what happened and made to see it with their own eyes, not only those who took part in the exploits but also those who did not, and their sympathies are moved so that rather than being the private misfortune of the mourners it appears to be the common misfortune of the whole people. After the burial and all the usual ceremonies they place

the image of the deceased in the most conspicuous spot in the house, enclosed in a wooden shrine. This image consists of a mask made to represent the deceased with extraordinary fidelity both in shape and complexion. These images they display at public sacrifices and decorate with much care and whenever any distinguished member of the family dies they take these masks to the funeral, putting them on those who seem to be as like the originals as possible in height and in general appearance. These men are dressed in appropriate clothes, a toga with a purple border if the deceased was a consul or praetor, one completely purple, if he had been a censor, and one embroidered with gold if he had celebrated a triumph or something similar. These men also all ride in chariots, while the fasces, axes and all the other customary insignia of the particular offices lead the way, according to the dignity of the rank in the state enjoyed by each in his lifetime, and on arriving at the rostra they all take their seats in turn on ivory chairs. It would be hard to imagine a more inspiring spectacle than this for a young man who aspires to fame and virtue. For who would not be inspired by the sight of the images of men famed for their excellence, all gathered together as if living and breathing? What could be a more glorious spectacle?

54. Besides, the one who delivers the oration over the man about to be buried, after he has finished speaking about this particular person, starts upon the others whose images are present, beginning with the most ancient, and recounts the successes and achievements of each. By this means as the glorious memory of brave men is continually renewed so the fame of those who have done any noble deed becomes immortal and the renown of those who have served their country well becomes a matter of common knowledge to the people and part of the heritage of posterity. But the chief benefit of the ceremony is that it inspires young men to endure every suffering for the general welfare in the hope of winning the glory that awaits the brave. What I say is confirmed by this fact. Many Romans have volunteered to decide a whole battle by single combat, not a few have chosen certain death, some in time of war to secure the safety of the rest, some in time of peace to preserve the safety of the state. There have also been instances of men in office putting their own sons to death, contrary to every custom and law, because they set a higher value on the interests of their country than their natural affinity to their closest relations. There are many stories told of this kind, related of many men in Roman history. But one will be enough for our present purpose and I will give the name as an instance to prove the truth of my words.

55. It is said that Horatius Cocles while fighting with two enemies at

the head of the bridge over the Tiber, which lies in front of the city, saw a large body of men advancing to support his enemies. Since he was afraid that they would force their way into the city, he turned round and shouted to those behind him to hasten back to the other side and break down the bridge. They obeyed him and while they were demolishing the bridge, he remained at his post receiving numerous wounds and held back the assault of the enemy, who were panic-stricken not so much by his strength as by his endurance and courage. When the bridge had been demolished, the enemy were thwarted in their attack, at which point Cocles threw himself into the river with his armour on and deliberately sacrificed his life, because he valued the safety of his country and his own future reputation more highly than his present life and the years that remained to him. Such, so it seems to me, is the enthusiasm and emulation for noble deeds that are engendered among the Romans by their customs.

F (9.10) The wealth of Syracuse comes to Rome, following Marcellus' capture of the city in 212 BC

The Romans, then, decided to transfer these things [the spoils of Syracuse] to their own city and to leave nothing behind. Whether their actions were right and to their advantage or the opposite is a matter admitting of much discussion, but the balance of the argument is in favour of believing it to have been wrong then and wrong now. If it had been from these kinds of starting points that they had advanced their country, it is clear that there would have been some reason for transferring to their own land those things through which they had become great. But if while leading lives of the greatest simplicity themselves, very remote from such luxury and extravagance, they nonetheless conquered men who had always possessed these things in the greatest abundance and of the finest quality, then how could we not think that they made a mistake? Surely it would be an indisputable error for a people to abandon the habits of conquerors and adopt the tastes of the conquered and at the same time attract that jealousy which is the most dangerous accompaniment of excessive prosperity. For the onlooker never feels moved to admire those who have taken possession of the property of others to the same extent that he is jealous of them, and that is combined with a certain pity for the original owners who have lost it. But when material wealth continues increasing and a people gather into their own hands all the possessions of everyone else and moreover invite in some way those who have been plundered to the spectacle, then it is twice as bad. For it is no longer the case of the spectators pitying their neighbours but themselves, as they recall the ruin of their own country. Such a sight produces an outburst not only of jealousy but also of rage against the victors. For the reminder of their own disaster serves to enhance their hatred of those responsible for it. To sweep the gold and silver, however, into their own coffers was perhaps reasonable. For it was impossible for them to aim at world empire without rendering everyone else powerless and securing such power and resources for themselves. But they might have left untouched things that had nothing to do with this build-up of power and thus at the same time avoided excessive jealousy and raised the reputation of their country, adorning it not with paintings and reliefs but with dignity of character and greatness of soul. I have said all this as a warning to those who lay claim to empire so that they may not imagine that, when they plunder cities, the misfortunes of others are an honour to their own country. The Romans, however, when they transferred these things to Rome, used such of them as were private property to increase the splendour of their own homes and such as belong to the state to adorn the city.

G (10.15.4–16.5) Scipio's sack of New Carthage in Spain, 209 BC

15. Scipio, when he thought that enough troops had entered the town, sent most of them, as is the Roman custom, against the inhabitants of the city ordering them to kill everyone they met and to spare no one and not to begin plundering until the signal had been given. They do this, it seems to me, in order to inspire terror. Consequently, when cities are captured by the Romans, one can often see not only humans slaughtered, but even dogs cut in two and the severed limbs of other animals. On this occasion the amount of such slaughter was exceedingly great because of the large size of the population. Scipio himself with about a thousand men pressed on to the citadel. When he arrived there, Mago at first thought of resistance but afterwards when he was sure that the city had already been captured he sent to demand a promise of his life and then surrendered the citadel. When this had happened, on the signal being given the soldiers stopped the killing and turned to plundering. When night fell, those of the soldiers who had been instructed to guard the camp remained there. Scipio with the thousand men encamped in the citadel and, summoning the rest from the houses by means of the tribunes, ordered them to gather together all the booty in the market square, doing this by maniples and taking up their quarters for the night by these several heaps. He then summoned the light-armed from the camp and stationed them

on the eastern hill. Thus did the Romans become masters of Carthage in Spain.

16. Next day once the baggage of those who had served in the Carthaginian ranks and the property of the townsmen and the workmen had been collected together in the marketplace, the tribunes divided it up among the several legions according to the Roman custom. The Roman procedure for dealing with booty after the capture of a city is as follows. Sometimes certain soldiers taken from each maniple are detailed for this duty, their number depending on the size of the city, sometimes maniples are detailed in turn for this task, but there are never more than half the whole number assigned to it. The rest remain in their own ranks in reserve, sometimes outside, at other times inside the city, as the occasion may demand. Sometimes, though rarely, four legions are massed together but generally speaking the army is divided into two legions of Romans and two of allies. All who are detailed for plundering bring the booty back, each to his own legion, and when it has been sold, the tribunes distribute the proceeds among all equally, including not only those held in the protecting force but also those who were guarding the tents or who were sick or who had been sent anywhere on any service.

H (11.5.1–6.4) An ambassador (possibly Rhodian) addresses the Aitolians, 207 BC

5. Put then before your eyes your own folly. You claim to be at war against Philip on behalf of the Greeks, so that they might escape from servitude to him, but your war is really for the enslavement and ruin of Greece. That is the story told by your treaty with Rome which earlier existed only in writing but now is seen in practice. Previously, the very words of it brought disgrace upon you, but now, through being put into action, this is clear to everyone. Furthermore, Philip only lends his name and serves as a pretext for the war. For he is not exposed to any attack. It is against his allies that you have made this treaty, namely the majority of the Peloponnesians, the Boiotians, the Euboians, the Phokians, the Lokrians, the Thessalians and the Epirotes, bargaining that their bodies and their goods shall belong to the Romans, their cities and their territories to the Aitolians. If you captured a city yourselves, you would not be prepared to violate the freeborn or to burn the buildings, because you look upon such conduct as cruel and barbarous. Yet, you have made a treaty by which you have handed over all other Greeks to the barbarians to be exposed to the most shameful violence and lawlessness. This was not recognised earlier but now the fate of the

people of Oreos and of the suffering Aiginetans has revealed you to everyone, fortune having, as though of set purpose, suddenly brought your folly onto the stage. So much for the origin of the war and what has happened up to now. But if everything goes exactly as you have in mind, what sort of conclusion must be expected? Will it not be the beginning of great miseries for all the Greeks?

6. For I assume that no one can fail to see that if the Romans get rid of the war in Italy – and this is imminent now that Hannibal has been confined to a narrow district in Bruttium – they will direct their whole power upon Greece, supposedly to help the Aitolians against Philip but in reality with a view to bringing Greece entirely under their own power. And if they decide to treat it well when they have conquered it, theirs will be the honour and the glory and if badly theirs too will be the plunder from those they destroy and the power over those who survive. By then you will be calling the gods as witnesses when no god will be any longer willing to help you and no man able to.

I (18.27.7–32) The Macedonian phalanx compared with the Roman legion

27. . . . Such was the outcome of the battle that was fought at Kynoskephalai in Thessaly between the Romans and Philip.

28. In my sixth book I made a promise that at a suitable opportunity I would make a comparison between the arms of the Romans and those of the Macedonians and the tactical formations of each, pointing out how they differ for better or worse from each other. Now I will try, considering what they actually did, to fulfil my promise. For in former times the Macedonian tactics proved themselves by experience capable of conquering those of Asia and Greece, while the Roman system could conquer those of Africa and of all the peoples of western Europe. In our day not once but on many occasions their tactics and men have challenged each other in battle. Therefore it will be, I think, a useful and worthwhile task to investigate their differences and discover why it is that the Romans always conquer and take the prize on the field of battle. If we do this, we shall not put it all down to fortune and congratulate them without giving reasons, as the thoughtless of mankind do, but instead, because we know the real causes, we shall give their leaders the tribute of praise and admiration they deserve.

Now as to the battles which the Romans fought against Hannibal and the defeats which they suffered in them I need say no more. For it was not owing to their arms or their tactics but to the skill and genius of Hannibal that they met with those defeats and that I made quite clear in my account of the battles then. My contention is supported by two facts. First is the conclusion of the war; for once the Romans got a general of ability comparable to Hannibal victory was soon theirs. Secondly Hannibal himself, being dissatisfied with the original equipment of his men and having immediately after his first victory furnished his troops with the weaponry of the Romans, continued to employ them until the end of the war. Pyrrhos, too, employed not only Italian weaponry but Italian forces, placing a maniple of Italians and a company of his own phalanx alternately in his battles against the Romans. Yet, even this did not enable him to win; the battles were somehow or another always indecisive. It was necessary to speak first on these points to anticipate any instances that might seem to contradict my theory. I will now return to my comparison.

29. Many factors make it easy to understand that so long as the phalanx maintains its proper formation and strength, nothing can resist it face to face or withstand its charge. For since a man in closed battle formation occupies a space of three feet and since the length of the sarissa [pike] is sixteen cubits [roughly 24 ft, 7.5 m] according to its original design, which has been reduced in practice to fourteen, and as of these fourteen cubits four must be deducted to allow for the distance between the two hands holding it and to balance the weight in front, it follows clearly that each hoplite will have ten cubits of sarissa projecting beyond his body, when he lowers it with both hands as he advances against the enemy. Hence, too, though the men of the second, third and fourth rank will have their sarissa projecting further beyond the front rank than the men of the fifth, yet even these last will have two cubits of their sarissas beyond the front rank, so long as the phalanx is properly formed and the men close up as regards both depth and breadth, as in the description in Homer [*Iliad* 13.131–3, omitted]. If my description is true and exact, it is clear that in front of each man of the first rank there will be five sarissas projecting to distances varying by a descending scale of two cubits.

30. From this description it is easy to imagine the appearance and strength of a charge by the whole phalanx as it advances sixteen deep. Of these sixteen ranks all above the fifth are unable to reach far enough with their sarissas to take part in the actual fighting. Therefore they do not level them man against man but hold them pointing upwards over the shoulders of the ranks in front of them, so as to shield the heads of the whole phalanx. For the sarissas are massed so closely that they repel missiles which have passed over the heads of the front ranks and might fall on those behind them. During an advance these rear ranks

press forward on those in front with the weight of their bodies and so give extra force to the charge while making it impossible for those at the front to turn round.

Such is the arrangement, general and detailed, of the phalanx. It remains now to compare with it the peculiarities and distinctive features of the arms and tactical formation of the Romans. A Roman soldier in full armour also requires a space of three feet. But their method of fighting involves individual motion for each man, because he defends his body with a shield which he moves about to any point from which a blow is coming and because he uses his sword for both cutting and thrusting. It is evident, therefore, that there should be a looser order and the men should be at an interval of at least three feet from each other, both on flank and rear, if they are to do what is necessary effectively. The result of this will be that each Roman soldier will face two of the front rank of a phalanx so that he has to encounter and fight against ten sarissas. It is not possible for one man to have time to cut through them once fighting is at close quarters nor is it easy to overpower them by force, seeing that the Roman front ranks are not supported by the rear ranks, either in respect of force or in the use of their swords. Therefore it may readily be understood that, as I said at the beginning, it is impossible to confront a charge of the phalanx so long as it retains its proper formation and strength.

31. What then is the reason for Roman victory in battle and what is it that undermines those who use the phalanx? It is because in war the times and places for action are unlimited whereas there is but one time and one type of ground that allows a phalanx to function properly. If then there were anything to compel the enemy to submit to the time and place that suited the phalanx when they were about to fight a decisive battle, it would be natural to expect that those who employed the phalanx would always carry off victory. But if the enemy finds it possible, and even easy, to avoid its attack, how would such a formation still be formidable? It is generally agreed that for its employment the phalanx needs terrain that is flat, bare and without such impediments as ditches, gullies, depressions, steep banks or beds of rivers, all of which are sufficient to hinder and break up such a formation. And everyone will also agree that it is almost impossible or at any rate exceedingly rare to find a stretch of land extending twenty stades [c. 2.5 miles] or more without any such obstacle. Let us suppose, however, that such a district has been found. If the enemy decline to come down into it but go round the country sacking the cities and land of the allies, what use will the phalanx be? For if it remains on ground suited to itself, it

will not only fail to aid its friends but it will be unable even to ensure its own safety. For the transport of supplies will easily be stopped by the enemy, seeing that they have undisputed possession of the open country. But if the phalanx leaves its own ground and attempts action elsewhere, it will be easy prey for the enemy. If, on the other hand, the enemy does descend into plain but, instead of committing the whole army to face the phalanx's single chance to charge, they withhold some of their forces from the conflict at the moment of engagement, it is easy to see what will happen from considering what the Romans are currently doing.

32. What I am now saying does not need to be established by argument but from what has already happened. For the Romans do not attempt to make their front equal to that of the phalanx and then charge directly against it with their whole force, but some of their divisions are kept in reserve while others join battle with the enemy at close quarters. Afterwards, whether the phalanx drives its opponents from their ground or is itself driven back, its peculiar formation is broken up. For whether it is following those who are retreating or flying from those who are advancing, it leaves the rest of its forces behind and when this happens the enemy's reserves can move into the space which the phalanx had previously been occupying and so no longer charge it head on but fall on its flank and rear. Since, then, it is easy to take precautions against the opportunities the phalanx requires and the advantages it enjoys but impossible to prevent the enemy from seizing the opportunity to act against it, how does it not follow that in practice the difference between these two systems is huge? Of course those generals who employ the phalanx must march over ground of every description, pitch camps, occupy points of advantage, besiege and be besieged and meet with unexpected appearances of the enemy. For all these are part and parcel of war and have an important and sometimes decisive effect on the final victory. In all these situations the Macedonian phalanx is difficult, and sometimes impossible, to handle, because the men cannot act either in squads or separately, whereas the Roman formation is flexible. Every Roman, once armed and on the field, is equally ready for every place and time and for any appearance of the enemy. He is equally well-prepared and needs to make no change, whether he is required to fight in the main body, or in a detachment, or in a single maniple or even by himself. Therefore, just as the effective use of the parts of the army is much superior, so the plans of the Romans are much more often attended by success than those of others. I thought it necessary to discuss this subject at some length, because at the very

moment of the Macedonian defeat many Greeks supposed what had happened was incredible and many will still be at a loss to explain the inferiority of the phalanx to the Roman system of arming their troops.

J (18.44.1–47.3) The freedom of the Greeks, 196 BC

44. At this time the ten commissioners arrived from Rome who were to handle the affairs of the Greeks, bringing with them the decree of the Senate on the peace with Philip. The main points of the decree were these: that all other Greeks, whether in Asia or Europe, were to be free and enjoy their own laws but that Philip should hand over to the Romans those at present under his authority and all towns in which he had a garrison before the Isthmian games and restore Euromos, Pedasa, Bargylia, Iasos, Abydos, Thasos, Marina and Perinthos to freedom and remove his garrisons from them; that Flamininus should write to Prusias about the liberation of Kios in accordance with the decree of the Senate; that Philip should hand over to the Romans within the same period all captives and deserters and likewise all decked ships, except five light ships and his sixteen-banked vessel and should pay a thousand talents, half at once and half by instalments spread over ten years.

45. When this decree was published in Greece, it created a feeling of confidence and joy among everyone with the sole exception of the Aitolians who were annoyed at not obtaining what they were hoping for and so complained about the decree saying that it was mere words with nothing practical in it. From the terms of the decree itself they constructed plausible arguments to unsettle those who were willing to listen. They said that there were two distinct propositions in the decree relating to the cities garrisoned by Philip, one ordering him to remove his garrisons and to hand over the cities to the Romans, the other to remove the garrisons and set the cities free. Those that were to be set free were clearly named and they were towns in Asia; it was plain therefore that those which were to be handed over to the Romans were those in Europe, namely Oreos, Eretria, Chalkis, Demetrias and Corinth. From this it was obvious to all that the Romans were receiving the fetters of Greece from Philip and that the Greeks were getting not freedom but a change of masters.

These arguments of the Aitolians were repeated *ad nauseam*. But, meanwhile, Flamininus left Elateia with the ten commissioners. After crossing to Antikyra, he sailed straight to Corinth and there sat in council with the commissioners and embarked on a comprehensive settlement. But as the slanders of the Aitolians gained currency and were believed by some, Flamininus was forced to enter upon many elaborate arguments at the commission meetings. He explained that if they wanted to acquire universal renown among the Greeks and to establish firmly in the minds of all that they had made the initial crossing of the sea not for the sake of their own advantage but for the freedom of the Greeks, then they must withdraw from every district and free all the cities which were now garrisoned by Philip. But this was just the point in dispute among the commissioners, since about all the other cities a decision had been reached in Rome and the ten commissioners had clear instructions from the Senate, but the power to decide about Chalkis, Corinth and Demetrias had been left to them because of Antiochos, so that, looking at the current situation, they might take what action they thought best about these cities. For it was clear that this king had for some time past been meditating interference in Europe. Nonetheless, as far as Corinth was concerned, Flamininus persuaded the commissioners to free it at once, but he retained the Acrocorinth, Demetrias and Chalkis.

46. When all this had been decided, the time for the celebration of the Isthmian games arrived. The expectation of what would happen there drew men of the highest rank from nearly every part of the world and many and varied were the stories circulating throughout the festival. Some said that it was impossible for the Romans to withdraw from some places and towns, while others asserted that they would withdraw from those they considered famous but would retain others that were less prominent yet equally serviceable. These people even took it upon themselves to name these places, rivalling each other in ingenuity. While people were still in this state of uncertainty and as the crowd gathered in the stadium to watch the games, the herald came forward and having proclaimed silence by the sound of a trumpet delivered this proclamation: 'The Senate of the Romans and Titus Quinctius [Flamininus] the proconsul, having conquered King Philip and the Macedonians in war, leave the following free, without a garrison, subject to no tribute and in full enjoyment of their ancestral laws, the Corinthians, Phokians, Lokrians, Euboians, Phthiotic Achaians, Magnesians, Thessalians and Perrhaibians.' The roar of the crowd was overwhelming from the very beginning, so that some did not hear the proclamation at all while others wanted to hear it again. The majority were unable to believe it and felt as if they had heard the words in a dream because of the unexpectedness of what had happened; everyone, each from a different impulse, shouted out for the herald and the trumpeter to come into the middle of the stadium and say it again.

They wanted, I suppose, not only to hear the speaker but also to see him because what he had to say was so unbelievable. So for a second time the herald came forward into the middle and silenced the clamour with his trumpeter. When he repeated exactly the same proclamation as before, so thunderous was the applause that it is difficult for those who hear of it today to imagine what happened. When at length the noise subsided, no one paid any attention whatever to the athletes but all were talking to each other or to themselves, and seemed like people bereft of their senses. Indeed, after the games were over, in the extravagance of their joy they came close to killing Flamininus with their effusive gratitude. Some wanted to look him in the face and call him their saviour, others were keen to touch his hand, and the majority threw garlands and fillets on him – between them they nearly crushed him to death. But although this expression of popular gratitude was thought to have been excessive, one may say with confidence that it fell short of the importance of the event itself. For it was an extraordinary thing that the Romans and their leader Flamininus should have deliberately incurred unlimited expense and danger for the sole purpose of freeing the Greeks. It was also a great thing that their power was equal to their intention. But the greatest thing of all was that there was no chance obstacle to their endeavour but every single thing came to a successful conclusion at the same time: so that all Greeks, Asiatic and European alike, by a single proclamation became free, without a garrison, subject to no tribute and enjoying their own laws.

47. When the festival was over, the first persons with whom the commissioners dealt were the ambassadors from Antiochos. They instructed them that the king must abstain from attacking those cities in Asia which were autonomous and go to war with none of them and must withdraw from those that had been subject to Ptolemy or Philip. In addition to this they forbade him to cross to Europe with an army. For none of the Greeks was any longer to be attacked by anyone or subject to anyone. Finally they said that some of their own number would go to visit Antiochos.

K (24.8–9) Kallikrates addresses the Senate, 180/79 BC
8. When Hyperbatos, the general of the Achaians, brought before the assembly the question of the letter from the Romans about the recall of the Spartan exiles, Lykortas [father of Polybios] recommended that no change should be made, on the grounds that the Romans were only acting as they were bound to do in listening, in so far as the petition was reasonable, to men who on the face of it were deprived of their rights.

But whenever it was explained to them that some elements of a petition were impossible and others would bring great disgrace and damage upon their friends, it was not the Roman practice to insist on them peremptorily or force their adoption. 'So in this case also,' he said, 'if it is shown that we Achaians by obeying their letter would be breaking our oaths, our laws and the inscribed agreements that hold our league together, the Romans will withdraw their orders and admit that we are right to hesitate and to ask to be excused from carrying out their instructions.' Such was the speech of Lykortas. But Hyperbatos and Kallikrates advised submission to the letter and that they should hold its authority superior to law, inscribed agreements or anything else. Such being the division of opinion, the Achaians voted to send ambassadors to the Senate to put before it the points contained in the speech of Lykortas. Straightaway they appointed Kallikrates of Leontion, Lydiades of Megalopolis and Aratos of Sikyon as ambassadors and sent them with instructions along the lines I have stated. But on their arrival in Rome, Kallikrates, going before the Senate, was so far from addressing it in accordance with his instructions that on the contrary he boldly denounced his political opponents and even undertook to lecture the Senate itself.

9. For he said that the Romans themselves were responsible for the way that the Greeks did not obey them and instead ignored their letters and orders. For in all democratic states at the time there were two parties, one recommending obedience to the written requests of the Romans and holding that neither law nor inscribed agreement nor anything else was superior to the will of the Romans, the other always quoting the laws, oaths and inscriptions and entreating the people not to break these lightly. This latter policy, he said, was by far the more popular in Achaia and the most influential with the multitude. As a result those who favoured Rome were discredited and denounced among the masses while it was the opposite for their opponents. If then some sign were to be given by the Senate, the political leaders would quickly change to the side of the Romans and the multitude would follow them out of fear. But if this were neglected by the Senate, the tendency towards the latter of the two parties would be universal, as the most creditable and honourable in the eyes of the populace. 'Even now,' he went on, 'certain people without any other claim to distinction have attained the highest offices in their own cities, simply because they are thought to speak against your instructions for the sake of maintaining the validity of their laws and decrees. If then you consider it a matter of indifference whether your letters are obeyed by

the Greeks, by all means go on as you have been. But if you wish your orders to be carried out and your letters to be despised by no one, you must give serious attention to this subject . . .'

L (31.10) Rome and the two Ptolemies, 163/2 BC

After the two Ptolemies had made their partition of the kingdom, the younger brother arrived in Rome wanting to have the division made between himself and his brother cancelled, on the ground that he had not agreed to the arrangement voluntarily but under compulsion and yielding to force of circumstances. He therefore begged the Senate to assign Cyprus to his portion; for even if that were done, his share would still be far inferior to that of his brother. Canuleius and Quintus supported Menyllos, the ambassador of the elder Ptolemy, by protesting that the younger Ptolemy owed his possession of Cyrene and his very life to them, so deep was the anger and hatred of the common people to him. Accordingly he had been only too glad to receive the government of Cyrene which he had not hoped for or expected and had exchanged oaths with his brother with the customary sacrifices. When Ptolemy denied all this, the Senate, seeing that the division was clearly an unsatisfactory one and at the same time wishing to make a division of the kingdom that would be politically effective since they were responsible for it, they granted the request of the younger Ptolemy with a view to their own interest. Measures of this type are now very common among the Romans, in which by taking advantage of the mistakes of others they effectively increase and strengthen their own rule, at the same time doing a favour and appearing to confer a benefit on those who are at fault. On this principle they acted now. They saw how great the power of the Egyptian kingdom was and, fearing lest if it ever acquired a competent leader he would grow too proud, they appointed Titus Torquatus and Gnaeus Merula to establish Ptolemy in Cyprus and so carry out their own policy while satisfying his.

M (31.21) Rome, Massinissa and Carthage, c. 161 BC

In Africa Massinissa saw how numerous the cities built along the lesser Syrtis were and how fertile the region was that they call Emporia and, casting an envious eye on the revenues which those places produced, he tried to seize it from the Carthaginians. He quickly gained possession of the open country because the Carthaginians were always averse to service in the field and were at that time seriously weakened by the long peace. But he was unable to gain possession of the cities because the Carthaginians guarded them carefully. Both parties referred their case to the Senate and embassies came many times to Rome from both sides, but it always happened that the Carthaginians got the worst of it in the judgement of the Romans, not for reasons of justice but because the judges were convinced that such a decision was in their interests.

N (36.9) Greek views on the Roman treatment of Carthage in the Third Punic War

There was a great deal of talk of all sorts in Greece, first as to the Carthaginians when the Romans conquered them and subsequently as to the question of the pseudo-Philip [in Macedon]. The opinions expressed in respect of the Carthaginians were widely divided and indicated entirely opposite views.

Some commended the Romans for adopting a policy that was wise and statesmanlike as regards their empire. By destroying this constant menace, a city that had many times disputed with them for supremacy and could do so again if the opportunity arose, they ensured dominion for their own country. This, it was said, was the action of sensible and far-sighted men.

Others contradicted this, saying that rather than adhering to the principles by which they acquired their supremacy they were little by little declining into that lust for power that characterised the Athenians and the Spartans and although they started later than them, the indications were that they were heading towards the same end. For in earlier times they had made war on everyone up to that point when they were victorious and their opponents had conceded that they had to obey the Romans and do as they were ordered. But nowadays they had given a foretaste of their policy by their conduct towards Perseus, when they destroyed the kingdom of Macedon root and branch, and had given the finishing stroke to that policy by the course adopted with regard to Carthage. For, although the Carthaginians had committed no irreversible offence, the Romans took steps against them that were irreversible and severe in spite of their accepting all conditions and submitting to all commands.

Others again said that the Romans were, generally speaking, a civilised people and they had a distinctive characteristic on which they prided themselves, that they conducted their wars in a straightforward and noble manner, not employing night attacks or ambushes and scorning every advantage to be gained by stratagem and deceit, and regarding battles that are fought openly and face to face as alone befitting their character. But in the present instance their whole campaign against the Carthaginians had been conducted by means of stratagem and deceit. Little by little, by holding out inducements here and prac-tising concealment there, they had deprived them of any hopes of assistance from their allies. This was a line of conduct more appropri-ate by rights to the intrigues of a monarchy than to a constitutional state like Rome and on any honest reckoning was virtually the same as impiety and treachery.

Again, there were some who took the opposite line to these. They said that if before the Carthaginians made their surrender the Romans had behaved in this way, holding out inducements here and making half-revelations there, they would be justly liable to such charges. If, on the other hand, the Carthaginians had already surrendered, so that the Romans could take whatever measures they chose concerning them, then the situation would be different. For if the Romans with this authority to act as it seemed good to them gave the orders and imposed the terms that they had decided upon, then what took place did not resemble an act of impiety and indeed fell far short of resembling an act of treachery. And some denied it was even an injustice. For these were the three categories into which every crime by nature must fall, but the conduct of the Romans fell into none of them. For impiety was an offence against the gods, one's parents or the dead, treachery was something done in violation of oaths or an inscribed agreement, and injustice was something done in violation of law and custom. But the Romans could not be charged on any of these counts. For they had not offended the gods, their parents or the dead, nor had they broken oaths or treaties, but on the contrary they had charged the Carthaginians with breaking them. Nor again had they violated laws, or customs or their own good faith; for having received a voluntary surrender, with the full power of doing what they pleased in the event of the submitting party not obeying their injunctions, they had, when that eventuality had arisen, applied force to it.

Pompeius Trogus

Pompeius Trogus was a historian from Gaul writing in Latin around the time of Augustus; his universal history survives in an abridgement by Justin. See further Chapter 4, section 1.

A (Justin 38.6.7–8) Extract from speech of Mithridates
This was the principle of hatred for all kings that they [the Romans] had established, doubtless because they themselves had such kings whose names were even enough to make them blush, either shepherds

from the aborigines, or soothsayers from the Sabines, or exiles from the Corinthians or captured and home-bred slaves from Etruria or what was the most honourable name among these, Superbi [the Proud]. And as they themselves say, their founders were suckled on the teats of a wolf, consequently their whole race has the mentality of wolves, with an insatiable lust for blood and eager and hungry for power and wealth.

B *(Justin 43.4.1–2) The Gauls and Massilia*
From these [the Greeks of Massilia], therefore, the Gauls learned to live a more civilised life, putting aside or moderating their barbarous ways; they learned to cultivate their lands and to enclose their cities with walls. They became accustomed to living according to the law rather than arms, to prune the vine and to plant the olive; and so splendid was its impact on men and things that it seemed not as if Greece had come to Gaul but as if Gaul had been transported to Greece.

C *(Justin 43.5.11) Trogus' family*
At the end of the book Trogus relates as follows: his ancestors were of Vocontian origin; his grandfather Pompeius Trogus received citizenship from Gnaeus Pompeius [Pompey] in the war against Sertorius; his uncle led a squad of cavalry under the command of the same Pompeius in the war with Mithridates; his father served under Gaius Caesar and was in charge of correspondence and embassies and also of his official seal.

D *(Justin 44.5.6–8) Spain from Hannibal to Augustus*
Hannibal, the son of Hamilcar, succeeded him, a general greater than either of them [Hasdrubal and Hamilcar]; for he surpassed the achievements of both and subdued the whole of Spain. Then he made war on the Romans and for sixteen years he tormented Italy with various disasters. Meanwhile, the Romans, once they had sent the Scipios to Spain, first drove the Carthaginians out of the region and afterwards waged bitter wars against the Spaniards themselves. Nor could the Spaniards submit to the yoke of a conquered province until Caesar Augustus after conquering the world directed his victorious arms against them; that barbarous and wild people, once they were brought to a more civilised life under the rule of law, he reduced into the form of a province.

Res Gestae

The *Res Gestae Divi Augusti* (Achievements of the Deified Augustus) was a record of the career of the Emperor Augustus in his own words that was inscribed outside his mausoleum in Rome. It survives, however, not from Rome but as a vast Latin inscription on the walls of the temple of Roma and Augustus in the Galatian city of Ankyra (Ankara), accompanied by a Greek translation.

A *(Heading)*

Below is a copy of the achievements of the divine Augustus, by which he brought the whole earth under the rule of the Roman people, and of his expenditure on behalf of the state and Roman people, inscribed on two bronze pillars that have been set up in Rome.

B *(RG 13)*

Our ancestors wanted the shrine of Janus Quirinus to be closed whenever throughout the whole empire of the Roman people by land and sea victories had brought peace. Although before I was born it is recorded as having been closed twice in total since the foundation of the city, the Senate decreed it to be closed three times while I was leader.

C *(RG 26–32)*

26. I extended the boundaries of all the provinces of the Roman people on which bordered peoples that did not obey our rule (*imperium*). I reduced to peace the Gallic and Spanish provinces and likewise Germany, an area bounded by the Ocean from Gades [Cadiz] to the mouth of the river Elbe. I imposed peace on the Alps from that region which is closest to the Adriatic as far as the Tyrrhenian Sea but did not wage an unjust war against any tribe. My fleet sailed from the mouth of the Rhine east to the region of the rising sun as far as the territory of the Cimbri, where, before that time, no Roman had ever been either by land or by sea; and the Cimbri and Charydes and Semnones and other German peoples of the same region sent embassies to ask for my friendship and that of the Roman people. On my orders and under my auspices two armies were led, at around the same time, into Ethiopia and that part of Arabia that is called 'Eudaemon', and sizeable forces of the enemy from both peoples were killed in battle and many towns were captured. The advance into Ethiopia reached as far as the town of Nabata, to which Meroe is closest. The army went into Arabia as far as the territory of the Sabaei to the town of Mariba.

27. I added Egypt to the empire of the Roman people. In the case of Greater Armenia, although I could have made it into a province after the assassination of its king Artaxes, I preferred, following the example of our ancestors, to hand that kingdom over to Tigranes [III], the son

of King Artavasdes and grandson of King Tigranes [II], acting through Tiberius Nero who was then my stepson. And afterwards when the same nation revolted and rebelled and was subdued by my son Gaius, I handed it over to King Ariobarzanes, the son of Artabazus, king of the Medes for him to rule, and after his death to his son Artavasdes. When he was killed, I sent into that kingdom Tigranes [V] who was descended from the royal family of the Armenians. I recovered all the provinces that extend eastwards beyond the Adriatic Sea and also Cyrene, all these being at that time mostly in the possession of kings, and previously Sicily and Sardina which had been occupied in the slave war.

28. I founded colonies of soldiers in Africa, Sicily, Macedonia, both Spanish provinces, Achaia, Asia, Syria, Gallia Narbonensis and Pisidia. Furthermore Italy has twenty-eight colonies founded under my authority, which during my lifetime have been very busy and well-populated.

29. After defeating the enemy I recovered from Spain, Gaul and the Dalmatians a number of military standards that had been lost by other generals. I compelled the Parthians to restore to me the spoils and standards of three Roman armies and to seek the friendship of the Roman people as suppliants. These standards I deposited in the inner sanctuary that is in the temple of Mars Ultor [the Avenger].

30. Before I became leader no Roman army had ever approached the tribes of the Pannonians. After they had been conquered through the agency of Tiberius Nero who was at that time my stepson and my legate, I made them subject to the rule of the Roman people and I advanced the frontier of Illyricum right up to the bank of the river Danube. An army of Dacians that crossed to this side of that river was, under my auspices, defeated and destroyed and afterwards my army, led across the Danube, compelled the tribes of the Dacians to submit to the commands of the Roman people.

31. Royal embassies were often sent to me from India, which had never before been seen in the presence of any general of the Romans. Ambassadors came seeking our friendship from the Bastarnae and the Scythians and the kings of the Sarmatians who occupy both sides of the river Tanais [Don] and the king of the Albani and of the Hiberi and of the Medes.

32. To me as suppliants fled the following kings: of the Parthians, Tiridates and later Phraates, son of King Phraates; of the Medes, Artavasdes; of the Adiabeni, Artaxares; of the Britons, Dumnobellaunus and Tincomarus; of the Sugambri, Maelo; of the Suebic Marcomanni

. . . [text missing]. To me in Italy Phraates, son of Orodes, king of the Parthians, sent all his sons and grandsons, although not defeated in war but seeking our friendship by pledging his own children. And, during my leadership, the good faith of the Roman people has been experienced by many other nations, who previously had had no exchange of embassies or friendship with the Roman people.

Sallust

Gaius Sallustius Crispus (c. 86–35 BC) was a Roman politician turned historian. His two short monographs, *The Catilinarian Conspiracy* and *The Jugurthine War*, survive complete but his *Histories* are known only from fragments.

A *(Catilinarian Conspiracy 7.3–7) The pursuit of glory*

But, once freedom was won, it is incredible how much the state grew in a short time: so great was the desire for glory. Now, for the first time, the young men, as soon as they were able to endure warfare, learned through hard work in the camps the skills of a soldier and took their pleasure more in fine arms and cavalry horses than in prostitutes and parties. As a result, for such men no labour was unaccustomed, no place was difficult or inaccessible, no armed enemy was terrifying; courage overcame everything. But the greatest battle for glory was with each other; each man made haste to strike the enemy, to climb the wall and to be seen while doing such a deed. This they considered to be riches, this a good reputation and great nobility. They were greedy for praise but generous with money; they wanted boundless glory and honourable riches. If it did not take us too far from our subject, I could mention the places in which the Roman people with a small force routed vast armies of their enemies and the cities which though forti- fied by nature they nonetheless captured in battle.

Schoolbook

Extract from a bilingual children's textbook in Latin and Greek, late third or fourth century AD (Dionisotti 1982: 104–5).

A *(lines 74–5 from the section on events in the forum)*

The governor's seat is set up. The judge mounts the tribunal and through the voice of the herald orders people to stand. The defendant, a bandit, stands. He is interrogated in accordance with his deserts. He is tortured, the torturer thrashes him, his chest becomes constricted, he is hung up, he is racked, he is beaten with clubs, he is flogged, he goes through the whole sequence of tortures and still he denies that he is guilty. He is to be punished; the punishment is death, he is led to the sword.

Strabo

Strabo of Amaseia in the Pontus (roughly 60s BC to 20s AD) wrote a *Geography*, a vast and ambitious account in seventeen books that covered the Mediterranean and beyond. Written in Greek, it was in many ways the geography of the Roman empire.

A (2.5.8) *The unattractiveness of Britain*
For governmental purposes there would be no advantage in being well-acquainted with such lands [i.e. Britain and the regions beyond it] and their inhabitants, especially if the islands they inhabit are such that their isolation prevents them from harming or benefiting us in any way. In spite of having the capacity to occupy Britain, the Romans dismissed the idea, because they realised that there was nothing at all to fear from the Britons (for they are not strong enough to cross the sea and attack us) and that there was no great benefit in taking possession of the place. For it seems that the revenue from customs duties is at present greater than could be raised through tribute if deductions for the cost of maintaining an army to guard the island and collect the tribute are taken into account. There would be even less advantage to be gained in the case of the other islands around this one.

B (3.2.15) *Roman ways come to Spain*
Along with the prosperity of their country, a civilised and urban way of life has come to the Turdetani and also to the Celts on account of their proximity, as Polybios has said, or on account of kinship, but it is less pronounced in the case of the Celts as they generally live in villages. The Turdetani, however, and especially those that live along the Baetis [Guadalquivir river], have completely changed over to the Roman way of living and no longer even remember their own language. The majority have become Latins and they have received Romans as colonists so that they are not far off all being Roman. The cities that are at present jointly settled, Pax Augusta among the Celts, Augusta Emerita among the Turduli, Caesar Augusta among the Celtiberians and some other settlements, make clear the change in civic life I have spoken of. All the

Iberians of this type are called 'togati' [toga-wearers]. Among these are the Celtiberians who were once considered the most uncivilised of all.

Tacitus

Cornelius Tacitus (c. 56 – after 118 AD) was a Roman senator and historian. His *Annals*, much of which survive, treated the Julio-Claudian dynasty from Tiberius onwards; the *Histories* covered the years from AD 69 to AD 96 but only the account of the civil wars of 69–70 survives. His early works include the *Agricola*, a biography of his father-in-law, who was governor of Britain.

A (Annals 4.15, 37, 55–6, selections) Cult honours for the Emperor Tiberius

15. At that time everything was still in the hands of the Senate and as a result Lucius Capito, the procurator of Asia, when the province brought charges against him, had to answer the case there, with the emperor insisting that he had given Capito no authority except over slaves and property belonging to the emperor; that if he had usurped the powers of a praetor and used military forces, he had ignored his instructions; that they should listen to the allies. So the case was heard and the defendant sentenced. Thanks to this retribution and because of the punishment of Gaius Silanus the previous year, the cities of Asia voted a temple to Tiberius, his mother and the Senate. Permission was granted. . . .

37. Further Spain sent a delegation to the Senate with a request that they be allowed to follow the example of Asia and erect a temple to Tiberius and his mother. On this occasion, the emperor, who had generally been firm in rejecting honours, thinking that he should reply to the rumours that criticised him for yielding to vanity, began his speech like this:

'I realise, conscript fathers, that many demand consistency from me because I did not oppose the very same request when the cities of Asia approached me recently. Therefore I shall put before you a defence of my earlier silence and at the same time what I have decided for the future. The divine Augustus did not prohibit the establishment of a temple to himself and the city of Rome at Pergamon and I treat all his actions and sayings as law. I followed this precedent all the more readily since worship of the Senate was joined with my own cult. But while it may be excusable to allow this once, to be consecrated in the image of the divine throughout all the provinces would be presumptuous arrogance; and the honour paid to Augustus will vanish if it is vulgarised by indiscriminate flattery.' . . .

55. In order to divert criticism, Tiberius attended the Senate frequently and for several days listened to embassies from Asia arguing about which city should erect his temple. Eleven cities competed, all equally ambitious but with varied resources. With little to set them apart from each other they recollected their ancient origins and their loyalty to the Roman people during the wars with Perseus, Aristonikos and the other kings. But the Hypaepians, Trallians, Laodicaeans and Magnesians were all passed over as not important enough. Not even the Ilians, although they referred to Troy as the forebear of the city of Rome, counted, apart from past glories. There was some hesitation because the Halikarnassians claimed that in twelve hundred years not a single earthquake had shaken their homes and the foundation of the temple would stand on natural rock. It was believed that the Pergamenes had achieved enough in having the temple of Augustus there, the very fact they based their case on. The Ephesians and Milesians seemed to have devoted their cities to the worship of Diana and Apollo respectively. So the debate was between Sardis and Smyrna. Those from Sardis read out a decree of the Etruscans with whom they claimed kinship. For, they said, Tyrrhenos and Lydos, the sons of king Atys, had divided their people because there were so many of them. Lydos had stayed in the land of his fathers, while Tyrrhenos was assigned the task of establishing new settlements, and these peoples, the former in Asia, the latter in Italy, took their names from their leaders. The wealth of the Lydians increased further when people were sent to that part of Greece that subsequently took its name from Pelops. At the same time they reminded their listeners of letters from generals, treaties struck with us at the time of the war with the Macedonians, the fullness of their rivers, their temperate climate and the rich surrounding land.

56. Those from Smyrna recalled their distant past, whether founded by Tantulus son of Jupiter or Theseus, also of divine birth, or one of the Amazons. Then they moved on to that which they mainly relied upon, their services to the Roman people, sending naval forces not only to help in foreign wars but also those endured in Italy. They added that they were the first to establish a temple of the city of Rome, in the consulship of Marcus Porcius Cato [195 BC], when the power of the Roman people was certainly great but not yet at its peak, since Carthage still stood and the kings of Asia were still powerful. At the same time they introduced Lucius Sulla as a witness, that when his army had been in a very serious situation on account of the harshness

of the winter and a lack of clothing and when this was announced at an assembly in Smyrna, everyone who was present took the clothes off their bodies and sent them to our legions. So the senators, when asked their opinion, preferred Smyrna and Vibius Marsus proposed that Marcus Lepidus, to whom that province [Asia] had been assigned, be given a special officer to look after the temple.

B (Annals 14.31–7) The revolt of Boudicca, AD *60–61*

31. Prasutagus, king of the Iceni, famous for his long prosperity, had made the emperor his heir together with his two daughters, believing that by such an act of submission he would protect his kingdom and his house from harm. But the opposite happened, so much so that his kingdom and house were devastated as if captured in war, the one by centurions, the other by slaves. It began with the flogging of his wife Boudicca and the rape of his daughters. All the leading men of the Iceni were deprived of their ancestral estates, as if Rome had been given the whole country, and the king's relatives were treated as slaves. At this outrage and fearing worse, since they had been reduced to the condition of a province, they took up arms and incited rebellion among the Trinovantes and others who, not yet broken by slavery and secretly plotting, had pledged to reclaim their freedom. Their bitterest hatred was directed against the veterans. Recently settled at the colony of Camulodunum [Colchester], the veterans were driving people from their homes and expelling them from the fields, 'captives' or 'slaves' as they called them. The lawlessness of the veterans was encouraged by the soldiers, since their way of life was similar and they hoped the same licence would one day be given to themselves. In addition to this the temple that had been built for the divine Claudius was viewed as if it were a citadel of everlasting despotism and those chosen as its priests were pouring away whole fortunes under the guise of religion. Nor did there appear to be any great difficulty in destroying the colony since it was surrounded by no fortifications. Too little forethought had been given to this by our commanders, more concerned as they were with aesthetics than usefulness.

32. Meanwhile, with no obvious cause, the statue of victory at Camulodunum fell over and turned around as though yielding to the enemy. Women, agitated into a frenzy, cried out that destruction was at hand and that foreign cries had been heard in their senate house; the theatre had been filled with howling and in the estuary of the Thames a vision of the ruined colony had been seen; the ocean had a bloody appearance and the ebbing tide had left behind it the likenesses of

human bodies, generating hope among the Britons and fear among the veterans. But as Suetonius [the governor] was far away, they sought help from Catus Decianus, the procurator. He sent no more than two hundred men inadequately armed. In the town there was a small unit of soldiers. Relying on the protection of the temple and hindered by secret adherents of the rebellion who sabotaged their plans, they prepared neither a ditch nor a rampart; nor did they move the women and the old so as to enable the young to resist alone. With no precautions, as if in the middle of peace, they were surrounded by a multitude of barbarians. Everything else was plundered or burnt in the assault, but the temple, in which the soldiers had gathered, was besieged for two days and then taken by storm. The victorious Britons met Petilius Cerialis, the commander of the ninth legion, as he was coming to the rescue, routed his legion and massacred the infantry. Cerialis escaped with the cavalry to the camp and found protection in the fortifications. Frightened by this disaster and by the hatred of a province which his greed had pushed into war, the procurator Catus crossed over to Gaul.

33. Suetonius, however, with remarkable resolution marched right through the enemy to Londinium, a town not distinguished by the title of 'colony' but nonetheless having a great reputation as a centre for businessmen and merchandise. Once there he was uncertain whether or not he should choose it as his base for the war, but on considering the small size of his forces and the sharp lessons meted out to Cerialis for his rashness, he decided to save the whole at the cost of a single town. Nor did the weeping and tears of those begging for his assistance deter him from giving the signal for departure and accepting into the column all those who would go with him. Any who were detained by their unwarlike gender, the infirmity of age or attachment to the place were slaughtered by the enemy. The same disaster happened at Verulamium [St Albans], since the barbarians, revelling in plunder and disliking effort, avoided the fortresses and military garrisons and instead sought out those places that offered the greatest riches for the plunderers and the least resistance. It is agreed that around seventy thousand citizens and allies were killed in the places I have mentioned. There was neither the taking of prisoners nor the selling of them nor any other commerce of war; instead they made haste with slaughtering, gibbets, burning and crosses, like men who are destined to pay the penalty but in the meantime seize their revenge.

34. Suetonius now had the fourteenth legion along with a detachment of the twentieth and auxiliaries from the neighbourhood, around ten thousand men in arms, when he prepared to fight a battle without

further delay. He chose a position approached by a narrow defile and closed in at the rear by a wood, once he was satisfied that there was no enemy except in front and that the plain was open without risk of ambushes. The legionary troops were drawn up in close order, light-armed at their sides and the cavalry massed on the wings. But the forces of the Britons, spread out in bands of infantry and cavalry, were exult-ant, in unprecedented numbers, and in so fierce a spirit that they even brought their wives with them as witnesses of their victory and put them on wagons which they had placed on the far edge of the plain.

35. Boudicca, carrying her daughters in front of her in a chariot, went up to each tribe, testifying that it was certainly usual for Britons to fight under the leadership of a woman; on this occasion, she told them, she was here not as one of noble ancestry fighting to avenge her kingdom and her wealth but as a woman of the people taking revenge for freedom lost, a body beaten with lashes and the violated chastity of her daughters; the lusts of the Romans had gone so far that there were no bodies that they spared, not even the old or the virgins. But the gods were at hand with just vengeance; a legion that had risked battle had met its end; the rest were hiding in the camp or considering flight; they would not even cope with the noise and shouting of so many thousands, much less the charge and close combat. If they weighed up in themselves the strength of the armies and the reasons for war, they must be victorious in this battle or die. That, she said, was the objective of a woman; the men could live and be slaves.

36. Nor did Suetonius stay silent at such a critical moment. Although he trusted in his men's courage, he still delivered a mixture of encour-agement and entreaties, that they might disregard the noise and empty threats of the barbarians; there were more women than young men to be seen facing them; unwarlike and unarmed they would give way as soon as they recognised the sword and the courage of the conquerors, routed as they had been so many times. Even when there were many legions, he said, it was only a few men that actually decided the battle; it would add to their glory that a small force should win the fame of a whole army. They should keep close order and once the javelins were discharged they should continue the bloodshed and slaughter with their shields and swords, giving no thought to plunder. When they had won their victory, everything would be theirs. Such was the enthusi-asm which followed the general's words, and so promptly did the old soldiers, with their long experience of battle, get ready to hurl their javelins that when Suetonius gave the signal for battle, he was already confident of the outcome.

37. . . . . The [Roman] soldiers did not even refrain from killing the women, while the baggage animals, shot through with missiles, added to the pile of corpses. Great was the glory won on that day and equal to the victories of former times. Certainly some say that not far short of eighty thousand Britons fell, while around four hundred of our soldiers died and not many more were wounded. Boudicca died by poison.

C (Agricola *19–21*) *Agricola brings civilisation to the Britons*
19. Agricola made the exaction of corn and tribute more bearable by distributing the burden equally, after he had got rid of those schemes for profit that were more resented than the tribute itself. For they [the Britons] were compelled to go through the farce of waiting outside locked granaries and buying grain unnecessarily and so paying their debt with money. Difficult routes and distant places were assigned for them, so that states with a winter camp nearby had to deliver the corn to remote and roadless districts, until what should have been easy for all became profitable for a few.

20. By suppressing these abuses in his first year in office he gave peace a good name; for, due to the negligence and unbearable conduct of his predecessors, it had come to be feared as much as war. But when summer arrived, with the army assembled he was present everywhere on the march, praising good discipline and keeping the stragglers in order. He chose the sites for the camp himself and he reconnoitred the estuaries and woods himself. Meanwhile he would give the enemy no rest, ravaging their lands with sudden attacks and when he had caused sufficient alarm he would show them in contrast the attractions of peace by sparing them. As a result many states which had up to that day acted on the basis of equality gave hostages and put aside their resentment. They were surrounded with garrisons and forts with such planning and care that no new part of Britain had previously come over so undamaged.

21. The following winter was used very productively. For, since the people were scattered and uncivilised and therefore inclined to war, Agricola sought to accustom them to tranquillity and leisure by showing what they could take pleasure in. Privately he encouraged them and publicly he assisted them in the building of temples, public squares (*fora*) and houses, praising those who showed readiness and rebuking those who did nothing. Thus competition for honour took the place of compulsion. Furthermore he educated the sons of the chieftains in the liberal arts, preferring the natural talent of the Britons over the studied skill of the Gauls so that those who only recently

had rejected the Latin language now desired eloquence. Hence too our dress became respectable and the toga commonplace. Gradually they yielded to the attractions of vice, the colonnade, the bath and the elegant banquet. This in their ignorance they called civilisation when it was really part of their enslavement.

D (Agricola 29.4–33.1) *Speech of Calgacus before battle of Mons Graupius, AD 84*

29. More than thirty thousand armed men were now to be seen and still all the young men flowed in, along with those whose old age was vigorous and full of life, men famous in war and each wearing their own decorations. Among the many leaders one stood out for courage and lineage. This was Calgacus who is said to have addressed the thronging crowds as they clamoured for battle in the following way:

30. 'When I consider the causes of the war and the critical position we are in, I have great confidence that this day and your unity will be the beginning of freedom for the whole of Britain. For all of you have come together and are untouched by slavery; there are no lands beyond us and, with the Roman fleet threatening us, not even the sea is safe. And so war and fighting, sources of honour for the brave, are now the safest path even for cowards to follow. Former battles, which were fought with varying fortune against the Romans, left hope of help in our hands, since as the most noble men of all Britain, dwelling in its inner sanctuary and with no view of the shores of the enslaved, we have kept even our eyes uncontaminated by the contagion of despotism. Here at the very limits of the earth and of freedom we have lived, defended to this day by our remoteness and our obscurity. Now the furthest part of Britain is exposed and what is unknown is always assumed to be valuable. But there is no people beyond us, nothing except waves and rocks, and the Romans, yet more deadly, from whose arrogance escape is vainly sought by obedience and submission. Plunderers of the world, after exhausting the land by their indiscriminate devastation, they now scrutinise the sea. If the enemy is rich, they are greedy, if poor, they are desirous of power; neither the East nor the West satisfies them. Whether there is wealth or poverty they alone will lust after it with equal enthusiasm. To plunder, to massacre, to seize they falsely call "empire" and where they create desolation they call it "peace".

31. Nature has willed it that every man's children and relatives are those dearest to him. These are torn from us by levies to slave away elsewhere; our wives and sisters, even if they escape the lust of the enemy, are dishonoured in the name of friends and guests. Our goods

and fortunes are used up for their tribute, our harvest for their granaries, our very hands and bodies are worn out amid flogging and insults
in the work of clearing a way through forests and marshes. Creatures
born to slavery are sold but once and are then fed by their masters;
but Britain buys her own slavery every day and every day she feeds it.
And as in a household the most recent addition among the slaves is
always a figure of fun for his fellow slaves, so in this long-established
slavery of the lands of the world it is us, new and worthless, who are
sought out for destruction. For we have no fertile lands, no mines and
no harbours, for the purpose of working which we might be spared.
Courage, too, and martial spirit in subjects are not welcome to rulers;
and distance and seclusion while they promote security also promote
suspicion. So since there is no hope of mercy, take courage, whether it
is safety or glory that is most dear to you. With a woman as leader the
Brigantes burnt a colony, stormed a camp, and if their good fortune
had not made them careless, they might have been able to throw off
the yoke. We, untouched and untamed, shall be fighting to keep our
freedom, not to reclaim it. Let us show in the very first encounter what
men Caledonia has kept in reserve.

32. Do you imagine that the Romans' bravery in war matches their
licentiousness in peace? It is to our quarrels and discords that they
owe their fame; they turn the faults of their enemy into the glory of
their army. Composed of so many diverse peoples, the army is held
together only by its success and will accordingly dissolve when things
go wrong. Unless you think that Gauls, Germans and (I am ashamed
to say) numerous Britons would be bound by loyalty and affection –
they do, I acknowledge, lend their blood to foreign despotism, but they
were enemies for longer than they have been slaves. Fear and terror
are weak bonds of attachment; when you remove them, those who
have ceased to fear will start to hate. Every incentive to victory is on
our side. There are no wives to fire up the Romans, no parents ready
to upbraid them for flight; for most of them there is no fatherland or
a different one. Few in number, terrified by the unfamiliarity of it all,
the sky itself, the sea and the forests, everything unfamiliar as they look
around, hemmed in and bound so to speak, the gods have delivered
them to us. Don't be frightened by empty appearances, by the flash of
gold and silver, because it does not protect and it does not wound. In
the very battleline of the enemy we will find our own forces. Britons
will recognise their cause, Gauls will remember their earlier freedom,
the remaining Germans will desert them just as the Usipi did recently.
Behind them there is nothing to fear, forts without garrisons, colonies

of old men, and municipal towns sick and discordant, caught between disobedient subjects and unjust rulers. Here you have a leader, here an army, there taxation and mines and all the other penalties of the enslaved. Whether you endure these forever or take instant revenge, this field will decide. As you advance into battle think of your ancestors and of your descendants.'

33. They received this speech with enthusiasm, expressed in the usual barbarian manner, with singing, shouts and discordant cries.

Tertullian

Tertullian (c. 160–c. 240 AD) was a Christian writer from North Africa; he wrote in Latin.

A (Apologeticus 25.12–17) Roman empire not due to religious merits
But how ridiculous it is to attribute the exalted status of the Roman name to religious merits, since it was only after the establishment of empire, or call it still a kingdom, that its religion made progress. For, although its fascination with superstition was first conceived by Numa, religion among the Romans was not yet a matter of images or temples. Religion was frugal, the rites were basic and there were no Capitoline temples reaching to the heavens, but altars were improvised ones of turf and vessels were still of Samian earthenware and vapours arose from these and the god was nowhere to be seen. For at that time the skill of the Greeks and Etruscans in shaping images had not yet overwhelmed the city. The Romans, therefore, were not religious before they were great and so it was not because they were religious that they are great. Indeed how can they be great on account of their religion, when their greatness was a consequence of their lack of religion? For, if I am not mistaken, every kingdom and empire is acquired by war and expanded by victories. But wars and victories usually involve the capture and destruction of cities. This whole business is not without harm to the gods; the destruction of fortifications and temples go together; there is slaughter for citizens and priests alike, nor is there any difference between the plundering of sacred or profane treasures. Therefore, the sacrileges of the Romans are as numerous as their victories, their triumphs over gods as many as those over peoples and booty won is matched by the images of captive gods. So not only do these gods endure being worshipped by their enemies, they even grant empire without limit to those whose wrongs they should be punishing rather than whose worship they should be rewarding. But beings that feel nothing are harmed with

impunity as much as they are worshipped in vain. Certainly it is hardly credible that religious merit has advanced to greatness a people who, as we said, have either grown by inflicting damage on religion or by the very process of their growth have damaged it. Besides, those whose kingdoms have been absorbed into the totality of the Roman empire were not without religions when they lost their kingdoms.

Third Sibylline Oracle

This is an enigmatic, apocalyptic text, written in Greek and mixing Jewish and Greek traditions, probably blending material from the second century BC to the first century AD (Gruen 1998).

A (ll. 350–55)
However much Rome received from tribute-paying Asia, three times that much money shall Asia receive in return from Rome and so take revenge for its destructive arrogance. However many people from Asia were servants in Italian homes, twenty times that many Italians shall labour in poverty in Asia and pay back their debt ten thousand times.

Tomb of the Scipios

The following are some of the epitaphs from the Tomb of the Scipios which was located by the Via Appia (*ILS* 1–6; Flower 1996: 159–80, 326–8). The Latin term *virtus* which is translated here as 'virtue' has connotations of manliness and courage which are not present in the English term.

A (ILS 1) Epitaph for L. Cornelius Scipio Barbatus (consul 298 BC)
L. Cornelius Scipio, son of Gnaeus
Cornelius Lucius Scipio Barbatus, born from his father Gnaeus, a brave and wise man, whose appearance was equal to his virtue; he was consul, censor and aedile among you; he captured Taurasia and Cisauna in Samnium and subjugated the whole of Lucania and brought back hostages.

B (ILS 2 and 3) Epitaph for L. Cornelius Scipio, son of Barbatus (consul 259 BC)
Lucius Cornelius Scipio, son of Lucius, aedile, consul, censor
Romans generally agree that this one man Lucius Scipio was the best of good men. Son of Barbatus, he was consul, censor and aedile among

you. He captured Corsica and the city of Aleria; he dedicated a temple to the storms in return for help.

C (ILS 4) P. Cornelius – not identified for certain, possibly the son of P. Scipio Africanus
The first line was inscribed in smaller text and was added later
You who wore the distinguished cap of the priest of Jupiter
As a result of your death everything was short-lived, honour, reputation and virtue, glory and talent. Had you been allowed to enjoy these things in a long life, you would easily have outstripped the glory of your ancestors by your deeds. For which reason the earth gladly receives you into its lap, Publius Cornelius Scipio, born of Publius.

D (ILS 5) Epitaph for Lucius Cornelius Scipio (quaestor 167 BC)
Lucius Cornelius Scipio, son of Lucius, grandson of Publius, quaestor, military tribune, died at thirty years of age. His father defeated Antiochus.

E (ILS 6) Epitaph for Gnaeus Cornelius Scipio Hispanus (praetor 139 BC)
Gnaeus Cornelius Scipio Hispanus, son of Gnaeus, praetor, curule aedile, quaestor, twice military tribune, member of the board of ten for judging lawsuits, member of the board of ten for sacred matters.

By my conduct I increased the virtues of my family, I begot offspring and I sought to equal the achievements of my father. I preserved the good reputation of my ancestors so that they are glad that I was their descendant. My honours have brought nobility to my family.

Valerius Maximus

A Latin writer in the reign of Tiberius about whom little is known with certainty.

A (Memorable Deeds and Sayings, 2.8.1)
Certain generals wanted triumphs to be decreed to themselves for trivial battles. In order to oppose them, legislation was passed preventing anyone from triumphing if they had not killed five thousand of the enemy in a single engagement. For our ancestors judged that it was not the number of triumphs but the glory of them that would most promote the honour of our city. But in order that so splendid a law was not erased by greed for laurels, it was supported by the assistance

of a second law, which L. Marius and M. Cato carried as tribunes of the people; for it threatens a penalty for generals who dare to report in dispatches to the Senate a false number of enemy killed in battle or citizens lost and orders them, when they first enter the city, to swear before the urban quaestors that each of the figures that they reported to the Senate was true.

Funeral stele of Regina

Fig. 7 Funeral Stele of Regina from Arbeia (South Shields) in northern England, set up by her husband Barates from Palmyra in Syria, third century AD (photo: Glenys Davies, University of Edinburgh Cast Collection, http://www.shc.ed.ac.uk/ undergraduate/collection/Casts/cast68.htm#)

Trajan's Column

Fig. 8 Trajan's Column, Rome AD 113 (photo: author)

Fig. 9 Detail of battle scenes on Trajan's Column (photo: author)

Colosseum

Fig. 10 Colosseum, Rome (photo: author)

Coins

Fig. 11 Denarius, 76–75 BC, showing globe between sceptre and ship's rudder (courtesy of Classical Numismatics Group, www.cngcoins.com)

Fig. 12 Denarius, 70 BC (Crawford 1974: no. 403): on one side two busts of personified Honour and Virtue, on the other figure of Italia (left) clasping the hand of Roma, who has foot resting on globe; held jointly in their hands is a cornucopia, symbolic of fruitfulness and fertility (courtesy of Classical Numismatics Group, www. cngcoins.com)

Fig. 13 Augustan as, minted Lugdunum (Lyons), showing Altar of Lugdunum above text 'ROM ET AUG' (Roma and Augustus) (courtesy of Classical Numismatics Group, www.cngcoins.com)

Victory temples

Fig. 14 The remains of a group of republican victory temples at Largo Argentina, Rome (photo: author)

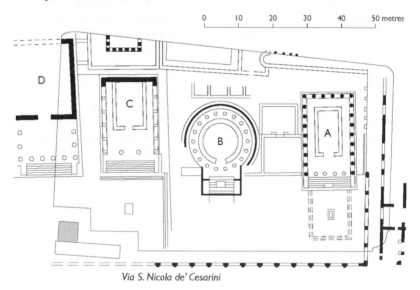

Fig. 15 Plan of the victory temples at Largo Argentina; as their identification is uncertain, they are usually known now only as Temples A, B, C and D (plan after Claridge 1998: 216).

Further Reading

Part 1 Debates

Chapter 1: Approaching Roman Imperialism

There are a number of excellent books covering different periods of Roman history which can be used to provide a broader context for the material discussed here. Early Rome up to 264 BC: Cornell 1995; Roman Republic: Crawford 1992, Bringmann 2007 and the essays in Rosenstein and Morstein-Marx 2006; Rome under the emperors: Millar 1981, Garnsey and Saller 1987, C. Wells 1992, Goodman 1997 and the essays in Potter 2006. The relevant volumes of the second edition of the *Cambridge Ancient History* are also valuable. Kelly 2006 is, as its title suggests, a very short introduction to the Roman empire but also a very good one. Roman imperialism should be studied with reference to a map; by far the best is the Barrington Atlas (Talbert 2000). For the Roman constitution, see Lintott 1999 and more briefly North 2006, the latter with a useful table of Roman magistrates and their powers on p. 264.

Brunt 1990 contains many of his key essays on the Roman empire and is essential reading. Richardson 2008 is a meticulous examination of the history of the two key terms, *imperium* and *provincia*. Champion 2004a is a useful reader on Roman imperialism with extracts from key contributions by modern scholars and a selection of source material in translation. Other collections of sources are Lewis and Reinhold 1990 (Republic and Empire), Dillon and Garland 2005 (Republic), Bagnall and Derow 2004 (Hellenistic), Sherk 1984 (Republic), Sherk 1988 (Empire), Levick 1985 (Empire). Further reading on ancient authors is to be found under each individual author in Part II. For ways of approaching source material, in particular numismatics, epigraphy and papyrology, see the essays in Crawford 1983 and Erskine 2009a. The fundamental study of Roman Republican coinage is Crawford 1974.

For various essays on the reception of Rome from Napoleon to Nazi Germany, see Edwards 1999. On Rome and the British empire, see especially Hingley 2000, though note the cautionary remarks of Bell 2007: 207–30. For an example of a late Victorian comparison between Roman and British empires see the study by the historian, jurist and politician, James Bryce (1901). Erskine 2009b covers uses of the ancient world in modern national identity and provides further bibliography.

There is an extensive modern literature on imperialism and empire; useful starting points are Doyle 1986 and the short introduction provided by Howe 2002. The history of the term 'imperialism' from its beginnings in the nineteenth century can be found in Koebner and Schmidt 1964. The study of Roman imperialism benefits from comparison with the other empires, both ancient and modern. Alcock et al. 2001 offers a wide-ranging set of comparative essays that extend up to the early modern period. On the Han dynasty see *The Cambridge History of China*, vol 1: *The Ch'in and Han Empires, 221 BC–AD 220* (1986). For the British empire, see Cain and Hopkins 2002 and Levine 2007. The United States and its worldwide influence has in recent times often be compared to Rome (cf. C. Murphy 2007, Münkler 2007); for a provocative examination of the American empire, Ferguson 2004, a book that significantly put the Colosseum on its cover (with a useful typology of empires on p. 11).

Chapter 2: From City to Empire

General accounts of Roman expansion can be found in the *Cambridge Ancient History*, 2nd edn, in particular vols 7.2 (The Rise of Rome to 220 BC) and 8 (Rome and Mediterranean to 133 BC); vol. 9 (The Last Age of the Roman Republic 146–43 BC) does treat the wars of the late second and first centuries BC but the emphasis tends to be on the collapse of the Republic. Errington 1971 provides one of the few sustained accounts of Rome's expansion but is now rather dated. Harris 1979: 175–254 reviews the origins of Roman wars from 320 BC to the Jugurthine War, arguing that the role of defensive thinking in such wars has been greatly exaggerated.

Cornell 1995 offers a full account of early Rome with Chapters 12 and 14 covering the conquest of Italy; the same author's chapters in *CAH*[2] 7.2 cover similar ground in a different form. For the conquest of Italy see also Oakley 1993 and David 1996; for relations with specific regions and peoples, Harris 1971a (Etruria and Umbria), Salmon 1967 (Samnites), Lomas 1993 (Greeks in South Italy), Bradley 2000

(Umbria), Dench 1995 (Central Apennines), Williams 2001 (Gauls in North Italy). Lomas 1996 has a good selection of relevant source material. For politics in Rome during the Republic, see Briscoe 1969 (on the East), Scullard 1973 (mid Republic), Gruen 1974 (on late Republic), Eckstein 1987 (mid Republic).

On Carthage, Lancel 1995, Scullard 1989a: 486–517, and for those who read German the writings of Huss 1985 and 1990. There are various narratives of the Punic Wars themselves; the *CAH²* version is to be found in Scullard 1989b and Briscoe 1989; Lazenby has written very clear accounts of each war (First in 1996; Second in 1978); Goldsworthy 2000 offers an accessible treatment of all three wars together. Hoyos 1998 covers the origins of the first two wars, while Hoyos 2003 deals with the Barcid dynasty; for a focus on Hannibal alone, see Lancel 1998; for the battle of Cannae, Daly 2002; Cornell et al 1996 reviews various aspects of the Second Punic War.

The best introduction to the early stages of Rome's conquest of the Greek world is Derow 2003 together with Derow 1989; for the later stages, McGing 2003 and Eilers 2003, who both draw attention to the Greek perspective. Holleaux's influential account first appeared in French in 1921, but his chapters in the first edition of the *Cambridge Ancient History* (vols. VII and VIII) reprise much of the material in English. Gruen 1984 has been the starting-point for much subsequent research, whether following on from it or in reaction to it. Eckstein 2008 tackles the period 230–170 BC, applying the Realist interpretation championed in Eckstein 2006. For the development of Roman power in the East in the late second and first centuries BC, see Sherwin-White 1993 and Kallet-Marx 1995 and under Augustus Bowersock 1965. McGing 1986 is an important study of Mithridates.

Rome's conquest of Spain up to 82 BC is well treated in Richardson 1986. There is no comprehensive account of the imperialism of the late Republic despite a significant expansion of Roman power over the course of the first century BC (though Badian 1968 is illuminating). Wars fought tend to be subsumed in the lives of commanders or histories of provinces, thus Caesar in Gaul: Goldsworthy 2006, Meier 1995; the essays in Griffin 2009 especially Rosenstein on Caesar as an imperialist; with Drinkwater 1983 on the broader provincial context. For Augustus, note C.Wells 1972 on the German wars; for Britain, Mattingly 2006; for Trajan's war in Parthia and Dacia, see Bennett 1997. Goodman 1997 provides useful coverage of the expansion and consolidation of Roman rule in the Principate.

Chapter 3: Explanations

It is Roman imperialism in the mid-Republic that has provoked the
most discussion (i.e. third to second centuries BC). Linderski 1984
reviews the work of Mommsen, Holleaux, Frank and de Sanctis in their
intellectual context. Harris 1979, replacing a defensive Rome with an
aggressive one, generated considerable debate; note in particular the
review articles of Sherwin-White 1980 and North 1981, Rich 1993 and
the essays in Harris 1984. Many of the issues are summed up concisely
in Beard and Crawford 1985: 72–84. Raaflaub 1996 seeks to explain
the origins of the Roman imperialism. Eckstein 2006 adds a new
dimension by introducing Realist political theory to interpret Roman
expansion. Very influential also has been Badian 1958 which argued
that Rome conceived of its relations with other states on the model of
the patron–client relationship that was such a feature of its domestic
sphere; Badian 1968 focuses on the late Republic. Note also the essay of
Veyne 1975 (in French).

Expansion may have become more restrained under the Empire (cf.
Cornell 1993), but some of the same issues inform debate; Luttwak
1976's grand strategy is a natural extension of earlier defensive arguments while Isaac 1992 presents a less centralised and more aggressive
Rome. A valuable contribution to our understanding of the Roman
conception of empire in the early centuries AD is Mattern 1999.

For warfare and the Roman army, see Sabin et al. 2007. The best
introduction to the Roman army is still Keppie 1984; fuller coverage
of most aspects can be found in the essays in the Erdkamp 2007, each
with further bibliography, and for source material on the army of the
Empire, Campbell 1994. Literature on the triumph is extensive. For
the early triumph Versnel 1970 and Bonfante Warren 1970; for the
developed triumph, Künzl 1988 (in German) and Beard 2007; specific studies include Favro 1994 (interaction with urban landscape),
Brilliant 1999, Holliday 2002 and Östenberg 2009, all treating the
triumph as spectacle in various ways. Rosenstein 1990 considers the
reverse, the implications of defeat for a Roman commander.

Economic motives for Roman imperialism have often been ruled
out; here Frank 1914's forceful rejection of commercial motives has
been influential and this line has been followed by many since, cf.
Badian 1968: 16–28, Gruen 1984: 288–315; the opposing case is made
by Harris 1971b and Crawford 1977. Certainly Romans did prosper
(see Shatzman 1975 for the wealth of senators in the Republic) and they
were perceived as greedy (cf. Erskine 1996). For the spread of Roman
businessmen in the wake of empire, Paterson 1998, Purcell 2005.

Chapter 4: The Subject

There is a considerable literature on the Greek reaction to Rome, both political and cultural. Forte 1972 brings together much material but is rather short on analysis. Gruen 1984: 316–56, Ferrary 1988: 223–494 (in French) and Erskine 1990: 181–204 examine the Greek, especially intellectual, views of Roman expansion. Still valuable is Fuchs 1938 (in German) which focuses on intellectual opposition to Rome. Greek attitudes to Rome form but one aspect of Momigliano 1975, a short yet fundamental treatment of Greek attitudes to others. Bowie 1970 is a pioneering study of the Second Sophistic; for more recent treatments, see Swain 1996 and Whitmarsh 2001; for the sophists themselves, Bowersock 1969. Woolf 1994 is an important study of the problems of Greek identity in the Roman empire, cf. also the essays in Goldhill 2001 and Konstan and Said 2006; for the specific role of athletics in Greek cultural identity, König 2005 and Newby 2005. For the Greek ideas of Rome's Trojan past, see Erskine 2001. Eilers 2002 examines the relationships between Roman aristocrats and Greek cities. Alcock 1993's use of survey archaeology offered a new way of approaching the impact of Rome on mainland Greece.

For individual Greek authors and their relationship with Rome, note in particular Polybios (Walbank 1972, Derow 1979, Eckstein 1995, Erskine 2000, Champion 2004b, the last two focusing on the Romans as barbarians), Diodoros (Sacks 1990), Dionysios of Halikarnassos (Gabba 1991), Strabo (Clarke 1999), Pausanias (Arafat 1996, Hutton 2005), Plutarch (Jones 1971, Duff 1999), Appian (Gowing 1992), Aelius Aristides (Oliver 1953), Dio Cassius (Millar 1964). Illuminating both Polybios and Roman expansion is Walbank's monumental commentary (1957-79).

The best approach to Jews and Judaea in the Roman empire is through the work of Goodman (esp. 1987 and 2007), always thought-provoking and accessible. Jewish attitudes to the Roman empire are surveyed briefly in de Lange 1978 and at much greater length in Hadas-Lebel 2006. Gruen 2002 and Barclay 1999 examine the Jewish diaspora throughout the Mediterranean. On 1 *Maccabees*, see Bartlett 1998, and for Josephus, note Bilde 1988, Rajak 2002 and the stimulating essays in Edmondson et al. 2005.

Some varied provincial perspectives on Rome are brought together in Yarrow 2006 which treats 1 *Maccabees*, Pompeius Trogus, Poseidonios, Diodoros, Nicolaus of Damascus and Memnon of Herakleia. On Trogus, see also Alonso-Núñez 1987. P.Wells 1999 is an attempt to recover the voice of the indigenous population of the West as they encountered Rome despite their lack of a literary record.

For other regions in the empire: Britain (Millett 1990, Mattingly 2006) Gaul (Drinkwater 1983, Woolf 1998), Spain (the well-illustrated Keay 1988, Curchin 1991 and 2004, Richardson 1996, Fear 1996); North Africa (Raven 1993, Whittaker 1996, Mattingly and Hitchner 1995, Bullo 2002 in Italian), Near East (Millar 1993), Anatolia (Mitchell 1993), Danube and Balkan provinces (Wilkes 1996), Bithynia and Pontus (Madsen 2009).

The contentious issue of romanisation and the processes of culture-change has been addressed in a good number of publications over the last twenty years or so, especially by archaeologists working on Britain, note in particular Millett 1990, the essays in Blagg and Millett 1990, Mattingly 1997, Woolf 1998: 1–23, MacMullen 2000 (on the Augustan empire), Fentress 2000, Keay and Terrenato 2001, Mattingly 2002 (proposing abandonment of concept), Merryweather and Prag 2003, Hingley 2005 (on globalisation), Wallace-Hadrill 2008; on creolisation, Webster 2001. The postcolonial perspective implicit in much recent work is explicit in Webster and Cooper 1996, a collection of papers on the theme. On the history of the concept of romanisation, see Hingley 2000 and Freeman 2007. For the relationship between Latin and the extension of Roman power, see the essays in Cooley 2002 and for a linguistic study of the use of Latin in the empire, Clackson and Horrocks 2007.

Romanisation also raises questions of resistance to Rome in its various forms, whether cultural or military. The work of Benabou (esp. 1976) on North Africa, a postcolonial perspective influenced by the French occupation of the region, is important for its emphasis on the way imperialism was experienced by the indigenous population (contextualising Benabou and other work on North Africa, Mattingly 1996). On revolts in the empire generally, note Dyson 1971 and 1975, both making comparisons with more recent colonial revolts. On resistance in the East and the Roman army as an occupying force, see Isaac 1992. Goodman 1987 and the essays in Berlin and Overman 2002 offer important treatments of the Jewish revolt; for the revolt of Boudicca, see Hingley and Unwin 2005.

On cults of Roman power (borrowing Simon Price's phrase), see Mellor 1975 for the goddess Roma in the Greek world, Price 1984 for imperial cult in Asia Minor and the extensive writings of Fishwick for the West (1987–2005).

Chapter 5: The Ruler

For Roman ideas of empire in the Republic see in particular Brunt 1978 but also Gruen 1984 and North 1993 (with an emphasis on religion);

for the Principate, see Mattern 1999 and, with its focus a little later, Lendon 1997. Nicolet 1991 offers an illuminating study of the relationship between geography and empire; note in particular his remarks on the symbolism of the globe (35–9) and on Agrippa's map (95–122), usefully complemented by T. Murphy 2004 on Pliny's *Natural History*. The imperial underpinning of Pliny's work has been a fruitful area for study recently as Carey 2003 with a focus on art and empire also shows.

The administration of the empire is the subject of a number of studies; the best starting point is Lintott 1993, cf. also Richardson 1994 and Ando 2006. Lintott 1993: 97–107 and Riggsby 1999: 120–50 offer accessible introductions to *repetundae* legislation, both stressing the role of the welfare of the subject; Richardson 1987, however, is sceptical. For the *publicani*, see Badian 1972 and under the Principate, Brunt 1990: 354–432; for their sometimes tense relationship with the governor, Kallet-Marx 1995: 138–48.

The essays in Rosenstein and Morstein-Marx 2006 give a good sense of how the development of Rome in the Republic was shaped by its empire; note in particular chapters by Patterson (on the city, together with his 1991 survey article), Hölkeskamp (on monuments and collective memory) and Welch (on manubial temples). For a more detailed account of the latter, Orlin 1997. Coulston and Dodge 2000 is a very useful collection of essays on the city of Rome itself, while the impact of empire is explored in the interdisciplinary collection of Edwards and Woolf 2003. On the seizure and display of art objects, see Gruen 1992: 84–129, Edwards 2003 and Miles 2008. For the development of city of Rome under Augustus, see Zanker 1988 (who notes its un-imperial appearance in the Republic, pp. 19–21) and Favro 2005. For foreigners in Rome and the process of migration, Noy 2000 and Morley 2003, the latter offering a rather different way of writing ancient history.

Brunt's interpretation of the impact of imperial expansion on the Italian countryside is summed up in Brunt 1971a (see also the essays in Brunt 1988); equally influential has been Hopkins 1978: 1–98. For an alternative view, see Rosenstein 2004. Brunt's arguments on population are to be found in his major study on Italian manpower and much else (1971b). For Lo Cascio's argument for the 'high' count see in particular his 1994 and 1999 papers together with Lo Cascio and Malanima 2005 which considers the development of the Italian population up to the beginning of the twentieth century. On the Italian population see now the wide-ranging set of essays in de Ligt and Northwood 2008. Lo Cascio's arguments have engendered considerable debate if not acceptance (cf. Scheidel 2008). For the changing nature of Roman citizenship, see Sherwin-White 1973, Lintott 1993: 161–7 and Dench 2005: 93–151; for its impact on the Senate in the late Republic and Principate, Wiseman 1971; on the Antonine Constitution, Hekster 2008: 45–55.

Part II Documents

For those wishing to read beyond the extracts, translations of most of these are available in a number of series. The extensive Loeb Classical Library gives both the original language and a translation on facing pages; there are also very good translations in the Oxford World Classics series and in Penguin Classics. Details of translations that are included on the Perseus website are given under Internet Resources.

Exceptions are the following:
Augustine, *The City of God*, R. W. Dyson, Cambridge, 1998.
Digest, A. Watson (ed.), *The Digest of Justinian*, 2 vols. Philadelphia, 1998 (earlier edition with Latin text, 1985).
Lactantius, *Lactantius: The Divine Institutes*, Anthony Bowen and Peter Garnsey, Liverpool, 2003.
Pompeius Trogus: the only modern translation is that of J. C. Yardley with introduction and notes by R. Develin, *Justin: the Epitome of the Philippic History of Pompeius Trogus*, American Philological Association, Classical Resources Series 3, Scholars Press, Atlanta, 1994.
Res Gestae: Cooley 2009 provides text, translation and commentary.
Sibylline Oracles, translated by J. J. Collins in Charlesworth 1983: 317–472.

Further bibliography on Greek and Jewish authors is given in the reading for Chapter 4 above. For Latin authors see in particular the following: Caesar (Riggsby 2006), Cicero (Steel 2001), Pliny the Elder (Carey 2003, Murphy 2004), Pliny the Younger (Woolf 2006, Madsen 2009), Livy (Luce 1977, Jaeger 1997), Tacitus (Syme 1958), Pompeius Trogus (Yarrow 2006), Sallust (Syme 1964), Suetonius (Wallace-Hadrill 1983). Note also the commentaries on Livy, Ogilivie 1965 for Books 1–5, Oakley 1997–2005 for Books 6–10, Briscoe 1973, 1981, 2008 for books 31–40.

Quotations introducing chapters

These come from the following sources:

Edward Gibbon, *The History of the Decline and Fall of the Roman Empire*, vol. 1, Chapter 2 (D. Womersley's Penguin abridged edition, 2000, p. 46); this classic work was first published in the eighteenth century and is available in numerous editions.

John Kerry: his speech accepting the Democratic nomination, text at http://www.washingtonpost.com/wp-dyn/articles/A25678-2004Jul29.html

George W. Bush: in his introduction to the *The National Security Strategy of the United States of America 2002*, which can be found at http://georgewbush-whitehouse.archives.gov/nsc/nss/2002/index.html and in a print edition by Frank H. Columbus (New York, 2003).

Mahatma Gandhi: *The Collected Works of Mahatma Gandhi*, vol. 28 (Delhi, 1968), 130.

Lord Rosebery: this quotation appears in a number of different forms; I have used T. F. G. Coates, *Lord Rosebery: His Life and Speeches* (London, 1900), 24.

Internet Resources

Gateways

The following two sites provide links to a wide range of Ancient History and Classics Resources and are well worth exploring:
www.rdg.ac.uk/classics/Link/index.php
www.tlg.uci.edu/index/resources.html

Roman History

www.romanimperialism.com
Neville Morley's website aims to provide resources for understanding Roman imperialism and its continuing influence.

www.attalus.org
A year-by-year list of events in Greek and Roman history from 322 to 48 BC with many links to relevant online source material.

www.livius.org
An extensive collection of articles and texts on Ancient History, fuller on the East than the West.

www.roman-emperors.org
An online encyclopedia of Roman rulers and their families from Augustus to 15th C Byzantium.

www.romanarmy.com
Much about the Roman army here including a database of Roman helmets.

Texts

www.perseus.tufts.edu
The Perseus digital library contains a considerable collection of Greek and Latin texts in translation and in the original. It includes Appian, Caesar, the speeches and letters of Cicero, Josephus, Livy, Pliny the Elder, Pliny the Younger, Plutarch's *Lives*, Polybios, Sallust, Strabo, Tacitus, Vergil. For copyright reasons the translations here and elsewhere on the internet are often fairly old.

Penelope.uchicago.edu/Thayer/E/Roman/home.html
Many texts in translation and also a good selection of photographs from around the Roman world, including a number tracing the Via Flaminia to Ariminum.

www.thelatinlibrary.com
A very full collection of Latin texts in the original, Christian as well as Classical, but without translations.

Numismatics

www.numismatics.org
This is the American Numismatic Society's website; it contains a searchable database with an increasing number of digital images.

www.wildwinds.com/coins
Excellent images of both Republican and Imperial Roman coins.

www.coinarchives.com
This is a searchable archive of images and information drawn from the electronic catalogues of major numismatics auctions.

http://www.cngcoins.com
Classical Numismatics Group with an extensive searchable archive from sales; the coin illustrations in this book are taken from there.

Epigraphy and Papyrology

www.csad.ox.ac.uk
Website of the Centre for the Study of Ancient Documents in Oxford, which specialises in epigraphy and papyrology. Note in particular Vindolanda Online, an illustrated online edition of the writing tablets from the Vindolanda fort near Hadrian's Wall. There are also links to many important epigraphic and papyrological sites.

www.epigraphische-datenbank-heidelberg.de
An online database of inscriptions.

www.users.drew.edu/~jmuccigr/papyrology
A useful collection of papyrology links

Maps

www.unc.edu/awmc
The website of the Ancient World Mapping Center.

http://mappinghistory.uoregon.edu/english/EU/eu.html
Dynamic maps of historical problems, including romanisation and the Roman conquest of Italy.

And one that defies categorisation:

www.ancientsites.com

Glossary

aedile	A junior magistrate, annually elected, whose duties largely concerned the administration of the city of Rome
as	Roman coin, made out of bronze or copper
censor	A senior magistrate whose responsibilities included conducting the census and so maintaining the list of Roman citizens. Two men were elected to this prestigious position from among the ex-consuls, normally every five years for a term of eighteen months
conscript fathers	Senators of Rome, common in addresses to the Senate; in Latin: *patres conscripti*
consul	One of two chief magistrates of Rome, elected annually, with both civil and military responsibilities
demos	Greek term for 'the sovereign people', hence its use in phrases such as 'the demos of the Ephesians', a common formulation in official documents
denarius	A Roman silver coin
dictator	A supreme magistrate at Rome with sole power appointed very occasionally in times of crisis as a short-term measure to deal with a specific situation. Its character changed in the late Republic, notably when C. Iulius Caesar was appointed dictator for life
drachma	Greek silver coin, roughly equivalent in value to a Roman denarius, see also 'talent'

fasces	A bundle of rods and a single-headed axe that was carried by lictors in front of Roman magistrates to symbolise their authority
fetiales	Priests who advised the Senate on matters of war and peace. This college of twenty priests had responsibility for the fetial ritual employed in the declaration of war, Chapter 3, section 2, with **Livy A, p. 112**
imperator	Title given to a victorious general by his soldiers and held until the end of his magistracy or until his triumph. It was used permanently by Caesar and later came to be a title by which the emperor was known
imperium	See Chapter 1, section 2
legion	Main unit of the Roman army. The Republican legion was made up of between 4,200 and 5,000 men; under the Principate the figure was probably closer to 5,000 Initially divided into thirty maniples, it was by the first century BC arranged in ten cohorts, see **Polybios I, p. 137**
lictors	A Roman magistrate's attendants
maniple	One of the thirty units of the Roman legion, see **Polybios I, p. 137**
phalanx	Greek infantry formation used by the Hellenistic kingdoms
pontifex maximus	Chief priest of Rome
praetor	A Roman magistrate below the level of consul, annually elected, with judicial responsibilities in Rome and military duties outside it. The numbers gradually increased as Rome's empire increased
Principate	The term used to describe the rule of the emperors from Augustus until the third century. 'Princeps' (first or leading man) was the word chosen by Augustus to describe his own constitutional position
proconsul	see pro-magistrate
procurator	An employee of the emperor, who managed his property and other business, often in the

	provinces; this could include the collection of taxes
pro-magistrate	An ex-magistrate (consul, praetor or quaestor) given the power to act as if he held the office of consul etc., hence proconsul etc. This was especially useful when a commander on campaign needed his term of office extended or when the position of provincial governor could not otherwise be filled
provincia	Two related meanings: the task assigned to a magistrate; a unit of empire administered by a governor, a province
publicani	public contractors, in particular used of those collecting state revenues such as taxes
quaestor	A junior magistrate, annually elected, whose duties largely, though not exclusively, concerned finance. Numbers increased from ten in 197 to forty under Caesar; reduced to twenty by Augustus
rostra	Speaker's platform at Rome
stele (pl. stelai or stelae)	Smooth stone slab, standing upright, on which texts such as decrees or epitaphs are inscribed
talent	The largest Greek unit of measurement, used for both weight or sums of money. On the Attic-Euboian standard it weighed 29.196 kg, roughly eighty Roman pounds of silver; 1 talent = 60 minai = 6,000 drachmai. Some examples may put its value into context. Estimates for the cost of building the Parthenon very between 340 and 500 talents (Neils 2005: 53–4); the three-year Athenian siege of Potidaia was put at 2,000 talents by Thucydides (2.70.2); Alexander's army is reckoned to have cost twenty talents a day to maintain (Hammond 1981: 156). The value of Persian treasure reported to have been captured by Alexander was huge: 50,000 talents at Susa and 120,000 at Persepolis (Arrian 3.16.7, Diodoros 17.71.1)

tribunes of the plebs	Officials elected annually by the plebeian assembly, ten in number, whose traditional duty was to protect members of the plebs. They had the right to propose laws and to veto the acts of other magistrates or even a decree of the Senate
tribune, military	Junior officers in the army, six tribunes to a legion

Bibliography

Alcock, S. E. 1993. *Graecia Capta: The Landscapes of Roman Greece.* Cambridge.

Alcock, S. E. et al. (ed.) 2001. *Empires: Perspectives from Archaeology and History.* Cambridge.

Alonso-Núñez, J. 1987 'An Augustan World History: The "Historiae Philippicae" of Pompeius Trogus', *Greece & Rome* 34: 56–72.

Anderson, P. 1974. *Passages from Antiquity to Feudalism.* London.

Ando, C. 2000. *Imperial Ideology and Provincial Loyalty in the Roman Empire.* Berkeley.

Ando, C. 2006. 'The Administration of the Provinces', in Potter 2006: 177–92.

Arafat, K. 1996. *Pausanias' Greece: Ancient Artists and Roman Rulers.* Cambridge.

Austin, M. M. 2006. *The Hellenistic World from Alexander to the Roman Conquest: A Selection of Ancient Sources in Translation*, 2nd edn. Cambridge.

Badian, E. 1958. *Foreign Clientelae (264–70 BC).* Oxford.

Badian, E. 1959. 'Rome and Antiochus the Great: A study in Cold War', *Classical Philology* 54: 81–99 (reprinted in E. Badian, *Studies in Greek and Roman History.* Oxford, 1964. 113–39).

Badian, E. 1968. *Roman Imperialism in the Late Republic.* Oxford.

Badian, E. 1972. *Publicans and Sinners: Private Enterprise in the Service of the Roman Republic.* Ithaca.

Bagnall, R. and Derow, P. 2004. *The Hellenistic Period: Historical Sources in Translation.* Oxford (earlier edn published as *Greek Historical Documents: The Hellenistic Period*, 1981).

Barclay, J. M. G. 1999. *Jews in the Mediterranean Diaspora: From Alexander to Trajan (323 BCE–117 CE).* Berkeley.

Barnes, T. D. 1975. 'Constans and Gratian in Rome', *Harvard Studies in Classical Philology* 79: 325–33.

Bartlett, J. R. 1998. *1 Maccabees.* Sheffield.

Beard, M. 2007. *The Roman Triumph.* Cambridge.

Beard, M. and Crawford, M. 1985. *Rome in the Late Republic*. London.

Beard, M., North, J. and Price, S. 1998. *The Religions of Rome*. 2 vols. Cambridge.

Bell, D. 2007. *The Idea of Greater Britain: Empire and the Future of World Order, 1860–1900*. Princeton.

Benabou, M. 1976. *La Résistance africaine à la romanisation*. Paris.

Bennett, J. 1997. *Trajan, Optimus Princeps: A Life and Times*. London.

Berlin, A. and Overman, J. A. (eds) 2002. *The First Jewish Revolt*. London.

Bilde, P. 1988. *Flavius Josephus between Jerusalem and Rome*. Sheffield.

Blagg, T. and Millett, M. (eds) 1990. *The Early Roman Empire in the West*. Oxford.

Bonfante Warren, L. 1970. 'Roman Triumphs and Etruscan Kings: The Changing Face of the Triumph', *JRS* 60: 49–66.

Booth, K. 2007. *Theory of World Security*. Cambridge.

Bowersock, G. 1965. *Augustus and the Greek World*. Oxford.

Bowersock, G. 1969. *Greek Sophists in the Roman Empire*. Oxford.

Bowie, E. 1970. 'The Greeks and their Past in the Second Sophistic', *Past & Present* 46: 3–41 (reprinted in M. I. Finley (ed.), *Studies in Ancient Society*. London, 1974. 166–209).

Bradley, G. 2000. *Ancient Umbria: State, Culture and Identity in Central Italy from the Iron Age to Augustus*. Oxford.

Braund, D. 1984. *Rome and the Friendly King: The Character of the Client Kingship*. Beckenham.

Braund, D. 1993. 'Piracy under the Principate and the Ideology of Imperial Eradication', in Rich and Shipley 1993: 195–213.

Briscoe, J. 1967. 'Rome and the Class Struggle in the Greek States, 200–146 BC', *Past and Present* 36: 3–20 (reprinted in M. I. Finley (ed.), *Studies in Ancient Society*. London, 1974. 53–73).

Briscoe, J. 1969. 'Eastern Policy and Senatorial Politics 168–146 BC', *Historia* 18: 49–70.

Briscoe. J. 1973, 1981, 2008. *A Commentary on Livy*. Books 31–3, 34–7, 38–40. Oxford.

Briscoe, J. 1989. 'The Second Punic War', in *CAH²* 8: 44–80.

Brilliant, R. 1999. '"Let the Trumpets Roar!" The Roman Triumph', in B. Bergmann and C. Kondoleon (eds), *The Art of Ancient Spectacle* (Studies in the History of Art 56). Washington. 221–9.

Bringmann, K. 2007. *A History of the Roman Republic*. Cambridge (first published in German 2002).

Brodersen, K. 1995. *Terra Cognita: Studien zur römischen Raumerfassung*. Hildesheim.

Brunt, P. A. 1961. 'Charges of Provincial Maladministration under the Early Principate', *Historia* 10: 189–227 (reprinted in Brunt 1990: 53–95).

Brunt, P. A. 1963. Review of H. D. Meyer, *JRS* 53: 170–6 (reprinted as 'Augustan Imperialism', in Brunt, 1988: 240–80).

Brunt, P. A. 1971a. *Social Conflicts in the Roman Republic.* London

Brunt, P. A, 1971b. *Italian Manpower, 225 BC–AD 14.* Oxford.

Brunt, P. A. 1978. 'Laus Imperii', in Garnsey and Whittaker 1978: 159–91 (reprinted in Brunt 1990: 288–323).

Brunt, P. A. 1988. *The Fall of the Roman Republic and related Essays.* Oxford.

Brunt, P. A. 1990. *Roman Imperial Themes.* Oxford.

Bryce, J. 1901. 'The Roman Empire and the British Empire in India', in J. Bryce, *Studies in History and Jurisprudence.* Oxford. 1–71.

Bullo, S. 2002. *Provincia Africa: Le città e il territorio dalla caduta di Cartagine a Nerone.* Rome.

Cain, P. J. and Hopkins, A. G. 2002. *British Imperialism 1688–2000.* 2nd edn. Harlow.

Campbell, J. B. 1994. *The Roman Army, 31 BC–AD 337: A Sourcebook.* London.

Carey, S. 2003. *Pliny's Catalogue of Culture: Art and Empire in the Natural History.* Oxford.

Champion, C. (ed.) 2004a. *Roman Imperialism: Readings and Sources.* Oxford.

Champion, C. 2004b. *Cultural Politics in Polybius's Histories.* Berkeley.

Charlesworth, J. H. (ed.) 1983. *The Old Testament Pseudepigrapha: Apocalyptic Literature and Testaments.* Vol. 1. Garden City.

Clackson, J. and Horrocks, G. 2007. *The Blackwell History of the Latin Language.* Oxford.

Claridge, A. 1998. *Rome: An Oxford Archaeological Guide.* Oxford.

Clarke, K. 1999. *Between Geography and History: Hellenistic Constructions of the Roman World.* Oxford.

Clarke, K. 2001. 'An Island Nation: Re-Reading Tacitus' "Agricola"', *JRS* 91: 104–12.

Clifton, R. 1999. '"An Indiscriminate Blackness"? Massacre, Counter-Massacre and Ethnic Cleansing in Ireland 1640–1660', in M. Levene and P. Roberts (eds), *The Massacre in History.* London. 107–26.

Coleman, K. 2000. 'Entertaining Rome', in Coulston and Dodge 2000: 210–58.

Cooley, A. E. (ed.) 2002. *Becoming Roman, Writing Latin. Literacy and Epigraphy in the Roman West.* Portsmouth.

Cooley, A. E. 2009. *Res Gestae Divi Augusti: Text, Translation and Commentary.* Cambridge.

Cooper, R. 2002. 'The Postmodern State', in M. Leonard, *Re-Ordering the World: The Long-Term Implications of September 11th.* London. 11–20 (http://fpc.org.uk/fsblob/36.pdf).

Cornell, T. J. 1993. 'The End of Roman Imperial Expansion', in Rich and Shipley 1993: 139–70.

Cornell, T. J. 1995. *The Beginnings of Rome: Italy and Rome from the Bronze Age to the Punic Wars (c. 1000–264 BC).* London.

Cornell, T. J. 1996. 'Hannibal's Legacy: The Effects of the Hannibalic War on Italy', in Cornell et al. 1996: 97–113.

Cornell, T. J. 2000. 'The City of Rome in the Middle Republic (400–100 BC)', in Coulston and Dodge 2000: 42–60.

Cornell, T. J., Rankov, B. and Sabin, P. (eds) 1996. *The Second Punic War: A Reappraisal.* London.

Coulston, J. and Dodge, H. (eds) 2000. *Ancient Rome: The Archaeology of the Eternal City.* Oxford.

Crawford, M. 1970. 'Money and Exchange in the Roman World', *JRS* 60: 40–8.

Crawford, M. 1974. *Roman Republican Coinage.* London.

Crawford, M. 1977. 'Rome and the Greek World: Economic Relationships', *Economic History Review* 30: 42–54.

Crawford, M. (ed.) 1983. *Sources for Ancient History.* Cambridge.

Crawford, M. 1992. *The Roman Republic.* 2nd edn. London.

Curchin, L. R. 1991. *Roman Spain: Conquest and Assimilation.* London.

Curchin, L. R. 2004. *The Romanization of Central Spain: Complexity, Diversity and Change in a Provincial Hinterland.* London.

Daly, G. 2002. *Cannae: The Experience of Battle in the Second Punic War.* London.

David, J.-M. 1996. *The Roman Conquest of Italy.* Oxford.

de Lange, N. R. M. 1978. 'Jewish Attitudes to the Roman Empire', in Garnsey and Whittaker 1978: 255–81.

de Ligt, L. and Northwood, S. (eds) 2008. *People, Land and Politics: Demographic Developments and the Transformation of Roman Italy 300 BC–AD 14.* Leiden.

Dench, E. 1995. *From Barbarians to New Men: Greek, Roman and Modern Perceptions of the Peoples from the Central Apennines.* Oxford.

Dench, E. 2005. *Romulus' Asylum: Roman Identities from the Age of Alexander to the Age of Hadrian.* Oxford.

Derow, P. S. 1979. 'Polybius, Rome, and the East', *JRS* 69: 1–15.

Derow, P. S. 1989. 'Rome, the Fall of Macedon and the Sack of Corinth', *CAH²* 8: 290–323.

Derow, P. S. 1991. 'Pharos and Rome', *ZPE* 88: 261–70

Derow, P. S. 2003. 'The Arrival of Rome. From the Illyrian Wars to the Fall of Macedon', in Erskine 2003: 51–70.

de Sanctis, G. 1923. *Storia dei Romani.* Vol. 4.1. Turin.

de Sanctis, G. 1964. *Storia dei Romani.* Vol. 4.3. Florence.

de Souza, P. 1999. *Piracy in the Graeco-Roman World.* Cambridge.

Dillon, M. and Garland, L. 2005. *Ancient Rome from the Early Republic to the Assassination of Julius Caesar.* London.

Dionisotti, A. C. 1982. 'From Ausonius' Schooldays? A Schoolbook and Its Relatives', *JRS* 72: 83–125.

Dmitriev, S. Forthcoming. *The Greek Slogan of Freedom and Early Roman Politics in Greece.* Oxford.

Dobson, M. 2008. *The Army of the Roman Republic: The Second Century BC, Polybius and the Camps at Numantia, Spain*. Oxford.

Dodge, H. 2000. '"Greater than the Pyramids": The Water Supply of Ancient Rome', in Coulston and Dodge 2000: 166–209.

Doyle, M. W. 1986. *Empires*. Ithaca.

Drinkwater, J. 1979. 'A Note on Local Careers in the Three Gauls under the Early Empire', *Britannia* 10: 89–100.

Drinkwater, J. 1983. *Roman Gaul: The Three Provinces, 58 BC–AD 260*. London.

Duff, T. 1999. *Plutarch's Lives: Exploring Virtue and Vice*. Oxford.

Dyson, S. 1971. 'Native Revolts in the Roman Empire', *Historia* 20: 239–74.

Dyson, S. 1975. 'Native Revolt Patterns in the Roman Empire', *Aufsteig und Niedergang der romischen Welt* 2.3: 138–75.

Eckstein, A. M. 1987. *Senate and General: Individual Decision Making and Roman Foreign Relations, 264–194 BC*. Berkeley.

Eckstein, A. M. 1995. *Moral Vision in the Histories of Polybius*. Berkeley.

Eckstein, A. M. 1999. 'Pharos and the Question of Roman Treaties of Alliance in the Greek East in the Third Century BCE', *Classical Philology* 94: 395–418.

Eckstein, A. M. 2006. *Mediterranean Anarchy, Interstate War, and the Rise of Rome*. Berkeley.

Eckstein, A. M. 2008. *Rome Enters the Greek East: From Anarchy to Hierarchy in the Hellenistic Mediterranean, 230–170 BC*. Oxford.

Edmondson, J. 2006. 'Cities and Urban Life in the Western Provinces', in Potter 2006: 250–80.

Edmondson, J., Mason, S. and Rives, J. (eds) 2005. *Flavius Josephus and Flavian Rome*. Oxford.

Edwards, C. (ed.) 1999. *Roman Presences: Receptions of Rome in European Culture, 1789–1945*. Cambridge.

Edwards, C. 2003. 'Incorporating the Alien: The Art of Conquest', in Edwards and Woolf 2003: 44–70.

Edwards , C. and Woolf, G. (eds) 2003. *Rome the Cosmopolis*. Cambridge.

Eilers, C. 2002. *Roman Patrons of Greek Cities*. Oxford.

Eilers, C. 2003. 'A Roman East: Pompey's Settlement to the Death of Augustus', in Erskine 2003: 90–102.

Erdkamp, P. (ed.) 2007. *A Companion to the Roman Army*. Oxford.

Errington, R. 1971. *The Dawn of Empire: Rome's Rise to World Power*. London.

Erskine, A. 1990. *The Hellenistic Stoa: Political Thought and Action*. London.

Erskine, A. 1995. 'Rome in the Greek World: The Significance of a Name', in A. Powell (ed.), *The Greek World*. London. 368–83.

Erskine, A. 1996. 'Money-Loving Romans', *Papers of the Leeds International Latin Seminar* 9: 1–11.

Erskine, A. 2000. 'Polybios and Barbarian Rome', *Mediterraneo Antico* 3: 165–82.

Erskine, A. 2001. *Troy between Greece and Rome: Local Tradition and Imperial Power*. Oxford.

Erskine, A. (ed.) 2003. *A Companion to the Hellenistic World*. Oxford.

Erskine, A. (ed.) 2009a. *A Companion to Ancient History*. Oxford.

Erskine, A. 2009b. 'Ancient History and National Identity', in Erskine 2009a: 555–63.

Favro, D. 1994. 'The Street Triumphant: The Urban Impact of Roman Triumphal Parades', in Z. Çelik, D. Favro and R. Ingersoll (eds), *Streets: Critical Perspectives on Public Space*. Berkeley. 151–64.

Favro, D. 2005. 'Making Rome a World City', in K. Galinsky (ed.), *The Cambridge Companion to the Age of Augustus*. Cambridge. 234–63.

Fear, A. T. 1996. *Rome and Baetica: Urbanization in Southern Spain 50 BC–AD 150*. Oxford.

Fentress, E. (ed.) 2000. *Romanization and the City: Creation, Transformations and Failures*. Portsmouth.

Ferguson, N. 2004. *Colossus: The Rise and Fall of the American Empire*. London.

Ferrary, J.-L. 1988. *Philhellénisme et impérialisme. Aspects idéologiques de la conquête romaine du monde hellénistique, de la seconde guerre de Macédoine à la guerre contre Mithridate*. BEFAR 271. Rome.

Finley, M. I. 1978. 'Empire in the Greco-Roman World', *Greece & Rome* 25: 1–15.

Fishwick, D. 1987–2005. *The Imperial Cult in the Latin West: Studies in the Ruler Cult of the Western Provinces of the Roman Empire*. 3 vols. Leiden.

Fishwick, D. 2002. *The Imperial Cult in the Latin West: Studies in the Ruler Cult of the Western Provinces of the Roman Empire*. Vol. 3: *Provincial Cult*. Part 1: *Institution and Evolution*. Leiden.

Fishwick, D. 2004. *The Imperial Cult in the Latin West: Studies in the Ruler Cult of the Western Provinces of the Roman Empire*. Vol. 3: *Provincial Cult*. Part 3: *The Provincial Centre*. Leiden.

Flower, H. 1996. *Ancestor Masks and Aristocratic Power in Roman Culture*. Oxford.

Fontana, S. 2001. 'Leptis Magna. The Romanization of a Major African City through Burial Evidence', in Keay and Terrenato 2001: 161–72.

Forte, B. 1972. *The Romans as the Greeks Saw Them*. Rome.

Frank, T. 1914. *Roman Imperialism*. Baltimore.

Frederiksen, M. 1970–1. 'The Contribution of Archaeology to the Agrarian Problem in the Gracchan Period', *Dialoghi di Archeologia* 4–5: 330–57.

Freeman, P. W. M. 2007. *'The Best Training Ground for an Archaeologist.' Francis Haverfield and the Invention of Romano-British Studies*. Oxford.

Fuchs, H. 1938. *Der geistige Widerstand gegen Rom in der antiken Welt*. Berlin.

Gabba, E. 1991. *Dionysius and the History of Archaic Rome*. Berkeley.

Garnsey, P. and Saller, R. 1987. *The Roman Empire: Economy, Society and Culture*. London.

Garnsey, P. and Whittaker, C. (eds) 1978. *Imperialism in the Ancient World.* Cambridge.

Gebhard, E. and Dickie, M. 2003. 'The View from the Isthmus, ca 200 to 44 BC', in C. K. Williams and N. Bookidis (eds), *Corinth, the Centenary, 1896–1996.* Athens. 261–78.

Gleason, M. 2006. 'Greek Cities under Roman Rule', in Potter 2006: 228–49.

Gold, B. 1985. 'Pompey and Theophanes', *American Journal of Philology* 106: 312–27.

Goldhill, S. (ed.) 2001. *Being Greek under Rome: Cultural Identity, the Second Sophistic and the Development of Empire.* Cambridge.

Goldsworthy, A. 2000. *The Punic Wars.* London (reprinted in 2003 as *The Fall of Carthage*).

Goldsworthy, A. 2006. *Caesar, Life of a Colossus.* New Haven.

González, J. 1986. 'The *Lex Irnitana*: A New Copy of the Flavian Municipal Law', *JRS* 76: 147–238.

Goodman, M. 1987. *The Ruling Class of Judaea: The Origins of the Jewish Revolt against Rome AD 66–70.* Cambridge.

Goodman, M. 1997. *The Roman World 44 BC–AD 180.* London.

Goodman, M. 2007. *Rome and Jerusalem: The Clash of Ancient Civilizations.* London.

Gowing, A. 1992. *The Triumphal Narratives of Appian and Cassius Dio.* Ann Arbor.

Griffin, M. (ed.) 2009. *A Companion to Julius Caesar.* Oxford.

Gruen, E. S. 1974. *The Last Generation of the Roman Republic.* Berkeley.

Gruen, E. S. 1984. *The Hellenistic World and the Coming of Rome.* Berkeley.

Gruen, E. S. 1992. *Culture and National Identity in Republican Rome.* Ithaca.

Gruen, E. S. 1998. 'Jews, Greeks, and Romans in the Third Sibylline Oracle', in M. Goodman (ed.), *Jews in a Graeco-Roman World.* Oxford. 15–36.

Gruen, E. S. 2002. *Diaspora: Jews amidst Greeks and Romans.* Cambrige.

Hadas-Lebel, M. 2006. *Jerusalem against Rome.* Leuven.

Hammond, M. 1957. 'Composition of the Senate, AD 68-235', *JRS* 47: 74–81.

Hammond, N. G. L. 1981. *Alexander the Great: King, Commander and Statesman.* London.

Hansen, W. 1996. *Phlegon of Tralles' Book of Marvels.* Exeter.

Harris, W. V. 1971a. *Rome in Etruria and Umbria.* Oxford.

Harris, W. V. 1971b. 'On War and Greed in the Second-Century BC', *American Historical Review* 76: 1371–85.

Harris, W. V. 1979. *War and Imperialism in Republican Rome: 327–70 BC.* Oxford.

Harris, W. V. (ed.) 1984. *The Imperialism of Mid-Republican Rome.* Rome.

Harris, W. V. 1989. 'Roman Expansion in the West', *CAH*[2] 8: 107–62.

Häussler, R. 2002. 'Writing Latin – From Resistance to Assimilation: Language, Culture and Society in N. Italy and S. Gaul', in Cooley 2002: 61–75.

Haverfield, F. 1905–6. 'The Romanization of Britain'. *Proceedings of the British Academy* 2: 185-217.

Hekster, O. 2008. *Rome and its Empire AD 193–284*. Edinburgh.

Hingley, R. 2000. *Roman Officers and English Gentlemen: The Imperial Origins of Roman Archaeology*. London.

Hingley, R. 2005. *Globalizing Roman Culture: Unity, Diversity and Empire*. London.

Hingley, R. and Unwin, C. 2005. *Boudica: Iron Age Warrior Queen*. London.

Hitchner, R. B. 2008. 'Globalization Avant la Lettre: Globalization and the History of the Roman Empire'. *New Global Studies* 2.2, Article 2. Available at: http://www.bepress.com/ngs/vol2/iss2/art2

Hölkeskamp, K.-J. 2006. 'History and Collective Memory in the Middle Republic', in Rosenstein and Morstein-Marx 2006: 478–95.

Holleaux, M. 1921. *Rome, la Grèce et les monarchies hellénistiques au IIIe siècle avant J.-C. (273–205)*. Paris.

Holliday, P. J. 2002. *The Origins of Roman Historical Commemoration in the Visual Arts*. Cambridge.

Hopkins, K. 1978. *Conquerors and Slaves*. Cambridge.

Hopkins, K. 1983. *Death and Renewal*. Cambridge.

Hornblower, J. 1981. *Hieronymus of Cardia*. Oxford.

Howe, S. 2002. *Empire: A Very Short Introduction*. Oxford.

Howgego, C. J. 1990. 'Why did Ancient States Strike Coins?', *Numismatic Chronicle* 150: 1–25.

Hoyos, B. D. 1998. *Unplanned Wars: The Origins of the First and Second Punic Wars, 247–183 BC* Berlin.

Hoyos, D. 2003. *Hannibal's Dynasty: Power and Politics in the Western Mediterranean, 247–183 BC* Oxford.

Huss, W. 1985. *Geschichte der Karthager*. Munich.

Huss, W. 1990. *Die Karthager*. Munich.

Hutton, W. 2005. *Describing Greece. Landscape and Literature in the Periegesis of Pausanias: Greek Culture in The Roman World*. Cambridge.

Isaac, B. H. 1992. *The Limits of Empire: the Roman Army in the East*. Revised edn. Oxford.

Isaac, B. H. 2004. *The Invention of Racism in Classical Antiquity*. London.

Jaeger, M. 1997. *Livy's Written Rome*. Ann Arbor.

James, S. 2001. '"Romanization" and the Peoples of Britain', in Keay and Terrenato 2001: 187–209.

Jones, C. P. 1971. *Plutarch and Rome*. Oxford.

Kallet-Marx, R. 1995. *Hegemony to Empire: The Development of the Roman Imperium in the East from 148 to 62 BC*. Berkeley.

Keay, S. 1988. *Roman Spain*. London.

Keay, S. and Terrenato, N. (eds) 2001. *Italy and the West: Comparative Issues in Romanization*. Oxford.

Kelly, C. 2006. *The Roman Empire: A Very Short Introduction*. Oxford.

Keppie, L. 1984. *The Making of the Roman Army: From Republic to Empire*. London.

Koebner, R. and Schmidt, H. D. 1964. *Imperialism: The Story and Significance of a Political Word, 1840–1960*. Cambridge.

König, J. 2005. *Athletics and Literature in the Roman Empire*. Cambridge.

Konstan, D. and Said, S. (eds) 2006. *Greeks on Greekness: Viewing the Greek Past under the Roman Empire*. Cambridge.

Künzl, E. 1988. *Der römische Triumph: Siegesfeiern in antiken Rom*. Munich.

Lancel, S. 1995. *Carthage: A History*. Oxford (French edition, 1992).

Lancel, S. 1998. *Hannibal*. Oxford (French edition, 1995)

Lazenby, J. F. 1978. *Hannibal's War*. Warminster.

Lazenby, J. F. 1996. *The First Punic War*. Stanford.

Lendon, J. E. 1997. *Empire of Honour. The Art of Government in the Roman World*. Oxford.

Levick, B. 1985. *The Government of the Roman Empire: A Sourcebook*. London.

Levine, P. 2007. *The British Empire: Sunrise to Sunset*. Harlow.

Lewis, N. and Reinhold, M. 1990. *Roman Civilization: Selected Readings*. 2 vols. 3rd edn. New York.

Linderski, J. 1984. '*Si vis pacem, para bellum*: Concepts of Defensive Imperialism', in Harris 1984: 133–64.

Lintott, A. W. 1972. 'Imperial Expansion and Moral Decline in the Roman Republic', *Historia* 21: 626–38.

Lintott, A. W. 1993. *Imperium Romanum: Politics and Administration*. London.

Lintott, A. W. 1999. *The Constitution of the Roman Republic*. Oxford.

lo Cascio, E. 1994. 'The Size of the Roman Population: Beloch and the Meaning of the Republican Census Figures', *JRS* 84: 23–40.

lo Cascio, E. 1999. 'The Population of Roman Italy in Town and Country', in J. Bintliff and K. Sbonias (eds), *Reconstructing Past Population Trends in Mediterranean Europe (3000 BC–AD 1800)*. Oxford. 161–71.

lo Cascio, E. 2001. 'Recruitment and the Size of the Roman Population from the Third to the First Century BCE', in W. Scheidel (ed.), *Debating Roman Demography*. Leiden.

lo Cascio, E. and Malanima, P. 2005. 'Cycles and Stability: Italian Population before the Demographic Transition (225 BC–AD 1900)', *Rivista di Storia Economica* 21: 197–232.

Lomas, K. 1993. *Rome and the Western Greeks 350 BC–AD 200: Conquest and Acculturation in Southern Italy*. London.

Lomas. K. 1996. *Roman Italy 338 BC–AD 200*. London.

Lomas, K. 2009. 'Italy beyond Rome', in Erskine 2009a: 248–59.

Luce, T. J. 1977. *Livy: The Composition of his History*. Princeton.

Luttwak, E. N. 1976. *The Grand Strategy of the Roman Empire*. Baltimore.

MacMullen, R. 2000. *Romanization in the Time of Augustus*. New Haven.

Madsen, J. M. 2009. *Eager to be Roman: Greek Response to Roman Rule in Pontus and Bithynia*. London.

Mattern, S. P. 1999. *Rome and the Enemy: Imperial Strategy in the Principate*. Berkeley.

Mattingly, D. 1996. 'From One Colonialism to Another: Imperialism and the Maghreb', in Webster and Cooper 1996: 49–69.

Mattingly, D. (ed.) 1997. *Dialogues in Roman Imperialism: Power, Discourse and Discrepant Experience in the Roman Empire*. Portsmouth.

Mattingly, D. 2002. 'Weak and Vulgar "Romanization"', or Time for a Paradigm Shift?' *Journal of Roman Archaeology* 15: 536–40.

Mattingly, D. 2006. *An Imperial Possession: Britain in the Roman Empire*. London.

Mattingly, D. and Hitchner, R. B. 1995. 'Roman Africa: An Archaeological Review', *JRS* 85: 165–213.

McGing, B. 1986. *The Foreign Policy of Mithridates VI Eupator, King of Pontus*. Leiden.

McGing, B. 2003. 'Subjection and Resistance: To the Death of Mithradates', in Erskine 2003: 71–89.

Meadows, A. and Williams, J. 2001. 'Moneta and the Monuments: Coinage and Politics in Republican Rome', *JRS* 91: 27–49.

Meier, C. 1995. *Caesar: A Biography*. London (first pub. in German, 1982).

Mellor, R. 1975. *Thea Rhome. The Worship of the Goddess Roma in the Greek World*. Gottingen.

Merryweather, A. and Prag, J. (eds) 2003. '*Romanization*'?, *Digressus* Supp. 1 (http://www.digressus.org/contents.html).

Miles, M. M. 2008. *Art as Plunder: The Ancient Origins of Debate about Cultural Property*. Cambridge.

Millar, F. 1964. *A Study of Cassius Dio*. Oxford.

Millar, F. 1981. *The Roman Empire and its Neighbours*. 2nd edn. London.

Millar, F. 1993. *The Roman Near East 31BC–AD 337*. Cambridge.

Millett, M. 1990. *The Romanization of Britain: An Essay in Archaeological Interpretation*. Cambridge.

Mitchell, S. 1993. *Anatolia: Land, Men and Gods in Asia Minor*. Oxford.

Mitchell, S. 1999. 'The Administration of Roman Asia from 133 BC to AD 250', in W. Eck and E. Müller-Luckner (eds), *Lokale Autonomie und römische Ordnungsmacht in den kaiserzeitlichen Provinzen vom 1. bis 3. Jahrhundert*. Munich. 17–46.

Momigliano, A. 1975. *Alien Wisdom: The Limits of Hellenization*. Cambridge.

Mommsen, T. 1887. *The Provinces of the Roman Empire from Caesar to Diocletian*. New York (first published in German, 1885)

Morley, N. 1996. *Metropolis and Hinterland: the City of Rome and the Italian Economy 200 BC–AD 200*. Cambridge.

Morley, N. 2001. 'The Transformation of Italy, 225–28 BC', *JRS* 91: 50–62.

Morley, N. 2003. 'Migration and the Metropolis', in Edwards and Woolf 2003: 147–76.

Morstein-Marx, R. and Rosenstein, N. 2006. 'The Transformation of the Republic', in Rosenstein and Morstein-Marx 2006: 625–37.

Münkler, H. 2007. *Empires: The Logic of World Domination from Ancient Rome to the United States*. Cambridge (first published in German in 2005).

Murphy, C. 2007. *Are We Rome? The Fall of an Empire and the Fate of America*. New York (published in the UK as *The New Rome: The Fall of an Empire and the Fate of America*, 2008).

Murphy, T. 2004. *Pliny the Elder's Natural History. The Empire in the Encyclopaedia*. Oxford.

Musti, D. 1978. *Polibio e l'imperialismo romano*. Naples.

Neils, J. 2005. *The Parthenon from Antiquity to the Present*. Cambridge.

Newby, Z. 2005. *Greek Athletics in the Roman World: Victory and Virtue*. Oxford.

Nicolet, C. 1991. *Space, Geography and Politics in the Early Roman Empire*. Ann Arbor.

North, J. 1981. 'The Development of Roman Imperialism', *JRS* 71: 1–9.

North, J. 1993. 'Roman Reactions to Empire', *Scripta Classica Israelica* 12: 127–38.

North, J. 2006. 'The Constitution of the Roman Republic', in Rosenstein and Morstein-Marx 2006: 256–77.

Noy, D. 2000. *Foreigners at Rome: Citizens and Strangers*. London.

Nye, J. 2002. *The Paradox of American Power: Why the World's Only Superpower Can't Go It Alone*. Oxford.

Oakley, S. 1993. 'The Roman Conquest of Italy', in Rich and Shipley 1993: 38–68.

Oakley, S. 1997–2005. *A Commentary on Livy: Books 6–10*, 4 vols. Oxford.

Ogilvie, R. M. 1965, *A Commentary on Livy: Books 1–5*. Oxford.

Oliver, J. H. 1953. *The Ruling Power: A Study of the Roman Empire in the Second Century after Christ through the Roman Oration of Aelius Aristides*. Philadelphia.

Orlin, E. 1997. *Temples, Religion and Politics in the Roman Republic*. Leiden.

Östenberg, I. 2009. *Staging the World: Spoils, Captives and Representations in the Roman Triumphal Procession*. Oxford.

Packer, J. E. 2001. *The Forum of Trajan in Rome: A Study of the Monuments in Brief*. Berkeley.

Parker, R. W. 1991. 'Potamon of Mytilene and his family', *ZPE* 85: 115–29.

Paterson, J. 1998. 'Trade and Traders in the Roman World: Scale, Structure and Organisation', in H. Parkins and C. Smith (eds), *Trade, Traders, and the Ancient City*. London. 149–67.

Patterson, J. 1992. 'The City of Rome: from Republic to Empire', *JRS* 82: 186–215.

Petit, P. 1976. *Pax Romana*. Berkeley (first published in French, 1967).

Petrochilos, N. 1974. *Roman Attitudes to the Greeks*. Athens.

Potter, D. 2004. 'The Roman Army and Navy', in H. Flower (ed.), *The Cambridge Companion to the Roman Republic*. Cambridge. 66–88.

Potter, D. (ed.) 2006. *A Companion to the Roman Empire*. Oxford.

Price, S. R. F. 1984. *Rituals and Power: The Roman Imperial Cult in Asia Minor*. Cambridge.

Purcell, N. 1990. 'The Creation of a Provincial Landscape: The Roman Impact on Cisalpine Gaul', in T. Blagg and M. Millett (eds), *The Early Roman Empire in the West*. Oxford. 7–29.

Purcell, N. 2005. 'Romans in the Roman World', in K. Galinsky (ed.), *The Cambridge Companion to Augustus*. Cambridge. 85–105.

Raaflaub, K. A. 1996. 'Born to be Wolves? The Origins of Roman Imperialism', in R. W. Wallace and E. M. Harris (eds), *Transitions to Empire: Essays in Greco-Roman History, 360–146 BC, in Honor of E. Badian*. Norman. 273–314.

Rajak, T. 2002. *Josephus*. 2nd edn. London.

Rathbone, D. 1981. 'The Development of Agriculture in the Ager Cosanus during the Republican Period: Problems of Evidence and Interpretation', *JRS* 71: 10–23.

Rathbone, D. 1996. 'The Imperial Finances', *CAH*² 10: 309–23.

Rauh, N. 1993. *The Sacred Bonds of Commerce: Religion, Economy, and Trade Society at Hellenistic Roman Delos, 166–87 BC* Amsterdam.

Raven, S. 1993. *Rome in Africa*. London. 3rd edn (first, 1969).

Rawson, E. 1990. 'The Antiquarian Tradition: Spoils and Representations of Foreign Armour', in W. Eder (ed.), *Staat und Staatlichkeit in der frühen römischen Republik*. Stuttgart. 157–73 (reprinted in E. Rawson, *Roman Culture and Society*. Oxford, 1991. 582–98).

Rich, J. 1976. *Declaring War in the Roman Republic in the Period of Transmarine Expansion*. Brussels.

Rich, J. 1993. 'Fear, Greed and Glory: The Causes of Roman War-Making in the Middle Republic', in Rich and Shipley 1993: 38–68.

Rich, J and Shipley, G. (eds) 1993. *War and Society in the Roman World*. London.

Richardson, J. S. 1976. 'The Spanish Mines and the Development of Provincial Taxation in the Second Century BC', *JRS* 66: 139–52.

Richardson, J. S. 1986. *Hispaniae: Spain and the Development of Roman Imperialism 218–82 BC*. Cambridge.

Richardson, J. S. 1987. 'The Purpose of the *Lex Calpurnia de repetundis*', *JRS* 77: 1–12.

Richardson, J. S. 1994. 'The Administration of the Empire', *CAH*² 9: 564–98.

Richardson, J. S. 1996. *The Romans in Spain*. Oxford.

Richardson, J. S. 2008. *The Language of Empire: Rome and the Idea of Empire from the Third Century BC to the Second Century AD*. Cambridge.

Riggsby, A. 1999. *Crime and Community in Ciceronian Rome*. Austin.

Riggsby, A. 2006. *Caesar in Gaul and Rome: A War in Words.* Austin.

Robert, L. 1969. 'Théophane de Mytilène à Constantinople', *Comptes rendus de l'Académie des Inscriptions et Belles-Lettres*, 42–64.

Rosenstein, N. 1990. *Imperatores Victi: Military Defeat and Aristocratic Competition in the Middle and Late Republic.* Berkeley.

Rosenstein, N. 2004. *Rome at War: Farms, Families and Death in the Middle Republic.* Chapel Hill.

Rosenstein, N. and Morstein-Marx, R. (eds) 2006. *A Companion to the Roman Republic.* Oxford.

Sabin, P., van Wees, H. and Whitby, M. (eds) 2007. *The Cambridge History of Greek and Roman Warfare.* 2 vols. Cambridge.

Sacks, K. S. 1990. *Diodorus Siculus and the First Century.* Princeton.

Saller, R. 1998. 'American Classical Historiography', in A. Molho and G. S. Wood (eds), *Imagined Histories: American Historians Interpret the Past.* Princeton. 222–37.

Salmon, E. T. 1967. *Samnium and the Samnites.* London.

Schatzman, I. 1975. *Senatorial Wealth and Roman Politics.* Brussels.

Scheidel, W. 2003. 'Germs for Rome', in Edwards and Woolf 2003: 158–76.

Scheidel, W. 2008. 'Roman Population Size: The Logic of the Debate', in de Ligt and Northwood 2008: 17–70.

Scobie, A. 1986. 'Slums, Sanitation and Mortality in the Ancient World', *Klio* 68: 399–433.

Scullard, H. H. 1973. *Roman Politics 220–150 BC.* 2nd edn. Oxford.

Scullard, H. H. 1980. *A History of the Roman World 753 to 146 BC.* 4th edn. London (first published 1935).

Scullard, H. H. 1989a. 'Carthage and Rome', in *CAH*[2] 7.1: 486–569.

Scullard, H. H. 1989b. 'The Carthaginians in Spain', in *CAH*[2] 8: 17–43.

Serrati, J. 2000. 'Garrisons and Grain: Sicily between the Punic Wars', in C. Smith and J. Serrati (eds), *Sicily from Aeneas to Augustus: New Approaches in Archaeology and History.* Edinburgh. 115–33.

Shatzman, I. 1975. *Senatorial Wealth and Roman Politics.* Brussels.

Shaw, B. D. 1984. 'Bandits in the Roman Empire', *Past & Present* 105: 3–52.

Shaw, B. D. 1990. 'Bandit Highlands and Lowland Peace: The Mountains of Isauria–Cilicia', *Journal of the Economic and Social History of the Orient* 33: 199–233.

Shaw, B. D. 1996. 'Seasons of Death: Aspects of Mortality in Imperial Rome', *JRS* 86: 100–38.

Sherk, R. K. 1969. *Roman Documents from the Greek East: Senatus Consulta and Epistulae to the Age of Augustus.* Baltimore.

Sherk, R. K. 1984. *Rome and the Greek East to the Death of Augustus.* Translated Documents of Greece and Rome 4. Cambridge.

Sherk, R. K. 1988. *The Roman Empire: Augustus to Hadrian.* Translated Documents of Greece and Rome 6. Cambridge.

Sherwin-White, A. N. 1967. *Racial Prejudice in Imperial Rome.* Cambridge.

Sherwin-White, A. N. 1973. *Roman Citizenship*. 2nd edn, Oxford.

Sherwin-White, A. N. 1980. 'Rome the Aggressor?', *JRS* 70: 177–81.

Sherwin-White, A. N. 1993. *Roman Foreign Policy in the East*. London.

Shuckburgh, E. S. 1889. *The Histories of Polybius*. London.

Shuckburgh, E. S. 1889–1900. *The Letters of Cicero: The Whole Extant correspondence in Alphabetical Order*. London.

Steel, C. E. W. 2001. *Cicero, Rhetoric and Empire*. Oxford.

Steinby, C. 2007. *The Roman Republican Navy: From the Sixth Century to 167 BC*. Helsinki.

Storey, G. 1997. 'The Population of Ancient Rome', *Antiquity* 71: 966–78.

Swain, S. 1996. *Hellenism and Empire: Language, Classicism and Power in the Greek World, AD 50–250*. Oxford.

Syme, R. 1958. *Tacitus*. Oxford.

Syme, R. 1964. *Sallust*. Berkeley.

Talbert, R. J. A. (ed.) 2000. *The Barrington Atlas of the Greek and Roman World*. Princeton.

Torelli, M. 2006. 'The Topography and Archaeology of Republican Rome', in Rosenstein and Morstein-Marx 2006: 81–101.

Toynbee, A. J. 1965. *Hannibal's Legacy: The Hannibalic War's Effects on Roman Life*. 2 vols. Oxford.

Versnel, H. S. 1970. *Triumphus: An Inquiry into the Origin, Development, and Meaning of the Roman Triumph*. Leiden.

Veyne, P. 1975. 'Y a-t-il eu un impérialisme romain?', *Mélanges de l'École Française de Rome* 87: 793–855.

Veyne, P. 1993. '*Humanitas*: Romans and non-Romans', in A. Giardina (ed.), *The Romans*. Chicago. 342–69.

Walbank, F. W. 1957–79. *A Historical Commentary on Polybius*. 3 vols. Oxford.

Walbank, F. W. 1963. 'Polybius and Rome's Eastern Policy', *JRS* 53: 1–13 (reprinted in F. W. Walbank, *Selected Papers*. Oxford, 1985. 138–56).

Walbank, F. W. 1972. *Polybius*. Berkeley.

Walbank, F. W. 1995. '"Treason" and Roman Domination: Two Case-Studies, Polybius and Josephus', in C. Schubert and K. Brodersen (eds), *Rom und der griechische Osten: Festschrift für Hatto H. Schmitt zum 65. Geburtstag*. Stuttgart. 273–85. (reprinted in F. W. Walbank, *Polybius, Rome and the Hellenistic World*. Cambridge, 2002. 258–76).

Wallace-Hadrill, A. 1983. *Suetonius: The Scholar and his Caesars*. London.

Wallace-Hadrill, A. 2008. *Rome's Cultural Revolution*. Cambridge.

Webster, J. 2001. 'Creolizing the Roman Provinces', *American Journal of Archaeology* 105: 209-25.

Webster, J. and Cooper, N. (eds) 1996. *Roman Imperialism: Post-Colonial Perspectives*. Leicester Archaeology Monographs 3. Leicester.

Welch, K. E. 2006. 'Art and Architecture in the Roman Republic', in Rosenstein and Morstein-Marx 2006: 496–542.

Wells, C. M. 1972. *The German Policy of Augustus: An Examination of the Archaeological Record.* Oxford.

Wells, C. M. 1992. *The Roman Empire.* 2nd edn. London.

Wells, P. S. 1999. *The Barbarians Speak: How the Conquered Peoples Shaped the Roman Empire.* Princeton.

Wesch-Klein, G. 2007. 'Recruits and Veterans', in P. Erdkamp (ed.), *A Companion to the Roman Army.* Oxford. 435–50.

Whitmarsh, T. 2001. *Greek Literature and the Roman Empire. The Politics of Imitation.* Oxford.

Whittaker, C. 1996. 'Roman Africa: Augustus to Vespasian', *CAH²* 10: 586–618.

Wilkes, J. J. 1996. 'The Danubian and Balkan Provinces', *CAH²* 10: 545–85.

Williams, J. 2001. *Beyond the Rubicon: Romans and Gauls in Republican Italy.* Oxford.

Wiseman, T. P. 1971. *New Men in the Roman Senate, 139 BC–AD 14.* Oxford.

Witcher, R. 2000. 'Globalisation and Roman Imperialism: Perspectives on Identities in Roman Italy', in E. Herring and K. Lomas (eds), *The Emergence of State Identities in Italy.* London. 213–26.

Witcher, R. 2005. 'The Extended Metropolis: *Urbs, Suburbium* and Population', *Journal of Roman Archaeology* 18: 120–38.

Woolf, G. 1994. 'Becoming Roman, Staying Greek: Culture, Identity and the Civilizing Process in the Roman East', *Proceedings of the Cambridge Philological Society* 40: 116–43.

Woolf, G. 1997. 'The Roman Urbanization of the East', in S. E. Alcock (ed.), *The Early Roman Empire in the East.* Oxford. 1–14.

Woolf, G. 1998. *Becoming Roman: The Origins of Provincial Civilization in Gaul.* Cambridge.

Woolf, G. 2006. 'Pliny's Province', in T. Bekker-Nielsen (ed.), *Rome and the Black Sea Region: Domination, Romanisation, Resistance.* Aarhus. 93–108.

Yarrow, L. M. 2006. *Historiography at the End of the Republic. Provincial Perspectives on Roman Rule.* Oxford.

Zanker, P. 1988. *The Power of Images in the Age of Augustus.* Ann Arbor.

Zetzel, J. E. G. 1999. *Cicero: On the Commonwealth and On the Laws.* Cambridge.

Ziolkowski, A. 1992. *The Temples of Mid-Republican Rome and their Historical and Topographical Context.* Rome.

Ziolkowski, A. 1993. '*Urbs Direpta*, or How the Romans Sacked Cities', in Rich and Shipley 1993: 69–91.

Index